C. WRIGHT MILLS

AND *THE POWER ELITE*

C. WRIGHT MILLS

AND

THE POWER ELITE

Compiled by

G. WILLIAM DOMHOFF

AND

HOYT B. BALLARD

Beacon Press

Boston

International Standard Book Number: 0–8070–4185–8

9 8 7 6 5 4

Frontispiece courtesy Hal McIntosh originally drawn for Saturday Review

The compilers gratefully acknowledge permission to republish the
following copyright material:
"C. Wright Mills" by Ralph Miliband from Monthly Review, September,
1962, by permission of the publisher. "The Sociology of C. Wright
Mills" originally published as "C. Wright Mills and The American Left"
by Eugene V. Schneider from Monthly Review, February, 1963, by
permission of the author and the publisher. "A Critique of the Ruling Elite
Model" by Robert A. Dahl from The American Political Science Review,
June, 1958, by permission of the author and the publisher, " 'Power Elite'
or 'Veto Groups'?" by William Kornhauser from Culture and Social
Character edited by Seymour Martin Lipset and Leo Lowenthal, © The
Free Press of Glencoe, Inc., 1961, reprinted by permission of The
Macmillan Company. "The Distribution of Power in American Society"
by Talcott Parsons from his volume Structure and Process in Modern
Societies, © The Free Press, a Corporation 1960, reprinted by permission
of The Macmillan Company. "Power in America" by Dennis Wrong from
Commentary, copyright © 1956 by the American Jewish Committee,
reprinted by permission of the author and the publisher. "Are the Blind
Leading the Blind?" by A. A. Berle, Jr., from the New York Times Book
Review, April 4, 1956, © by The New York Times Company, reprinted
by permission of the author and the publisher. "Power in the United
States" by Robert S. Lynd from The Nation by permission of the
publisher. "Power Elite or Ruling Class" by Paul M. Sweezy from
Monthly Review, September, 1956, by permission of the publisher. "Power
in America" by Herbert Aptheker from his volume The World of
C. Wright Mills, Copyright © 1960 by Herbert Aptheker, by permission
of the author and Marzani and Munsell. "Socialism and Sociology" by
Philip Rieff from Partisan Review, Summer 1956, © 1956 by Partisan
Review, reprinted by permission of the author and the publisher. "The
Interlocking Overlappers" by Richard Rovere from his volume The
American Establishment and Other Reports, Opinions, and Speculations,
© 1956 by Richard Rovere, reprinted by permission of Harcourt, Brace &
World, Inc. "The Power Elite Reconsidered" by Daniel Bell from
American Journal of Sociology, November, 1958, Copyright 1958 by the
University of Chicago Press, reprinted by permission of the publisher.
"Comment on Criticism" by C. Wright Mills from Dissent by permission
of the publisher.

CONTENTS

C. WRIGHT MILLS AND *THE POWER ELITE*

INTRODUCTION

C. Wright Mills (1916–1962) was the most controversial and hard-hitting sociologist of the post-World-War-II era. He disrupted the general academic complacency of that generation by saying disturbing things about the new middle class of white collar workers, about the sociological imagination, and about the American response to the Cuban revolution. But his most provocative comments were on the structure of power in American society. The appearance of his *The Power Elite* in 1956 reopened the study of the upper reaches of American society in a social science that had lost interest in such a controversial topic. The provocative nature of *The Power Elite* is attested to by the considered reviews it elicited from leading social scientists on the American and British scenes.

The purpose of this book is to bring together some of the most thoughtful and representative of these many reviews in order to continue the discussion on power and social structure that was initiated by the publication of *The Power Elite*. While this book is first and foremost directed to a consideration of the substantive ideas put forth by Mills, it also presents some of the ideas and methods of the various reviewers, and reveals in part the underlying values of both Mills and his critics.

The book is divided into five sections. The first serves to introduce Mills and his ideas. Sections two, three, and four place Mills' critics in the categories utilized by him in his little-known answer to some of the reviews of *The Power Elite*. Mills classified his critics as Liberal, Radical, and Highbrow in the rejoinder which is reprinted in the fifth and final section. Liberal and Radical are clear enough, and by Highbrow Mills described those sophisticates who were seemingly above it all. They paid as much attention to Mills and his motives as they did to the content of the book, viewing it "as an event and a stratagem," in Mills' words.

Mills' rejoinder to critics appeared about a year after *The Power Elite*. While it contains answers to some of the questions raised in sections two through four, it was in fact written before many of the best reviews appeared. In order to provide comment on the later reviews, and to survey the discussion from a perspective of ten years and recent research, the book concludes with an essay by one of the editors, *"The Power Elite* and Its Critics."

G. William Domhoff
UNIVERSITY OF CALIFORNIA, SANTA CRUZ

Hoyt B. Ballard
TEXAS A. & I. UNIVERSITY, KINGSVILLE

ACKNOWLEDGMENTS

We would like to express our thanks to David Horowitz, Ralph Miliband, and Addison Potter for editorial suggestions, to Joan Hodgson for tracking down a great many hard-to-find references, and to Happy Hunter, Sharon Overgaard, and Grace Stall for typing the manuscript. Our thanks also to our colleagues Benjamin Smith and Robert Simmons for stimulating our thinking on this topic.

G.W.D.
H.B.B.

PART I

C. Wright Mills and His Sociology

It is often easier to understand a theoretical controversy when the principal figure is thoroughly familiar. But C. Wright Mills is no easy person to characterize. An angry, politically oriented social scientist, he never voted. A sparkling popularizer, he was at the same time a well-trained and well-read professor of sociology who did a great deal of original research.[1] A man who felt totally alienated from the American system, he was yet a 100 percent American who could live nowhere else. An advocate of socialism, he was also a devastating and amusing critic of Soviet Russia without being an "anti-communist." Called by some a Marxist, others thought him un-Marxist or even anti-Marxist. In 1957 he said he had never been a Marxist; in 1962 he wrote as a "plain Marxist" in criticizing "vulgar" and "sophisticated" Marxists for trying to rationalize and repair Marx's outmoded model rather than using Marx's method to construct a new and credible picture of a changed reality.[2]

Ralph Miliband's article in this section portrays Mills in all his complexity. The article by Eugene V. Schneider is a concise and readable summary of Mills' thought.

[1] Mills received his Ph.D. in sociology and anthropology from the University of Wisconsin. He was, at his death, associate professor of sociology at Columbia University.

[2] C. Wright Mills, *The Marxists* (New York: Dell, 1962), pp. 96–104.

C. Wright Mills

BY RALPH MILIBAND

I mourn the death of C. Wright Mills, bitterly and personally. We had, in the last five years of his life, become close friends. I am not minded to write a detached appraisal of his work and thought. But I think I can write about the man he was, and what he was about.

Mills was forty-five years old when he died of a second heart attack last March, at his home in West Nyack, near New York. He had by then long established himself as the most interesting and controversial sociologist writing in the United States. With books like *White Collar, The Power Elite,* and *The Sociological Imagination,* he had succeeded in proving to a new generation of students what most of their teachers had managed to conceal from them: that social analysis could be probing, tough-minded, critical, relevant, and scholarly; that ideas need not be handled as undertakers handle bodies, with care but without passion; that commitment need not be dogmatic; and that radicalism need not be a substitute for hard thinking. With what he called "pamphlets," like *The Causes of World War III* and *Listen, Yankee,* he had wanted, and managed, to reach a wider public, in the hope of doing what one man could against the brainwashing and intimidation to which his fellow Americans were, and are, exposed from all sides, day in and day out.

Ralph Miliband teaches political sociology at the London School of Economics. He is the author of Parliamentary Socialism *and co-editor of three volumes of* The Socialist Register. *This article appeared first in the* New Left Review, *May–June, 1962, and then in the* Monthly Review, *September, 1962.*

C. WRIGHT MILLS AND *THE POWER ELITE*

Mills was as American as could be. He was born in Texas, and liked to recall that his grandfather, in the old days of one man one gun, had died, shot in the back. However, he not only fled from the intellectual desert of Texas as soon as he had graduated from its University: let his enemies make of it what they will, he also came to feel a deep alienation from America, its ethos, its politics, its way of life. His was not the snob dislike which some Americans feel for a country incapable of matching the hierarchical graces of Europe, nor the alienation which often accompanies the romantic vision of vanished America, rural, small-town, face-to-face. Mills' interest in Europe was strictly sociological. Nor did he feel the need to look for radical inspiration outside America: the Wobblies would do quite well. And he was not, as some critics alleged, an *égaré* Jeffersonian, hankering for a pre-industrial age: he liked stainless steel, efficient heating systems, fast motorcycles. He was an excellent mechanic and professional with a camera. He would have made a first-class engineer. What he loathed about America was not its industrial strength, but the mess which a profit-oriented society has made, and cannot but make, of its human and material powers; not America's cars, but their built-in shoddiness, not television, but its commercialized misuse. *Caveat Emptor* did not strike him as the last word in social wisdom.

Enters *The Power Elite.* It is easy but dishonest to attribute the corruption of a society to its people. Rousseau was right: the people is never corrupt. But it is often corrupted—by those whom it pays to corrupt, by those who have the power to do it. In *White Collar,* which he thought his best book, he had analyzed the various kinds of corruption which had affected the middle layers of American society. In *The Power Elite,* he went on to locate the corrupters-in-chief, the men of the "higher immorality," and found them in three interlocking

4

groups: the corporate rich and the "warlords" (those whom an unexpected disciple, Eisenhower by name, has called the "industrial-military complex") and the political directorate.

The Power Elite is a rich and intricate book, written, like all that Mills wrote, in a compelling style—intense, muscular, alive. It is one of the very few books to glitter among the grey mass of what, in the United States, passed for social analysis in the frightened fifties. There is room for debate about much of its detail. But I don't think there is much room for serious debate about the book's general thesis, namely, that in America some men have enormous power denied to everyone else; that these men are, increasingly, a self-perpetuating elite; that their power is, increasingly, unchecked and irresponsible; and that their decision-making, based on an increasingly "military definition of reality" and on "crackpot realism," is oriented to immoral ends.

Mills was an angry man, with the disciplined, directed anger of the humanist in an irrational society—for what is humanism if not anger with unreason? His fiercest anger, however, was not with the Power Elite: for they were merely acting out the role cast for them by the social setting in which they were allowed to wield power; nor with American labor leaders, the men whom he had, in one of his first books, hopefully called the "New Men of Power." True, they had failed to form an effective counterweight to the Power Elite; worse, they had adopted its ethos and its purposes. But then, Mills had long given up (mistakenly, I think) the belief that organized labor could ever, in an advanced capitalist society, be the maker of radical history—the "labor metaphysic," he called that belief. It was not the Power Elite, Labor, or White Collar which angered him most, but defaulting academics and intellectuals.

To an extraordinary degree, Mills had something which is

not very common among academics and intellectuals: an intense respect for the intellectual craft; for the world of ideas, knowledge, and scholarship; for the intellectual as the high priest of reason and truth. He really liked only two kinds of people: those who were good with their hands, a carpenter, a mechanic, a gunsmith; and those who were possessed by the intellectual passion, as he was himself. He never made the vulgar mistake of taking seriously only those who shared his view of the world. Unlike many radicals (not to speak of anti-radicals), he was an intensely listening man. The basic requirement was not shared opinions, but honesty and knowledge, scholarship and relevance. Every working day (and every day was a working day), he was engaged, through books, essays, articles, newspapers, in a silent but active debate with fellow writers, anywhere. I have never seen anyone read as creatively as Mills did. He couldn't even read a detective story without pencil in hand.

"All social scientists," he wrote, "by the fact of their existence, are involved in the struggle between enlightenment and obscurantism." But he knew that there was an "ought" missing from that proposition, that many social scientists, in the struggle between enlightenment and obscurantism, are on the wrong side, or refuse to be involved, which comes to the same. This is what roused him to indignation—conformist unthinking, reason at the eager service of unreasonable kings, sophisticated apologetics for the inexcusable, social scientists as shields of orthodoxy and bellboys of authority.

It is from that indignation that stemmed *The Sociological Imagination.* That book was both a denunciation and a plea: a denunciation of social science as abstracted triviality, as windy pretension allied to timid respectability, of the uses of social science for the purpose, not of challenge, but of adjustment; and a plea—for the big probe, for a social science "of direct relevance to urgent public issues and insistent human trouble," for the social scientist as a man fired with the will "to make a difference in the quality of human life in our time."

The trouble with Mills was that he never managed to emancipate himself from a view of the intellectual as the free man, in duty bound to help make others free. Such a romantic, naive belief is inconvenient; it poses a threat. No wonder he made enemies in the academic fraternity.

It was only in 1956 that Mills, on leave from Columbia University, first came to Europe. He had, until then, been very America-oriented. In April 1957 he came to a weekend seminar in Surrey, organized by the Students' Union of the London School of Economics. He was a big man, who looked bigger, reserved but intensely alert, deliberate in speech and coolly appraising, unassumingly at ease with the students, whom he bowled over, quite unselfconsciously. Shortly after, in July, he and I went to Poland, where Adam Schaff as the philosopher of official Poland, and Leszek Kolakowski as the most acute of the young Polish "revisionists," showed us two parts of an equation, to which neither had the complete answer, nor could have.

Until then, Mills had generally shared the outlook of that particular stream of American radicalism which views the Soviet regime as inherently evil, and present-day Communism as the frozen caricature of a uniquely penetrating body of thought. For the record, I might as well add here that the label "Texas Trotskyite" which some people stupidly tried to pin on him was doubly inaccurate: he was born in Texas but he was not a Texan; nor did he ever identify himself with any of the fifty-seven varieties of American Trotskyism. He simply thought

Trotsky one of the most remarkable minds of the Marxist tradition—who but a fool or an ignoramus does not? His visit to
Poland, two subsequent visits to Russia, in 1960 and 1961,
and much talk and debate with intellectuals in the Communist
bloc, left him intensely interested and pondering, "ambiguous," as he put it, about much of Soviet society, better aware
of its problems, its evils, *and* its promise. Unlike the dogmatic
anti-Communists of the American Left, whom he now saw as
"members of the old futilitarians of the dead Left," Mills did
not react to the Soviet bloc as if he had a vested intellectual
and political interest in the perpetuation of all that was evil in
it: *his* world would not be shattered by the humanization of
Soviet society and by the unfreezing of its Stalinist mold. Some
of his friends thought and said that he had "gone soft" on the
Stalinists. It was an absurd charge which deeply distressed
him, more than any other attack from any other quarter ever
distressed him. He was the last man to surrender his judgment
and his perception to the dogmatists of either camp. He was
still "working on" Communism and the Soviet bloc when he
died: his last book, *The Marxists,* published shortly after his
death, is the last testimony to the rare honesty he brought to
that effort. One of his unfinished manuscripts was a *Letter to a
Russian Intellectual,* a book in which he hoped to enter into a
thorough examination of the problems, common and dissimi-
lar, which intellectuals of East and West confront, or ought to
confront.

Some men are pamphleteers by vocation. Mills was not. He
became one in the late fifties, reluctantly, out of a deeply felt
need to present, to as wide an audience as could be reached,
alternatives to the military definition of reality which he believed to be at the center of his country's foreign policies. What
he was concerned with, he wrote about. By the late fifties, he

had come to be haunted (as only idiots are not) by the fear that East and West were trapped in a terrible dialectic, which would ultimately turn the planet into a thermonuclear crematorium. (Not voting discuss)

The detailed analysis and prescriptions of *The Causes of World War III* matter less here than its insistence on "the wholesale cultural and political default of NATO intellectuals during the past decade and a half" as one of the causes of World War III. He had no illusions as to the likelihood of his proposals being acted upon "this week by the power elite of the United States," the more so since, from their standpoint, these proposals "were indeed utopian, expensive, idealistic, unsound and, for all I know, traitorous." Mills was speaking above all to intellectuals, "scientists and artists, ministers and scholars . . . those who represent the human intellect . . . who are part of the great discourse of inquiry and reason, of sensibility and imagination." I don't know how many were persuaded, but I know that many listened, and drew strength from what they heard. He had, in those last years, become a voice and was becoming the spokesman of a movement, "the big daddy of the New Left," as someone sneered. He did not relish the role. For all his intensity and impatience, he was a singularly modest, unpretentious man. He was embarrassed by the fan mail which poured into his letter box, and he hated being distracted from the big books he wanted to write. But there was no surcease. For suddenly, there was Cuba.

As Mills wrote in *Listen, Yankee,* he had not thought much about Cuba until the summer of 1960—eighteen months after Fidel Castro took power in Havana. Cuba was forced upon his attention by visits to Brazil in the autumn of 1959 and to Mexico in the spring of 1960. "In both Rio de Janeiro and Mexico City," he recalled, "Cuba was of course a major topic of discussion. But I did not know what was happening there, much less what I might think about it, and I was then busy with other studies." He decided to "look into" Cuba: by the time he went there in the late summer of 1960, he had set up one of his beloved "files" and had read voraciously on Cuba and Latin America. The book which came out of that trip was written in six weeks, at white heat, the way Tom Paine must have written *Common Sense,* for another revolution.

Mills was rather detached about his previous books: the next ones would be *much* better. But he was proud of *Listen, Yankee,* and with good reason. For it is a good and brave book, in which one Yankee tried to explain, well and bravely, through the fog of misrepresentation with which the American press had shrouded the island, why the Cuban Revolution was by far the best and most decent thing that had ever happened in and to Latin America. Mills did not go into Cuba gooey-eyed, nor did he come out of Cuba gooey-eyed. As he wrote, "I am for the Cuban Revolution. I do not worry about it. I worry for it and with it." He did believe that Castro, having been his own Kerensky and Lenin, could avoid becoming his own Stalin as well. His desperate anxiety to persuade his countrymen that the Cuban Revolution should be helped stemmed from his conviction that nothing was more likely to make the moustache and not the beard the symbol of the revolution than the United States' attempt to destroy it. Long before it happened, he had come to believe that the United States *would* attempt to destroy the Revolution by force. It filled him with bitter, helpless shame. In fact, it broke his heart. It was in December 1960 that he suffered his first major heart attack. It was altogether fitting that, when Mills died fifteen months later, Fidel Castro should have sent a wreath to the funeral. For Mills was a casualty of the Cuban Revolution, and of the revolution of our times.

10

C. Wright Mills

C. Wright Mills cannot be neatly labeled and cataloged. He never belonged to any party or faction; he did not think of himself as a "Marxist"; he had the most profound contempt for orthodox Social Democrats and for closed minds in the Communist world. He detested smug liberals and the kind of radical whose response to urgent and uncomfortable choices is hand wringing. He was a man on his own, with both the strength and also the weakness which go with that solitude. He was on the Left, but not of the Left, a deliberately lone guerrilla, not a regular soldier. He was highly organized, but unwilling to *be* organized, with self-discipline the only discipline he could tolerate. He had friends rather than comrades. Despite all this, perhaps because of it, he occupied a unique position in American radicalism. He was desperately needed by socialists everywhere, and his death leaves a gaping void. In a trapped and inhumane world, he taught what it means to be a free and humane intellect. "Get on with it," he used to say. "Work." So, in his spirit, let us.

The Sociology of C. Wright Mills

BY EUGENE V. SCHNEIDER

Men of sensibility, as Mills would say, may agree on the nature of present-day society, and yet disagree on the process by which this society was brought into being and in what direction it will develop. And if there is such disagreement, then it is virtually certain that there will be disagreement on what must be done, on what *can* be done, by those who wish to change the drift of things. The aim of this article is not to offer a critique of Mills—that would be quite impossible in the space of a few pages—but to present in highly condensed form the main features of his beliefs about modern society.

Theoretical Approach

Mills was above all a social scientist, that is, he believed that society could be made the object of rational inquiry. It is important to keep this in mind precisely because Mills leveled such bitter attacks on present-day social science, whether of the academic or "Marxist" varieties. Those who doubt that society can be studied scientifically are going to be disappointed in Mills, no matter how much they may enjoy his attacks on current social sciences.

Eugene V. Schneider is a professor of sociology at Bryn Mawr College. He is the author of Industrial Sociology. *This paper, which appeared in the* Monthly Review, *February, 1963, has been retitled and the first and last sections condensed (with the permission of the author) because they were addressed only to political leftists, telling them that Mills had many ideas not shared by the traditional Left about which they would have to make up their minds.*

But he was a social scientist of his own kind. He rejected most academic social science on two grounds. First, he scornfully rejected that social science which lacks historical perspective of any kind, which views society as essentially an equilibrium, maintained by a set of functioning institutions. For such social science there are no internal contradictions, only deviance; there are no long-term forces of social change, only variations about equilibrium; there is no succession of historically unique societies, only variations of "society." Second, he rejected academic social science because it refused to take a moral stand on what it was studying. For Mills this was not only a moral fault, it was a sin against science, for it confined the social sciences to studying things as they are, without ever coming to grips with things as they might be. Yet the potentialities in any given situation are also real. By failing to recognize this fact, academic social science doomed itself to a static view of society, to the trivial, the obvious, the half-baked. Even worse, it seemed to justify the present, with all its absurdity, inhumanity, and danger, as somehow necessary or even right.

It might seem that this position must lead Mills to the acceptance of Marxism as the only possible valid social science. And in a certain sense, it did; Mills explicitly labeled himself a "plain Marxist." But it is necessary to understand what Mills meant by this term.

For Mills, Marxism was three things: an approach to social phenomena, a method for studying them, and a system of values by which to judge societies and to formulate programs of action. The Marxist approach to the study of society was an historical and a functional one. It held that all societies were constantly changing, by evolution or by revolution, into new forms. Each form was marked by specific types of social structure, human personalities, processes of change and resistance

13

to change, and specific functional relationships between all of these. Each society, then, was governed by "laws" specific to itself. As a method, Marxism demanded that once a model of any specific society was constructed, deductions be made from this model which could be used to predict the course of events, but only until such time as the model would be rendered obsolete by evolution or revolution. As a philosophy, Marxism judged each society in terms of its capacity to provide the basic elements of a truly human condition, by which Marx meant not only material necessities, but the widest possible opportunity for the exercise of reason and freedom.

Marxism, in Mills' view, did *not* mean that one set of "laws," deducted from one master model, was applicable to all types and stages of capitalist society, let alone other types of society. The trouble with almost all the existing varieties of Marxism was that they sought to use a model which Marx derived largely from one form of capitalist society to analyze quite different types of society. Because these models are obsolete, the predictions derived from them about the course of modern history have been fallacious. Thus they have led to what Mills regarded as fallacious predictions about the increasing alienation and pauperization of the working class, the constant worsening of economic crises and ultimate stagnation, the ever constant and sharpening class struggle, and the outbreak of revolutions in advanced capitalist societies.

Mills believed that underlying these fallacies is a false model of modern society. Thus he denies that in our time men are dominated by their relationships to the means of production. He asks, can the behavior of blue-collar workers, white-collar workers, capitalists, managers, generals, Negroes, be understood in these terms? He denies that the "superstructure" of society—the prevailing ideas and institutions—is always the reflection of the economic base. Is it true, for instance, that the state has always been the servant of the capitalist class, that it is never able to restrain its capitalists? He denies that, today, social being always determines consciousness. How, he asks, can one account for "false consciousness"? What about the ability of the mass media to *create* consciousness in relation to certain issues and objects? He denies that men in our time can make history only within the limits set by changes in the economic base of society. This, he argues, is gravely to underestimate the role of leaders and men of power in the making of modern history. Mills did not deny that all of these assumptions of the classical Marxist model may have been valid in another period; but he held that they are not eternal principles of society and that they certainly do not adequately describe our own times.

At this time the reader may be left wondering in what sense Mills was a Marxist. Perhaps instead of calling himself a "plain Marxist," Mills should have said along with Marx and in the precise sense that Marx meant it: "I, at least, am not a Marxist."

Society

Using what he considered to be the Marxian approach, method, and philosophy, Mills set about constructing what he thought was a more adequate model of advanced industrial society. It is possible here only to indicate briefly some of the major elements in this model. It will be found described in detail in his trilogy, *New Men of Power, White Collar,* and *The Power Elite.*

First, it must be understood that Mills believed that all advanced industrial societies, capitalist or non-capitalist, are subject to many of the same dynamic forces. Above all, modern

15

society is marked by a process of rationalization (which is not the same thing as ordinary rationality). Rationalization is manifest in the growth of large-scale bureaucracies, revolutions in technology, developing techniques for the manipulation of people, the great growth of science. In the economic sphere, the result has been the bureaucratization and concentration of many phases of production. In the military sphere, the result has been the modern military machine—vast, bureaucratized, armed with the weapons of mass destruction. In the political sphere, there has appeared the state bureaucracy and the mass media as a means of manipulating people. Only society as a whole, at least in the capitalist countries, has resisted this process of rationalization.

From these central conditions of advanced industrial society flows a train of consequences, of which the most fateful are (1) the rise of an elite of powerful men who are in control of the means of death, production, and political power; and (2) below them an unorganized "mass" ruled over and controlled by this elite to an extent unique in human history.

The power elite are those who control the great organizations; they are the men at the head of the great corporations, the armed forces, the state, the mass media of communication. They are the men who make the "big decisions"—whether to go to war, to drop a bomb, to make peace, to join an alliance, to adopt a new economic policy. And they have the power to make sure that the rest of society accepts their decisions, if, indeed, they bother to secure assent at all. Their appearance is inevitable in advanced industrial society, but in the United States their position is, for a variety of reasons, peculiarly invulnerable: there is the absence of competing elites, the lack of a civil service, the sudden rise of America to a position of world power without the traditions or institutions to play such a role.

The power elite is *not* an economic class, based on ownership of property. Those who control the military forces have no property rights in their organization, and the same is true of the political directorate. Nor does the capitalist class simply control the giant economic bureaucracies. It is more accurate to say that the corporations have reorganized the capitalist class; its wealth is now largely corporate wealth. It is the interests and programs of the corporate elite which dominate the capitalist class more than the other way about. But who are the members of this elite? Some of them, to be sure, are drawn from the capitalist class; their wealth and connections have been their tickets of admission to the world of corporate power. Some of them have come up through their own organizations. Some have come in from other giant organizations, particularly the military. This shift of power from the capitalist class to the economic elite is reflected in the declining prestige of the "very rich," the legendary families, the "400's." For members of these declining elites to wield power, they must enter the corporate world, or one of the other great organizations.

Yet to some degree this power elite does form a unified group, with a similarity of outlook, programs, and values. They have similar interests, first of all in maintaining themselves in power and then in substantive matters of policy. Thus a permanent war economy reflects the interests of the economic elite in an assured and profitable market; at the same time it guarantees the position of the military elite, and provides the state with the necessary leverage for conducting foreign policy. Unity is also based on the similarity of the types of men who make up the elite. As heads of large-scale organizations, they have a great deal of experience in common. They have had similar educational and occupational careers. They tend to come from the same religious, ethnic, and occupational backgrounds. Because they are the same type of men, and because their interests coincide at many points, they find it easy and profitable to interchange positions, and this serves to unify them further. Probably they are not formally organized; their unity is achieved by go-betweens, through informal associations, through the interchange of positions.

The state plays a peculiar role in Mills' model. The state is, of course, one of the great organizations of advanced industrial society, and as such it forms a major source of power in society. But the state has now spawned an independent elite. There is no civil service, independent of passing administrations, on the level of policy decisions. Most professional politicians operate on the middle levels of power. Rather, the political elite is composed of a mixture of top-level politicians and members of the military and economic elites. Yet this does not mean that the state is merely the tool of the economic-military elite, much less of the capitalist class. No matter what the source of the political elite, the state remains, to some degree, an independent source of power and policy. There is certainly much coincidence of interest and outlook between the political directorage and the other elites; but this does not mean that the political elite is not able to initiate and pursue a policy of its own.

Forming a sort of penumbra to the power elite are the go-betweens, the advisers and consultants of the elite, powerful politicians, local and regional upper classes, and celebrities whose faces are known to the general public. On occasion members of these groups may be raised into the power elite.

Below this elite of powerful men are the middle levels of power where various special interest groups struggle among themselves for advantage and position. Occasionally the powerful may intervene in their struggles for tactical reasons and, of course, the power elite will brook no opposition from that quarter. But within these limits, the middle levels are quite free to carry on their struggles. It is here that are found the labor unions, the farm organizations, the Congress, and all the myriad of special local or regional interests that it represents. These groups have readily abdicated from making the big decisions; they have traded national power for immediate advantage and, from this point of view, many of them have done well.

Below these top and middle levels of power is the "mass society." It includes all those who have little or no power over the decision-makers at the top, those who receive from the top orders, information, interpretations of events, sometimes in recognizable form, sometimes not. On the one hand, the mass is more or less firmly controlled, depending on the needs of the power elite, by various institutions such as education, religion, unions, the press, the movies, radio, and TV. On the other hand, the mass lacks its own organizations, leadership, or ideology. As a result, the mass can be manipulated by the top for whatever purposes it chooses: to secure assent for a decision . . . a market . . . a source of military manpower, or for whatever other reason.

It should be noted that by a "mass society" Mills does not necessarily mean a homogeneous society. There may be plenty of distinctions within a mass society; distinctions of age, sex, race, occupation, religion, even class. The point is that in a mass society these distinctions do not and cannot serve as a basis for organization to counter the power of the elite.

The mass society, like the power elite, has risen from forces lying deeply imbedded within the social structure. First, mass society is the obverse of the power elite; as power has been concentrated at the top, the mass has been denuded of it. But, second, mass society is the outcome of certain changes in the class structure. The old middle class of small property and wealth, which at one time supported populist or even anti-capitalist movements, has decreased in numbers and largely lost whatever organization and influence it once possessed. In its place has appeared a very numerous and growing class of white-collar workers, clinging frantically to the prestige of the older middle class, but without even its economic base. This class has no traditions, no organizations, no unity. It is probably the most easily controlled group in society; given a small amount of status, the opportunity to remain distinct from the working class, even a vague hope of "rising," it will remain quiescent.

What has happened to the working class, the class upon which Marxists everywhere have placed their hopes, and which Mills himself at one time (in *The New Men of Power*) considered the only bar to slump and war? Organized labor has, of course, entered the middle levels of power; it has become bureaucratized and its leaders quite happily abdicate any claims to positions within the power elite in return for freedom of action within their own little spheres. Organized labor has, in fact, become one of the institutions of mass society; its function there is to control the working class in behalf of the power elite. At the same time, the rank and file of the working class has lost much of whatever unity and militancy (which was never very much, in Mills' estimate) it once possessed. In numbers, it is a declining class; it is split by ethnic and racial divisions; those sections which are employed and organized are smug, those which are neither shattered; it has accepted the values of the "mass society" and yearns vaguely for the white collar for itself or its children, for a home in the suburbs. It possesses virtually no organizations outside of its unions, and it has lost control even of them.

The institutions of society have lost or abdicated whatever position they once had as centers of rational thought, freedom, and initiative. The schools long ago abandoned any opposition to the Establishment. Religion has traded its concern with the freedom and development of the human soul for a mess of comfort and respectability. The universities have been lulled or forced into quietude by liberal grants for research in behalf of the interests of the power elite, by the rise of the academic bureaucrat, by a relentless war against their independent teachers. Science has become a machine in the service of the power elite.

Mills' Program of Action

Who then, according to Mills, has the will and the capacity to oppose the power elite, the mass society, the inexorable drift toward slump and war? Mills argues that the only group in society with at least the will, if not the power, is the intelligentsia. Intellectuals are defined as all those whose concern is with discovering and articulating the meaning and development of societal forces, and in relating these forces to the personal problems that people face; intellectuals are those who offer alternatives for the development of society and thus for the self, and who suggest programs of action for attaining these alternatives. Insofar as intellectuals function as intellectuals, they cannot help but realize and oppose the role of the power elite in this society and the drift toward slump and war that it has set in motion. By the same token, the intellectuals cannot help but oppose the mass society, with its denial of rationality and freedom to all but a very few, with the limited and distorted selves that it produces. The mere dealers in ideas—those who have become technicians in the service of the Establishment, or those who have, through disgust or disillusionment, ceased to face these problems—are not intellectuals; they have forfeited their right to that name.

PART II

Liberal Critics of THE POWER ELITE

The Power Elite *was received by its liberal critics as a provocative but mistaken analysis of the American polity. The liberals disliked Mills' methodological approach as well as his rejection of several generally held convictions in American social science. They criticized Mills for bypassing the study of the decision-making process to look instead at the decision makers and for failing to distinguish between corporate owners and corporate managers to the degree that liberals are wont to do. Futhermore, they questioned the relatively impotent role attributed to the political directorate and the relegation of such groups as farmers, workers, small businessmen, and professionals to the middle levels of power.*

The liberal critics realized that The Power Elite*'s bitter criticisms were directed against liberal intellectuals fully as much as the elites of power. It was no secret that Mills charged them with defending established authority. He wrote of their "celebration" of American government and their teaching of "national patriotism." The liberals, as might be expected, reacted strongly.*

A Critique of the Ruling Elite Model

BY ROBERT A. DAHL

A great many people seem to believe that "they" run things: the old families, the bankers, the City Hall machine, or the party boss behind the scene. This kind of view evidently has a powerful and many-sided appeal. It is simple, compelling, dramatic, "realistic." It gives one standing as an inside-dopester. For individuals with a strong strain of frustrated idealism, it has just the right touch of hard-boiled cynicism. Finally, the hypothesis has one very great advantage over many alternative explanations: It can be cast in a form that makes it virtually impossible to disprove.

Consider the last point for a moment. There is a type of quasi-metaphysical theory made up of what might be called an infinite regress of explanations. The ruling elite model *can* be interpreted in this way. If the overt leaders of a community do not appear to constitute a ruling elite, then the theory can be saved by arguing that behind the overt leaders there is a set of covert leaders who do. If subsequent evidence shows that this covert group does not make a ruling elite, then the theory can be saved by arguing that behind the first covert group there is another, and so on.

Now whatever else it may be, a theory that cannot even in principle be controverted by empirical evidence is not a scientific theory. The least that we can demand of any ruling elite theory that purports to be more than a metaphysical or polemi-

Robert A. Dahl is professor of political science at Yale University. Among his books are Congress and Foreign Policy, Modern Political Analysis, *and* Who Governs? *This paper appeared in* The American Political Science Review, *June, 1958.*

cal doctrine is, first, that the burden of proof be on the proponents of the theory and not on its critics; and, second, that there be clear criteria according to which the theory could be disproved.

With these points in mind, I shall proceed in two stages. First, I shall try to clarify the meaning of the concept "ruling elite" by describing a very simple form of what I conceive to be a ruling elite system. Second, I shall indicate what would be required in principle as a simple but satisfactory test of any hypothesis asserting that a particular political system is, in fact, a ruling elite system. Finally, I shall deal with some objections.

I. A Simple Ruling Elite System

If a ruling elite hypothesis says anything, surely it asserts that within some specific political system there exists a group of people who to some degree exercise power or influence over other actors in the system. I shall make the following assumptions about power:[1]

1. In order to compare the relative influence of two actors (these may be individuals, groups, classes, parties, or what not), it is necessary to state the scope of the responses upon which the actors have an effect. The statement, "A has more power than B," is so ambiguous as to verge on the meaningless, since it does not specify the scope.

2. One cannot compare the relative influence of two actors who always perform identical actions with respect to the group influenced. What this means as a practical matter is that ordinarily one can test for differences in influence only where there are cases of differences in initial preferences. At one ex-

[1] See Robert A. Dahl, "The Concept of Power," *Behavioral Science,* Vol. 2 (July, 1957), pp. 201–215.

treme, the difference may mean that one group prefers alternative A and another group prefers B, A and B being mutually exclusive. At the other extreme, it may mean that one group prefers alternative A to other alternatives, and another group is indifferent. If a political system displayed complete consensus at all times, we should find it impossible to construct a satisfactory direct test of the hypothesis that it was a ruling elite system, although indirect and rather unsatisfactory tests might be devised.

˙ Consequently, to know whether or not we have a ruling elite, we must have a political system in which there is a difference in preferences, from time to time, among the individual human beings in the system. Suppose, now, that among these individuals there is a set whose preferences regularly prevail in all cases of disagreement, or at least in all cases of disagreement over key political issues (a term I propose to leave undefined here). Let me call such a set of individuals a "controlling group." In a full-fledged democracy operating strictly according to majority rule, the majority would constitute a controlling group, even though the individual members of the majority might change from one issue to the next. But since our model is to represent a ruling elite system, we require that the set be *less than a majority in size.*

However, in any representative system with single member voting districts where more than two candidates receive votes, a candidate *could* win with less than a majority of votes; and it is possible, therefore, to imagine a truly sovereign legislature elected under the strictest "democratic" rules that was nonetheless governed by a legislative majority representing the first preferences of a minority of voters. Yet I do not think we would want to call such a political system a ruling elite system. Because of this kind of difficulty, I propose that we exclude

27

from our definition of a ruling elite any controlling group that is a product of rules that are actually followed (that is, "real" rules) under which a majority of individuals could dominate if they took certain actions permissible under the "real" rules. In short, to constitute a ruling elite a controlling group must not be *a pure artifact of democratic rules.*

A ruling elite, then, is a controlling group less than a majority in size that is not a pure artifact of democratic rules. It is a minority of individuals whose preferences regularly prevail in cases of differences in preference on key political issues. If we are to avoid an infinite regress of explanations, the composition of the ruling elite must be more or less definitely specified.

II. Some Bad Tests

The hypothesis we are dealing with would run along these lines: "Such and such a political system (the U.S., the U.S.S.R., New Haven, or the like) is a ruling elite system in which the ruling elite has the following membership." Membership would then be specified by name, position, socio-economic class, socio-economic roles, or what not.

Let me now turn to the problem of testing a hypothesis of this sort, and begin by indicating a few tests that are sometimes mistakenly taken as adequate.

The first improper test confuses a ruling elite with a group that has a high *potential for control.* Let me explain. Suppose a set of individuals in a political system has the following property: there is a very high probability that if they agree on a key political alternative, and if they all act in some specified way, then that alternative will be chosen. We may say of such a group that it has a *high potential for control.* In a large and complex society like ours, there may be many such groups. For example, the bureaucratic triumvirate of Professor Mills would appear to have a high potential for control.[2] In the city of New Haven, with which I have some acquaintance, I do not doubt that the leading business figures together with the leaders of both political parties have a high potential for control. But a potential for control is not, except in a peculiarly Hobbesian world, equivalent to actual control. If the military leaders of this country and their subordinates agreed that it was desirable, they could most assuredly establish a military dictatorship of the most overt sort; nor would they need the aid of leaders of business corporations or the executive branch of our government. But they have not set up such a dictatorship. For what is lacking are the premises I mentioned earlier, namely agreement on a key political alternative and some set of specific implementing actions. That is to say, a group may have a high potential for control and a *low potential for unity*. The actual *political effectiveness* of a group is a function of its potential for control *and* its potential for unity. Thus a group with a relatively low potential for control but a high potential for unity may be more politically effective than a group with a high potential for control but a low potential for unity.

The second improper test confuses a ruling elite with a group of individuals who have more influence than any others in the system. I take it for granted that in every human organization some individuals have more influence over key decisions than do others. Political equality may well be among the most Utopian of all human goals. But it is fallacious to assume that the absence of political equality proves the existence of a ruling elite.

The third improper test, which is closely related to the preceding one, is to generalize from a single scope of influence. Neither logically nor empirically does it follow that a group with a high degree of influence over one scope will necessarily

[2] C. Wright Mills, *The Power Elite* (New York, 1956), *passim*.

have a high degree of influence over another scope within the same system. This is a matter to be determined empirically. Any investigation that does not take into account the possibility that different elite groups have different scopes is suspect. By means of sloppy questions one could easily seem to discover that there exists a unified ruling elite in New Haven; for there is no doubt that small groups of people make many key decisions. It appears to be the case, however, that the small group that runs urban redevelopment is not the same as the small group that runs public education, and neither is quite the same as the two small groups that run the two parties. Moreover the small group that runs urban redevelopment with a high degree of unity would almost certainly disintegrate if its activities were extended to either education or the two political parties.

III. A Proposed Test

If tests like these are not valid, what can we properly require?

Let us take the simplest possible situation. Assume that there have been some number—I will not say how many—of cases where there has been disagreement within the political system on key political choices. Assume further that the hypothetical ruling elite prefers one alternative and other actors in the system prefer other alternatives. Then unless it is true that in all or very nearly all of these cases the alternative preferred by the ruling elite is actually adopted, the hypothesis (that the system is dominated by the specified ruling elite) is clearly false.

I do not want to pretend either that the research necessary to such a test is at all easy to carry out or that community life lends itself conveniently to strict interpretation according to the requirements of the test. *But I do not see how anyone can suppose that he has established the dominance of a specific group in a community or a nation without basing his analysis on the careful examination of a series of concrete decisions.* And these decisions must either constitute the universe or a fair sample from the universe of key political decisions taken in the political system.

Now it is a remarkable and indeed astounding fact that neither Professor Mills nor Professor Hunter has seriously attempted to examine an array of specific cases to test his major hypothesis.[3] Yet I suppose these two works more than any others in the social sciences of the last few years have sought to interpret complex political systems essentially as instances of a ruling elite.

To sum up: The hypothesis of the existence of a ruling elite can be strictly tested only if:

1. The hypothetical ruling elite is a well-defined group.
2. There is a fair sample of cases involving key political decisions in which the preferences of the hypothetical ruling elite run counter to those of any other likely group that might be suggested.
3. In such cases, the preferences of the elite regularly prevail.

IV. Difficulties and Objections

Several objections might be raised against the test I propose.

First, one might argue that the test is *too weak*. The argument would run as follows: If a ruling elite *doesn't* exist in a community, then the test is satisfactory; that is, if every hypothetical ruling elite is compared with alternative control groups, and in fact no ruling elite exists, then the test will in-

---

[3] Mills, *op. cit.;* Floyd Hunter, *Community Power Structure* (Chapel Hill, 1953).

deed show that there is no minority whose preferences regularly prevail on key political alternatives. But—it might be said—suppose a ruling elite *does* exist. The test will not *necessarily* demonstrate its existence, since we may not have selected the right group as our hypothetical ruling elite. Now this objection is valid; but it suggests the point I made at the outset about the possibility of an infinite regress of explanations. Unless we use the test on every possible combination of individuals in the community, we cannot be certain that there is not some combination that constitutes a ruling elite. But since there is no more *a priori* reason to assume that a ruling elite does exist than to assume that one does not exist, the burden of proof does not rest upon the critic of the hypothesis, but upon its proponent. And a proponent must specify what group he has in mind as his ruling elite. Once the group is specified, then the test I have suggested is, at least in principle, valid.

Second, one could object that the test is *too strong*. For suppose that the members of the "ruled" group are indifferent as to the outcome of various political alternatives. Surely (one could argue) if there is another group that regularly gets its way in the face of this indifference, it is in fact the ruling group in the society. Now my reasons for wishing to discriminate this case from the other involve more than a mere question of the propriety of using the term "ruling elite," which is only a term of convenience. There is, I think, a difference of some theoretical significance between a system in which a small group dominates over another that is opposed to it, and one in which a group dominates over an indifferent mass. In the second case, the alternatives at stake can hardly be regarded as "key political issues" if we assume the point of view of the indifferent mass; whereas in the first case it is reasonable to say that the alternatives involve a key political issue from the standpoint of both groups. Earlier I refrained from defining the concept "key political issues." If we were to do so at this point, it would seem reasonable to require as a necessary although possibly not a sufficient condition that the issue should involve actual disagreement in preferences among two or more groups. In short, the case of "indifference vs. preference" would be ruled out.

However, I do not mean to dispose of the problem simply by definition. The point is to make sure that the two systems are distinguished. The test for the second, weaker system of elite rule would then be merely a modification of the test proposed for the first and more stringent case. It would again require an examination of a series of cases showing uniformly that when "the word" was authoritatively passed down from the designated elite, the hitherto indifferent majority fell into ready compliance with an alternative that had nothing else to recommend it intrinsically.

Third, one might argue that the test will not discriminate between a true ruling elite and a ruling elite together with its satellites. This objection is in one sense true and in one sense false. It is true that on a series of key political questions, an apparently unified group might prevail who would, according to our test, thereby constitute a ruling elite. Yet an inner core might actually make the decisions for the whole group.

However, one of two possibilities must be true. Either the inner core and the front men always agree at all times in the decision process, or they do not. But if they always agree, then it follows from one of our two assumptions about influence that the distinction between an "inner core" and "front men" has no operational meaning; that is, there is no conceivable way to distinguish between them. And if they do not always agree, then the test simply requires a comparison at those points in time when they disagree. Here again, the advantages of concrete cases are palpable, for these enable one to discover who initiates or vetoes and who merely complies.

Fourth, it might be said that the test is either too demanding or else it is too arbitrary. If it requires that the hypothetical elite prevails in *every single case,* then it demands too much. But if it does not require this much, then at what point can a ruling elite be said to exist? When it prevails in 7 cases out of 10? 8 out of 10? 9 out of 10? Or what? There are two answers to this objection. On the one hand, it would be quite reasonable to argue, I think, that since we are considering only key political choices and not trivial decisions, if the elite does not prevail in *every* case in which it disagrees with a contrary group, it cannot properly be called a ruling elite. But since I have not supplied an independent definition of the term "key political choices," I must admit that this answer is not wholly satisfactory. On the other hand, I would be inclined to suggest that in this instance as in many others we ought not to assume that political reality will be as discrete and discontinuous as the concepts we find convenient to employ. We can say that a system approximates a true ruling elite system, to a greater or lesser degree, without insisting that it exemplify the extreme and limiting case.

Fifth, it might be objected that the test I have proposed would not work in the most obvious of all cases of ruling elites, namely in the totalitarian dictatorships. For the control of the elite over the expression of opinion is so great that overtly there is no disagreement; hence no cases on which to base a judgment arise. This objection is a fair one. But we are not concerned here with totalitarian systems. We are concerned with the application of the techniques of modern investigation to American communities, where, except in very rare cases, terror is not so pervasive that the investigator is barred from discovering the preferences of citizens. Even in Little Rock, for example, newspaper men seemed to have had little difficulty in finding diverse opinions; and a northern political scientist of my acquaintance has managed to complete a large number of productive interviews with white and Negro Southerners on the touchy subject of integration.

Finally one could argue that even in a society like ours a ruling elite might be so influential over ideas, attitudes, and opinions that a kind of false consensus will exist—not the phony consensus of a terroristic totalitarian dictatorship but the manipulated and superficially self-imposed adherence to the norms and goals of the elite by broad sections of a community. A good deal of Professor Mills' argument can be interpreted in this way, although it is not clear to me whether this is what he means to rest his case on.

Even more than the others this objection points to the need to be circumspect in interpreting the evidence. Yet here, too, it seems to me that the hypothesis cannot be satisfactorily confirmed without something equivalent to the test I have proposed. For once again either the consensus is perpetual and unbreakable, in which case there is no conceivable way of determining who is ruler and who is ruled. Or it is not. But if it is not, then there is some point in the process of forming opinions at which the one group will be seen to initiate and veto, while the rest merely respond. And we can only discover these points *by an examination of a series of concrete cases where key decisions are made:* decisions on taxation and expenditures, subsidies, welfare programs, military policy, and so on.

It would be interesting to know, for example, whether the initiation and veto of alternatives having to do with our missile program would confirm Professor Mills' hypothesis, or indeed any reasonable hypothesis about the existence of a ruling elite. To the superficial observer it would scarcely appear that the military itself is a homogeneous group, to say nothing of their supposed coalition with corporate and political executives. If the military alone or the coalition together is a ruling elite, it is either incredibly incompetent in administering its own fundamental affairs or else it is unconcerned with the success of its policies to a degree that I find astounding.

However I do not mean to examine the evidence here. For the whole point of this paper is that the evidence for a ruling elite, either in the United States or in any specific community, has not yet been properly examined so far as I know. And the evidence has not been properly examined, I have tried to argue, because the examination has not employed satisfactory criteria to determine what constitutes a fair test of the basic hypothesis.

"Power Elite" or "Veto Groups"?

BY WILLIAM KORNHAUSER

I

In the fifties two books appeared purporting to describe the structure of power in present-day America. They reached opposite conclusions: where C. Wright Mills found a "power elite," David Riesman found "veto groups." Both books have enjoyed a wide response, which has tended to divide along ideological lines. It would appear that *The Power Elite* has been most favorably received by radical intellectuals, and *The Lonely Crowd* has found its main response among liberals. Mills and Riesman have not been oblivious to their differences. Mills is quite explicit on the matter: Riesman is a "romantic pluralist" who refuses to see the forest of American power inequalities for the trees of short-run and discrete balances of power among diverse groups (244).[1] Riesman has been less explicitly polemical, but he might have had Mills in mind when he spoke of those intellectuals "who feel themselves very much out of power and who are frightened of those who they think have the power," and who "prefer to be scared by the power structures they conjure up than to face the possibility

William Kornhauser is professor of sociology at the University of California, Berkeley. He is the author of The Politics of Mass Society *and* Scientists in Industry. *This paper appeared as a chapter in* Culture and Social Character, *a set of essays in honor of David Riesman, edited by Seymour M. Lipset and Leo Lowenthal* (New York: The Free Press, 1961).

[1] Page references in the text for remarks by C. Wright Mills refer to *The Power Elite* (New York: Oxford University Press, 1956).

37

that the power structure they believe exists has largely evaporated" (257–258).[2]

I wish to intervene in this controversy just long enough to do two things: (1) locate as precisely as possible the items upon which Riesman and Mills disagree; and (2) formulate certain underlying issues in the analysis of power that have to be met before such specific disagreements as those between Riesman and Mills can profitably be resolved.

We may compare Mills and Riesman on power in America along five dimensions:

1. Structure of power: how power is distributed among the major segments of present-day American society.
2. Changes in the structure of power: how the distribution of power has changed in the course of American history.
3. Operation of the structure of power: the means whereby power is exercised in American society.
4. Bases of the structure of power: how social and psychological factors shape and sustain the existing distribution of power.
5. Consequences of the structure of power: how the existing distribution of power affects American society.

1. Structure of Power

It is symptomatic of their underlying differences that Mills entitles his major consideration of power simply "the power elite," whereas Riesman has entitled one of his discussions "who has the power?" Mills is quite certain about the location of power, and so indicates by the assertive form of his title. Riesman perceives a much more amorphous and indeterminate

[2] Page references in the text for remarks by David Riesman refer to *The Lonely Crowd* (New York: Doubleday Anchor, 1953).

power situation, and conveys this view in the interrogative form of his title. These contrasting images of American power may be diagrammed as two different pyramids of power. Mills' pyramid of power contains three levels:

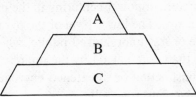

The apex of the pyramid (A) is the "power elite": a unified power group composed of the top government executives, military officials, and corporation directors. The second level (B) comprises the "middle levels of power": a diversified and balanced plurality of interest groups, perhaps most visibly at work in the halls of Congress. The third level (C) is the "mass society": the powerless mass of unorganized and atomized people who are controlled from above.

Riesman's pyramid of power contains only two major levels:

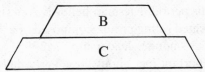

The two levels roughly correspond to Mills' second and third levels, and have been labeled accordingly. The obvious difference between the two pyramids is the presence of a peak in the one case and its absence in the other. Riesman sees no "power elite," in the sense of a single unified power group at the top of the structure, and this in the simplest terms contrasts his image of power in America with that of Mills. The upper level of Riesman's pyramid (B) consists of "veto groups": a diversified and balanced plurality of interest groups, each of which is primarily concerned with protecting its jurisdiction by blocking efforts of other groups that seem to threaten that jurisdiction. There is no decisive ruling group here, but rather an amorphous structure of power centering in the interplay among these interest groups. The lower level of the pyramid (C) comprises the more or less unorganized public, which is sought as an ally (rather than dominated) by the interest groups in their maneuvers against actual or threatened encroachments on the jurisdiction each claims for itself.

2. *Changes in the Structure of Power*

Riesman and Mills agree that the American power structure has gone through four major epochs. They disagree on the present and prospective future in the following historical terms: Mills judges the present to represent a fifth epoch, whereas Riesman judges it to be a continuation of the fourth.

The first period, according to Mills and Riesman, extended roughly from the founding of the republic to the Jacksonian era. During this period, Riesman believes America possessed a clearly demarcated ruling group, composed of a "landed-gentry and mercantilist-money leadership" (239). According to Mills, "the important fact about these early days is that social life, economic institutions, military establishment, and political order coincided, and men who were high politicians also played key roles in the economy and, with their families, were among those of the reputable who made up local society" (270).

The second period extended roughly from the decline of Federalist leadership to the Civil War. During this period power became more widely dispersed, and it was no longer possible to identify a sharply defined ruling group. "In this society," Mills writes, "the 'elite' became a plurality of top groups, each in turn quite loosely made up" (270). Riesman notes that farmer and artisan groups became influential, and "occasionally, as with Jackson, moved into a more positive command" (240).

The third period began after the Civil War and extended through McKinley's administration in Riesman's view (240) and until the New Deal according to Mills (271). They agree that the era of McKinley marked the high point of the unilateral supremacy of corporate economic power. During this period, power once more became concentrated, but unlike the Federalist period and also unlike subsequent periods, the higher circles of economic institutions were dominant.

The fourth period took definite shape in the 1930's. In Riesman's view this period marked the ascendancy of the "veto groups," and rule by coalitions rather than by a unified power group. Mills judges it to have been so only in the early and middle Roosevelt administrations: "In these years, the New Deal as a system of power was essentially a balance of pressure groups and interest blocs" (273).

Up to World War II, then, Mills and Riesman view the historical development of power relations in America along strikingly similar lines. Their sharply contrasting portrayal of present-day American power relations begins with their diverging assessments of the period beginning about 1940. Mills envisions World War II and its aftermath as marking a new era in American power relations. With war as the major problem, there arises a new power group composed of corporate, governmental, and military directors.

> The formation of the power elite, as we may now know it, occurred during World War II and its aftermath. In the course of the organization of the nation for that war, and the consequent stabilization of the war-like posture, certain types of man have been selected and formed, and in the course of these

institutional and psychological developments, new opportunities and intentions have arisen among them.[3]

Where Mills sees the ascendancy of a power elite, Riesman sees the opposite tendency toward the dispersal of power among a plurality of organized interests:

> There has been in the last fifty years a change in the configuration of power in America, in which a single hierarchy with a ruling class at its head has been replaced by a number of "veto groups" among which power is dispersed (239).

> The shifting nature of the lobby provides us with an important clue as to the difference between the present American political scene and that of the age of McKinley. The ruling class of businessmen could relatively easily (though perhaps mistakenly) decide where their interests lay and what editors, lawyers, and legislators might be paid to advance them. The lobby ministered to the clear leadership, privilege, and imperative of the business ruling class. Today we have substituted for that leadership a series of groups, each of which has struggled for and finally attained a power to stop things conceivably inimical to its interests and, within far narrower limits, to start things (246–247).

In short, both Mills and Riesman view the current scene from an historical perspective; but where one finds a hitherto unknown *concentration* of power, the other finds an emerging *indeterminacy* of power.

3. *Operation of the Structure of Power*

Mills believes the power elite sets all important public policies, especially foreign policy. Riesman, on the other hand, does not believe that the same group or coalition of groups sets

[3] C. Wright Mills, "The Power Elite," in A. Kornhauser (ed.), *Problems of Power in American Society* (Detroit: Wayne State University Press, 1957), p. 161.

all major policies, but rather that the question of who exercises power varies with the issue at stake: most groups are inoperative on most issues, and all groups are operative primarily on those issues that vitally impinge on their central interests. This is to say that there are as many power structures as there are distinctive spheres of policy (256).

As to the modes of operation, both Mills and Riesman point to increasing *manipulation,* rather than command or persuasion, as the favored form of power play. Mills emphasizes the secrecy behind which important policy-determination occurs. Riesman stresses not so much manipulation under the guise of secrecy as manipulation under the guise of mutual tolerance for one another's interests and beliefs. Manipulation occurs, according to Riesman, because each group is trying to hide its concern with power in order not to antagonize other groups. Power relations tend to take the form of "monopolistic competition": "rules of fairness and fellowship [rather than the impersonal forces of competition] dictate how far one can go" (247). Thus both believe the play of power takes place to a considerable extent backstage; but Mills judges this power play to be under the direction of one group, while Riesman sees it as controlled by a mood and structure of accommodation among many groups.

Mills maintains that the mass media of communication are important instruments of manipulation: the media lull people to sleep, so to speak, by suppressing political topics and by emphasizing "entertainment." Riesman alleges that the mass media give more attention to politics and problems of public policy than their audiences actually want, and thereby convey the false impression that there is more interest in public affairs than really exists in America at the present time. Where Mills judges the mass media of communication to be powerful political instruments in American society (315–316), Riesman argues that they have relatively little significance in this respect (228–231).

4. Bases of the Structure of Power

Power tends to be patterned according to the structure of interests in a society. Power is shared among those whose interests coincide, and divides along lines where interests diverge. To Mills, the power elite is a reflection and solidification of a *coincidence of interests* among the ascendant institutional orders. The power elite rests on the "many interconnections and points of coinciding interests" of the corporations, political institutions, and military services (19). For Riesman, on the other hand, there is an amorphous power structure, which reflects a *diversity of interests* among the major organized groups. The power structure of veto groups rests on the divergent interests of political parties, business groups, labor organizations, farm blocs, and a myriad of other organized groups (247).

But power is not a simple reflex of interests alone. It also rests on the capabilities and opportunities for cooperation among those who have similar interests, and for confrontation among those with opposing interests. Mills argues in some detail that the power elite rests not merely on the coincidence of interests among major institutions but also on the "psychological similarity and social intermingling" of their higher circles (19). By virtue of similar social origins (old family, upper-class background), religious affiliations (Episcopalian and Presbyterian), education (Ivy League college or military academy), and the like, those who head up the major institutions share codes and values as well as material interests. This makes for easy communication, especially when many of these people already know one another, or at least know many people in common. They share a common way of life, and therefore possess both the will and the opportunity to integrate their lines of action as representatives of key institutions. At times this integration involves "explicit co-ordination," as during war (19–20). So much for the bases of power at the apex of the structure.

At the middle and lower levels of power, Mills emphasizes the lack of independence and concerted purpose among those who occupy similar social positions. In his book on the middle classes,[4] Mills purports to show the weakness of white-collar people that results from their lack of economic independence and political direction. The white-collar worker simply follows the more powerful group of the moment. In his book on labor leaders,[5] Mills located the alleged political impotence of organized labor in its dependence on government. Finally, the public is conceived as composed of atomized and submissive individuals who are incapable of engaging in effective communication and political action (302 ff.).

Riesman believes that power "is founded, in large measure, on interpersonal expectations and attitudes" (253). He asserts that in addition to the diversity of interest underlying the pattern of power in America there is the psycho-cultural fact of widespread feelings of weakness and dependence at the top as well as at the bottom of the power structure: "If businessmen feel weak and dependent they do in actuality become weaker and more dependent, no matter what material resources may be ascribed to them" (253). In other words, the amorphousness of power in America rests in part on widespread feelings of weakness and dependence. These feelings are found among those whose position in the social structure provides resources that they could exploit, as well as among those whose position provides less access to the means of power. In fact, Riesman is

[4] *White Collar* (New York: Oxford University Press, 1951).
[5] *The New Men of Power* (New York: Harcourt, Brace and Company, 1948).

concerned to show that people at all levels of the social structure tend to feel weaker than their objective position warrants.

The theory of types of conformity that provides the foundation of so much of Riesman's writings enters into his analysis of power at this point. The "other-directed" orientation in culture and character helps to sustain the amorphousness of power. The other-directed person in politics is the "inside-dopester," the person who possesses political competence but avoids political commitment. This is the dominant type in the veto groups, since other-direction is prevalent in the strata from which their leaders are drawn. "Both within the [veto] groups and in the situation created by their presence, the political mood tends to become one of other-directed tolerance" (248). However, Riesman does not make the basis of power solely psychological:

> This does not mean, however, that the veto groups are formed along the lines of character structure. As in a business corporation there is room for extreme inner-directed and other-directed types, and all mixtures between, so in a veto group there can exist complex "symbiotic" relationships among people of different political styles. . . . Despite these complications I think it fair to say that the veto groups, even when they are set up to protect a clearcut moralizing interest, are generally forced to adopt the political manners of the other-directed (249).

Riesman and Mills agree that there is widespread apathy in American society, but they disagree on the social distribution of political apathy. Mills locates the apathetic primarily among the lower social strata, whereas Riesman finds extensive apathy in higher as well as lower strata. Part of the difference may rest on what criteria of apathy are used. Mills conceives of apathy as the lack of political meaning in one's life, the failure to think of personal interests in political terms, so that what happens in politics does not appear to be related to personal troubles.[6] Riesman extends the notion of apathy to include the politically uninformed as well as the politically uncommitted.[7] Thus political indignation undisciplined by political understanding is not a genuine political orientation. Riesman judges political apathy to be an important *basis* for amorphous power relations. Mills, on the other hand, treats political apathy primarily as a *result* of the concentration of power.

5. Consequences of the Structure of Power

Four parallel sets of consequences of the structure of power for American society may be inferred from the writings of Mills and Riesman. The first concerns the impact of the power structure on the interests of certain groups or classes in American society. Mills asserts that the existing power arrangements enhance the interests of the major institutions whose directors constitute the power elite (276 ff.). Riesman asserts the contrary: no one group or class is decisively favored over others by the culminated decisions on public issues (257).

The second set of consequences concerns the impact of the structure of power on the quality of politics in American society. Here Mills and Riesman are in closer agreement. Mills maintains that the concentration of power in a small circle, and the use of manipulation as the favored manner of exercising power, lead to the decline of politics as public debate. People are decreasingly capable of grasping political issues, and of relating them to personal interests.[8] Riesman also believes that politics has declined in meaning for large numbers of people.

---

[6] *White Collar,* p. 327.

[7] David Riesman and Nathan Glazer, "Criteria for Political Apathy," in Alvin W. Gouldner (ed.), *Studies in Leadership* (New York: Harper & Brothers, 1950).

[8] *White Collar,* pp. 342–350.

This is not due simply to the ascendancy of "veto groups," although they do foster "the tolerant mood of other-direction and hasten the retreat of the inner-directed indignants" (251). More important, the increasing complexity and remoteness of politics make political self-interest obscure and aggravate feelings of impotence even when self-interest is clear.[9]

The third set of consequences of the American power structure concerns its impact on the quality of power relations themselves. Mills contends that the concentration of power has taken place without a corresponding shift in the bases of legitimacy of power: power is still supposed to reside in the public and its elected representatives, whereas in reality it resides in the hands of those who direct the key bureaucracies. As a consequence, men of power are neither responsible nor accountable for their power (316–317). Riesman also implies that there is a growing discrepancy between the facts of power and the images of power, but for the opposite reason from Mills: power is more widely dispersed than is generally believed (257–258).

Finally, a fourth set of consequences concerns the impact of the power structure on democratic leadership. If power tends to be lodged in a small group that is not accountable for its power, and if politics no longer involves genuine public debate, then there will be a *severe weakening of democratic institutions,* if not of leadership (the power elite exercises leadership in one sense of the term, in that it makes decisions on basic policy for the nation). Mills claims that power in America has become so concentrated that it increasingly resembles the Soviet system of power:

> Official commentators like to contrast the ascendancy in totalitarian countries of a tightly organized clique with the American system of power. Such comments, however, are easier to

[9] "Criteria for Political Apathy," p. 520.

sustain if one compares mid-twentieth-century Russia with mid-nineteenth-century America, which is what is often done by Tocqueville-quoting Americans making the contrast. But that was an America of a century ago, and in the century that has passed, the American elite have not remained as patrioteer essayists have described them to us. The "loose cliques" now head institutions of a scale and power not then existing and, especially since World War I, the loose cliques have tightened up (271).

If, on the other hand, power tends to be dispersed among groups that are primarily concerned to protect and defend their interests rather than to advance general policies and their own leadership, and if at the same time politics has declined as a sphere of duty and self-interest, then there will be a *severe weakening of leadership*. Thus Riesman believes that "power in America seems to [be] situational and mercurial; it resists attempts to locate it" (257). This "indeterminacy and amorphousness" of power inhibits the development of leadership: "Where the issue involves the country as a whole, no individual or group leadership is likely to be very effective, because the entrenched veto groups cannot be budged" (257). "Veto groups exist as defense groups, not as leadership groups" (248). Yet Riesman does not claim that the decline of leadership directly threatens American democracy, at least in the short run: the dispersion of power among a diversity of balancing "veto groups" operates to support democratic institutions even as it inhibits effective leadership. The long-run prospects of a leaderless democracy are of course less promising.

II

In the second part of this paper, I wish to raise certain critical questions about Riesman's and Mills' images of power.

TWO PORTRAITS OF THE AMERICAN POWER STRUCTURE

	MILLS	RIESMAN
LEVELS	a. Unified power elite b. Diversified and balanced plurality of interest groups c. Mass of unorganized people who have practically no power over elite	a. No dominant power elite b. Diversified and balanced plurality of interest groups c. Mass of unorganized people who have some power over interest groups
CHANGES	a. Increasing concentration of power	a. increasing dispersion of power
OPERATION	a. One group determines all major policies b. Manipulation of people at the bottom by group at the top	a. Who determines policy shifts with the issue b. Monopolistic competition among organized groups
BASES	a. Coincidence of interests among major institutions (economic, military, governmental)	a. Diversity of interests among major organized groups b. Sense of weakness and dependence among those in higher as well as lower status
CONSEQUENCES	a. Enhancement of interests of corporations, armed forces, and executive branch of government b. Decline of politics as public debate c. Decline of responsible and accountable power—loss of democracy	a. No one group or class is favored significantly over others b. Decline of politics as duty and self-interest c. Decline of capacity for effective leadership

One set of questions seeks to probe more deeply the basic area of disagreement in their views. A second set of questions concerns their major areas of agreement.

Power usually is analyzed according to its distribution among the several units of a system. Most power analysts construe the structure of power as a *hierarchy*—a rank-order of units according to their amount of power. The assumption often is made that there is only one such structure, and that all units may be ranked vis-à-vis one another. Units higher in the hierarchy have power over units lower in the structure, so there is a one-way flow of power. Mills tends to adopt this image of the structure of power.

Riesman rejects this conception of the power structure as mere hierarchy:

> The determination of who [has more power] has to be made all over again for our time: we cannot be satisfied with the answers given by Marx, Mosca, Michels, Pareto, Weber, Veblen, or Burnham (255).

> The image of power in contemporary America presented [in *The Lonely Crowd*] departs from current discussions of power which are usually based on a search for a ruling class (260).

Riesman is not just denying the existence of a power elite in contemporary American society; he is also affirming the need to consider other aspects of power than only its unequal distribution. He is especially concerned to analyze common responses to power:

> If the leaders have lost the power, why have the led not gained it? What is there about the other-directed man and his life situation which prevents the transfer? In terms of situation, it seems that the pattern of monopolistic competition of the veto groups resists individual attempts at power aggrandizement. In terms of character, the other-directed man simply

does not seek power; perhaps, rather, he avoids and evades it (275).

Whereas Mills emphasizes the *differences* between units according to their power, Riesman emphasizes their *similarities* in this respect. In the first view, some units are seen as dominated by other units, while in the second view, all units are seen as subject to constraints that shape and limit their use of power *in similar directions.*

The problem of power is not simply the differential capacity to make decisions, so that those who have power bind those who do not. Constraints also operate on those who are in decision-making positions, for if these are the places where acts of great consequence occur, so are they the targets for social pressures. These pressures become translated into restrictions on the alternatives among which decision-makers can choose. Power may be meaningfully measured by ascertaining the range of alternatives that decision-makers can realistically consider. To identify those who make decisions is not to say how many lines of action are open to them, or how much freedom of choice they enjoy.

A major advance in the study of power is made by going beyond a formal conception of power, in which those who have the authority to make decisions are assumed to possess the effective means of power and the will to use it. Nor can it be assumed that those not in authority lack the power to determine public policy. The identification of effective sources of power requires analysis of how *decision-makers are themselves subject to various kinds of constraint.* Major sources of constraint include (1) opposing elites and active publics; and (2) cultural values and associated psychological receptivities and resistances to power. A comparison of Mills and Riesman with respect to these categories of constraint reveals the major area of disagreement between them.

Mills implies that both sources of constraint are by and large inoperative on the highest levels of power. (1) There is little opposition among the top power-holders. Since they are not in opposition to one another, they do not constrain one another. Instead, they are unified and mutually supportive. Furthermore, there are few publics to constrain the elite. Groups capable of effective participation in broad policy determination have been replaced by atomized masses that are powerless to affect policy, since they lack the social bases for association and communication. Instead, people in large numbers are manipulated through organizations and media controlled by the elite. (2) Older values and codes no longer grip elites, nor have they been replaced by new values and codes that could regulate the exercise of power. Top men of power are not constrained either by an inner moral sense or by feelings of dependence on others. The widespread permissiveness toward the use of expedient means to achieve success produces "the higher immorality," that is to say, elites that are irresponsible in the use of power.

In sharp contrast to Mills, Riesman attaches great importance to both kinds of constraints on decision-makers. (1) There is a plethora of organized groups, "each of which has struggled for and finally attained a power to stop things conceivably inimical to its interests" (247). Furthermore, there is extensive opportunity for large numbers of people to influence decision-makers, because the latter are constrained by their competitive relations with one another to bid for support in the electoral arena and more diffusely in the realm of public relations. (2) The cultural emphasis on "mutual tolerance" and social conformity places a premium on "getting along" with others at the expense of taking strong stands. People are psychologically disposed to avoid long-term commitments as a result of their strong feelings of dependence on their immediate peers. "Other-directed" persons seek approval rather than power.

In general, the decisive consideration in respect to the restraint of power is the presence of multiple centers of power. Where there are many power groups, not only are they mutually constrained; they also are dependent on popular support, and therefore responsive to public demands. Now, there are many readily observable cases of institutionalized opposition among power groups in American society. In the economic sphere, collective bargaining between management and labor is conflict of this kind; and to the extent that "countervailing power" among a few large firms has been replacing competition among many small firms in the market place, there is a *de facto* situation of opposition among economic elites. In the political sphere, there is a strong two-party system and more or less stable factionalism within both parties, opposition among interest blocs in state and national legislatures, rivalry among executive agencies of government and the military services, and so forth.

Mills relegates these conflicting groups to the middle levels of power. Political parties and interest groups, both inside and outside of government, are not important units in the structure of power, according to Mills. It would seem that he takes this position primarily with an eye to the sphere of foreign policy, where only a few people finally make the big decisions. But he fails to put his argument to a decisive or meaningful test: he does not examine the pattern of decisions to show that foreign policy not only is made *by* a few people (this, after all, is a constitutional fact), but that it is made *for their particular interests*. Mills' major premise seems to be that all decisions are taken by and for special interests; there is no action oriented toward the general interests of the whole community. Furthermore, Mills seems to argue that because only a very few people occupy key decision-making *positions,* they are free to decide on whatever best suits their particular interests. But the degree of *autonomy* of decision-makers cannot be inferred from the *number* of decision-makers, nor from the *scope* of their decisions. It is determined by the character of decision-making, especially the dependence of decision-makers on certain kinds of *procedure* and *support.*

Just as Mills is presenting a distorted image of power in America when he fails to consider the pressures on those in high positions, so Riesman presents a biased picture by not giving sufficient attention to *power differentials* among the various groups in society. When Riesman implies that if power is dispersed, then it must be relatively equal among groups and interests, with no points of concentration, he is making an unwarranted inference. The following statement conjures up an image of power in America that is as misleading on its side as anything Mills has written in defense of his idea of a power elite.

> One might ask whether one would not find, over a long period of time, that decisions in America favored one group or class . . . over others. Does not wealth exert its pull in the long run? In the past this has been so; for the future I doubt it. The future seems to be in the hands of the small business and professional men who control Congress, such as realtors, lawyers, car salesmen, undertakers, and so on; of the military men who control defense and, in part, foreign policy; of the big business managers and their lawyers, finance-committee men, and other counselors who decide on plant investment and influence the rate of technological change; of the labor leaders who control worker productivity and worker votes; of the black belt whites who have the greatest stake in southern politics; of the Poles, Italians, Jews, and Irishmen who have stakes in foreign policy, city jobs, and ethnic, religious and cultural organizations; of the editorializers and storytellers

who help socialize the young, tease and train the adult, and amuse and annoy the aged; of the farmers—themselves a warring congeries of cattlemen, corn men, dairymen, cotton men, and so on—who control key departments and committees and who, as the living representatives of our inner-directed past, control many of our memories; of the Russians and, to a lesser degree, other foreign powers who control much of our agenda of attention; and so on (257).

It appears that Riesman is asking us to believe that power differentials do not exist, but only differences in the spheres within which groups exercise control.

If Riesman greatly exaggerates the extent to which organized interests possess equal power, nevertheless he poses an important problem that Mills brushes aside. For Riesman goes beyond merely noting the existence of opposition among "veto groups" to suggest that they operate to smother one another's initiative and leadership. It is one thing for interest groups to constrain one another; it is something else again when they produce stalemate. Riesman has pointed to a critical problem for a pluralist society: the danger that power may become fragmented among so many competing groups that effective general leadership cannot emerge.

On Mills' side, it is indisputable that American political institutions have undergone extensive centralization and bureaucratization. This is above all an *institutional* change wrought by the greatly expanded scale of events and decisions in the contemporary world. But centralization cannot be equated with a power elite. There can be highly centralized institutions and at the same time a fragmentation of power among a multiplicity of relatively independent public and private agencies. Thus Riesman would appear to be correct that the substance of power lies in the hands of many large organizations, and these organizations are not unified or coordinated in any firm fashion. If they were, surely Mills would have been able to identify the major mechanisms that could produce this result. That he has failed to do so is the most convincing evidence for their nonexistence.

To complete this analysis, we need only remind ourselves of the fundamental area of agreement between our two critics of American power relations. Both stress the *absence of effective* political action at all levels of the political order, in particular among the citizenry. For all of their differences, Mills and Riesman agree that there has been a decline in effective political participation, or at least a failure of political participation to measure up to the requirements of contemporary events and decisions. This failure has not been compensated by an increase in effective political action at the center: certainly Riesman's "veto groups" are not capable of defining and realizing the community's general aspirations; nor is Mills' "power elite" such a political agency. Both are asserting the inadequacy of political associations, including public opinion, party leadership, Congress, and the Presidency, even as they see the slippage of power in different directions. In consequence, neither is sanguine about the capacity of the American political system to provide responsible leadership, especially in international affairs.

If there is truth in this indictment, it also may have its sources in the very images of power that pervade Mills' and Riesman's thought. They are both inclined toward a negative response to power; and neither shows a willingness to confront the idea of a political system and the ends of power in it. Riesman reflects the liberal suspicion of power, as when he writes "we have come to realize that men who compete primarily for wealth are relatively harmless as compared with men who compete primarily for power." That such assertions as this may very well be true is beside the point. For certainly negative consequences of power can subsist alongside of positive ones. At times Riesman seems to recognize the need for people to seek and use power if they as individuals and the society as a whole are to develop to the fullest of their capacities. But his dominant orientation toward power remains highly individualistic and negative.

Mills is more extreme than Riesman on this matter, since he never asks what is socially required in the way of resources of power and uses of power, but instead is preoccupied with the magnitude of those resources and the (allegedly) destructive expropriation of them by and for the higher circles of major institutions. It is a very limited notion of power that construes it only in terms of coercion and conflict among particular interests. Societies require arrangements whereby resources of power can be effectively used and supplemented for public goals. This is a requirement for government, but the use of this term should not obscure that fact that government either commands power or lacks effectiveness. Mills does not concern himself with the *ends* of power, nor with the conditions for their attainment. He has no conception of the bases of political order, and no theory of the functions of government and politics. He suggests nothing that could prevent his "power elite" from developing into a full-blown totalitarianism. The logic of Mills' position finally reduces to a contest between anarchy and tyranny.

The problem of power seems to bring out the clinician in each of us. We quickly fasten on the pathology of power, whether we label the symptoms as "inside-dopesterism" (Riesman) or as "the higher immorality" (Mills). As a result, we often lose sight of the ends of power in the political system under review. It is important to understand that pivotal decisions increasingly are made at the national level, and that this poses genuine difficulties for the maintenance of democratic control. It is also important to understand that a multiplicity of public and private agencies increasingly pressure decision-makers, and that this poses genuine difficulties for the maintenance of effective political leadership. But the fact remains that there have been periods of centralized decision-making *and* democratic control, multiple constraints on power *and* effective leadership. There is no simple relationship between the extent to which power is equally distributed and the stability of democratic order. For a democratic order requires strong government as well as public consent by an informed citizenry. Unless current tendencies are measured against both sets of needs, there will be little progress in understanding how either one is frustrated or fulfilled. Finally, in the absence of more disciplined historical and comparative analysis, we shall continue to lack a firm basis for evaluating such widely divergent diagnoses of political malaise as those given us by Mills and Riesman.

The Distribution of Power in American Society

BY TALCOTT PARSONS

I

It has been remarked that it is relatively rare, in the United States at least, for social scientists to attempt interpretive analyses of major aspects of the total society in which they live. This is particularly true of sociologists, unlike economists, who have made notable attempts in recent years to interpret their societies—for example, Schumpeter's *Capitalism, Socialism and Democracy* and Galbraith's *American Capitalism*. The main exception is Robin M. Williams, whose *American Society* is excellent. If for this reason alone, Professor Mills' book, *The Power Elite*, which must be understood as one of a series as yet far from complete, would be worthy of serious attention.

In the nature of the case, to produce such a study is a very difficult enterprise. However operationally useful precise data may be—and Mr. Mills makes copious and, with some exceptions, relatively good use of them—they cannot suffice for a full empirical grounding of interpretive conclusions, not only because on their own level they are fragmentary and incomplete, but because many of the crucial empirical questions arise on a level at which available operational procedures are not of much or any use. This is not in the least to say that

Talcott Parsons is a sociologist at Harvard University. His books include Economy and Society, The Social System, *and* The Structure of Social Action. *This review first appeared in* World Politics, *October, 1957, and was then included in a collection of his own essays,* Structure and Process in Modern Societies *(New York: The Free Press, 1960), from which this version is reprinted.*

observation is not feasible, but rather that it cannot be precise observation in the usual operational sense.

I am referring to questions of the type which are central to Mr. Mills' argument, as to whether and in what sense a relatively small group of the occupants of "command posts" in the society has acquired a paramount position of power, as to whether the relative power of such a group has greatly increased in the last twenty years, as to how unified such a group is, and the like.

There are technical ways of reducing the element of arbitrariness in such judgments and protecting them against at least the grosser sorts of ideological distortion. Checking against all the available precise data is one such method; viewing the problem from the perspective given by wide and deep knowledge, not only of our own society but of others, is another. But I think the most important is exercising control through the use of a relatively well-integrated and technical theoretical scheme. Undertaking as a professional sociologist to review Mr. Mills' book, I am motivated largely by the opportunity to test some of his main conclusions against expectations derived from a type of technical theory that is at best only partially shared by the author of the book. In these terms I wish to take serious issue with Mr. Mills' position on a number of very important points and to outline an alternative interpretation of what I take to be the salient facts of the situation. There are some points at which I differ from Mills on simple questions of fact, but for the most part my criticisms will deal with empirical generalizations and their theoretical background.[1] These generalizations concern not only the facts he

[1] Mr. Mills is clearly writing only partly for an audience of technical social scientists. Though my own argument will be largely based on considerations of technical theory, I shall not introduce explicit justification of my theoretical judgments into this review, but will try to state my case in relatively non-technical terms.

chooses to state and emphasize but others he omits or treats as unimportant.

What is the gist of Mills' argument? I am able here to give only a very brief summary. The reader should not depend on this review alone for his information about the contents of the book itself, but should go directly to Mills' own statement of his case.

Mills' central theme is the contention—in contrast to what he refers to as the traditional view of the political pluralism of American society—that there has developed to an unprecedented degree, in the last generation or so, a concentration of power in the hands of a small, relatively tightly integrated group of people. These are defined as the people occupying the institutional "command posts" of the society, the places where the decisions are made that have the greatest immediate and direct influence on the course of events in the society and on the shaping of its future and that of the rest of the world, so far as that future is dependent on what happens in the United States. Mills argues that the power of this group has grown disproportionately to the growth in size and power of the society as a whole.

The "command posts" in question are centered in large-scale organizations, which are certainly a prominent feature of American society. The power elite are in general those who occupy the decision-making positions in these large organizations. Mills identifies these in only two basic areas, business and government—although for his purposes the field of government is subdivided into the military and the political sectors; indeed, he almost tends to treat the military as independent of the rest of government. He clearly is thinking of the centralized type of organization where a few "top executives" exercise the main immediate decision-making power, in contrast to the democratic association with a somewhat more de-centralized structure of authority and influence. It seems to be largely on this ground that he contends that the executive branch of the federal government has gained a pronounced ascendancy over the legislative. He relegates Congress—even the most influential group of Senators—to what he calls the "middle level" of the power structure; such people do not belong to the "power elite."

Mills broadly identifies the power elite with the "upper class." But he does not agree with Lloyd Warner and his group that the primary element of this upper class is a hereditary group of families or lineages; its position clearly depends on occupational status, though there is also emphasis on the importance within it of the "very rich," the majority of whom have inherited their wealth. Contrary to most sociological usage, Mills restricts the term "class" to an economic meaning, so that by "upper class" he means, essentially, the rich. But this still leaves open the question of the substantive relations between inherited and newly acquired wealth, family status relatively independent of at least very large wealth, occupational status within various income ranges, and similar problems.

Generally, Mills is rather vague on the relations between the power elite and other elements which in some sense enjoy rather high prestige. He emphasizes the prominence of lawyers among the "political directorate," but there is no clear analysis of the role of professional groups in the occupational structure generally; one presumes that except for a few lawyers who are successful in politics or business, and perhaps some engineers, professional people do not belong to the power elite. Similarly he emphasizes that members of the power elite have more than the average amount of education, and in particular he stresses the proportion who have been to select private schools and to

"Ivy League" colleges. In general, he is greatly concerned about the fact that the power elite are not "representative" of the population as a whole in the sense of constituting a random sample by socio-economic origin, by education, by ethnic group, etc. This is a point to which I shall return.

Neither the "higher circles" generally nor the component of the "very rich" (Mills' term) are a leisure class in Veblen's sense; many, if not most of them, "work" in various fields of business and financial management. Furthermore, the processes of recruitment are about what social scientists have come to expect. Mills does not give any exact criteria for what he considers to be "upper class" as a category of social origin, but I have the impression that he puts the line somewhat lower than most sociologists would. But, however that may be, it is clear that there is a considerable element of stability from generation to generation in the higher-status groups in American society. Thus, if, to employ a pattern used by Mills, we take a group of prominent persons, the family origin of from two-thirds to three-fourths of them will be the upper third of the American status structure. It is not these essential facts but the interpretation placed upon them which raises questions for us. The only point of fact I would question is whether the recruitment of the very rich has shown a sharper increase through the process of inheritance than through self-earning. It is possible that this is so, but I am inclined to doubt it, and in any case their position does not depend only on the process which Mills calls "cumulative advantage."

Mills radically denies that the group he calls the "very rich" and the "corporate rich" are distinct "classes," in his sense. He explicitly lumps them together and on the whole gives the very rich a greater position of influence than they are usually accorded or than, I think, they actually enjoy. This is in line with his thesis that there is a single, unified power elite.

Clearly, it is his contention that the base of the (business) group as a whole lies in command of the very large business enterprises—somewhat erroneously, or at least ambiguously, he puts the primary emphasis on control of property in accounting for this power.

Of the three main subgroups, Mills treats the "political directorate" as by far the weakest. It has, according to him, been greatly infiltrated by the business element, so that it can scarcely be treated as independent. Hence virtually the only element independent of what might be called the business oligarchy is the military—and this, he holds, is coming increasingly to fuse with the business group, or at least to form a close community of interest with it.

The pluralistic components of our older political traditions, Mills feels, are rooted primarily in local groupings—partly, of course, through the constitutional provisions which establish federalism and make Congressional representation dependent on local constituencies. But the operations of the big organizations have become national in scope and often international. Hence structures rooted in localism have simply been pushed into a secondary position.

But at the same time Mills contends that the structural base of authentic localism has been progressively atrophied through the development of what he calls the "mass society." The most conspicuous phenomena of the mass society are the prevalence and characteristics of the media of mass communication, which tend to serve as instruments of the power elite out of the reach of locally based "publics" and influential elements in them. The theory of the mass society is only very sketchily presented in one chapter near the end of the book, but is clearly meant to provide one of the main components of the total picture of American society which Mills is presenting.

In terms of recent history, one of Mills' main contentions

is that the New Deal period did not represent a turning point in social development, but rather a superficial flurry which only momentarily disturbed the process of emergence of the power elite and the dominance of the business contingent within it. Thus Mills speaks of the economic elite as in due course coming "to control and to use for their own purposes the New Deal institutions whose creation they had so bitterly denounced" (272–73).

Mills repeatedly disavows any intention of presenting a "conspiratorial" interpretation of American social and political development. He stresses the institutional positions occupied by his elite rather than their personalities and conspiratorial activities. Nevertheless he often comes very close to this implication because of his special theory that a peculiar irresponsibility attaches to the elite and their actions. By this he seems to mean the absence or relative ineffectiveness of formal legal restraints or of a system of "checks and balances" of the sort which has traditionally been associated with our political system. His contention, thus, is that the power elite has been freed from the historic restraints of our society and uses its power in terms of what he calls a "higher immorality"—a conception which is not very clearly explained.

Finally, it should be mentioned that in this, as in some of his previous writings, Mills' general tone toward both men and institutions is sharply caustic. *The Power Elite* certainly purports to be an exposition and an explanation of what has been happening in American society, but it is equally an indictment. There is no pretense of even trying to maintain a scientific neutrality; the book is a fiery and sarcastic attack on the pretensions of the "higher circles" in America, either to competence in exercise of their responsibilities, or to moral legitimation of their position. In such a case, the critic must ascertain the moral position from which the indictment is formulated; I shall have something to say about this later. In his combination of often insightful exposition and analysis, empirical one-sidedness and distortion, and moral indictment and sarcasm, Mills reminds one more of Veblen than of any other figure; that he has attained the stature of Veblen I question, but the role he is cutting out for himself is similar.

II

As I have said, the Mills analysis presents what, to me, is a subtle and complex combination of acceptable and unacceptable elements. Let me now attempt, at some of the most important points, to unravel these elements from each other. I want to try this first on the level of empirical generalization and then to raise one or two more strictly theoretical problems. I shall do so more in my own terms than in those employed by Mills.

In my opinion, two salient sets of processes have been going on in American society during the past half-century, the combination of which encompasses the main facts which are essential to our problem. The first of these is the dynamic of a maturing industrial society, including not only the highly industrialized economy itself but its setting in the society as a whole —notably, its political system and class structure (in a wider sense of the term "class" than Mills')—and the repercussions of the industrial development on the rest of the society. The second concerns the altered position of the United States in world society, which is a consequence in part of our own economic growth, in part of a variety of exogenous changes, including the relative decline of the Western European powers, the rise of Soviet Russia, and the breakup of the "colonial" organization of much of the nonwhite world. The enormous enhancement of American power and responsibility in the world has taken place in a relatively short time and was bound to have profound repercussions on the characteristics of our own society. Our old political isolation has disappeared and given way to the deepest of involvements.

My first thesis is that these two processes *both* work in the direction of increasing the relative importance of government in our society and, with it, of political power. But their impact has been all the greater because of the extent to which the United States has been an almost specifically nonpolitical society. This has been evidenced above all in the institutions and tradition of political decentralization already mentioned, one aspect of which is the localism which Mills discusses. A second, however, has been a cultural tradition which has emphasized economic values—an emphasis on enterprise and production in an activist sense, not a merely passive hedonistic valuation of the enjoyment of material well-being. Moreover, the virtually unimpeded process of settlement of a continent in political isolation from the main system of world powers has favored maintenance of this emphasis to a greater extent than would otherwise have readily been possible.

At some points in his discussion, Mills seems to look back to the Jeffersonian picture of a system of economic production consisting mainly of small farmers and artisans, with presumably a small mercantile class mediating between them and consumers. Clearly this is not a situation compatible with high industrial development, in either of two respects. First, the order of decentralization of production, where the standard unit is a family-size one, is incompatible with either the organization or the technology necessary for high industrialism. Second, the "Jeffersonian" economy is not one in which economic production is differentiated from other social functions in specialized organizations; instead, the typical productive unit is at the same time a kinship unit and a unit of citizenship in the community.

In all salient respects, the modern economy has moved very far from the Jeffersonian ideal. The pace-setting units have become both large and specialized. Their development has been part of a general process of structural differentiation in the society which has led to greater specialization in many fields. An essential aspect of the process of development of the economy as a system in *both* these senses is greater specialization on at least three levels: first, the specialization of organizations in the functions of economic production as distinguished from other functions; second, the specialization of functions within the economy; and third, the specialization of the roles of classes of individuals within the organization.

Leadership is an essential function in all social systems which, with their increase of scale and their functional differentiation, tend to become more specialized. I think we can, within considerable limits, regard the emergence of the large firm with operations on a nationwide basis as a "normal" outcome of the process of growth and differentiation of the economy. Similarly, the rise to prominence within the firm of specialized executive functions is also a normal outcome of a process of growth in size and in structural differentiation. The question then arises whether the process of concentration of firms, and of executive power within firms, has "gone too far" because it has been greatly influenced by factors extraneous to the process of economic development itself.

Mills makes the assertion that the size of the large firm has exceeded the limits of economic efficiency. He presents no evidence, and I think most competent persons would regard this as an exceedingly difficult question. There is, however, one line of evidence not cited by Mills which has a bearing on it. It is true that the absolute size of firms has steadily increased

—General Motors today is larger than any firm of the 1920's. But the *relative* share of the largest firms in the production of the economy has remained essentially stable for more than a generation, a fact which points to some kind of equilibrium condition with respect to the degree of concentration in the system as a whole.

A cognate question is whether the power of the executive or managerial class within industry, and particularly within the large firms, has increased inordinately, which, if true, would indicate that factors other than the functional needs of the productive process were operating to skew the internal power structure of firms in favor of the executive groups.

Generally speaking, Mills' argument is that the power of the very rich and the corporate rich *within* the economy is inordinately great and, by virtue of the factor of cumulative advantage, is becoming continually greater. At the very least, I think, it can be said that his case is not proved and that there is equally good, if not better, evidence for an alternative view, particularly with reference to the trend.

First, I am not able to accept Mills' close identification of the very rich (i.e., the holders of "great fortunes") with the "corporate rich" (the primary holders of executive power in business organizations) as a single class in any very useful sense. Certainly, in the "heroic age" of American capitalism, from the Civil War to just after the turn of the century, the dominant figures were the entrepreneurs who, mainly as the founders of great enterprises and as the bankers and promoters concerned with mergers and reorganizations and the like, came to control these great organizations. But the dominant sociological fact of the outcome of that era was that these owning groups did not, as a group, succeed in consolidating their position precisely *within* their own enterprises and in the economy. It is a notorious fact that the *very* large enterprise, still largely under family control through property holdings, is much more the exception than the rule. Instead, the control has passed— by no means fully but for the most part—to professional career executives, who have not reached their positions through the exercise of *property* rights but through some sort of process of appointment and promotion.

Mills concedes the main facts of this situation but fails, in my opinion, to evaluate them properly. It seems to be clear that the original "captains of industry," the makers of the great fortunes, *failed* to achieve or to exercise sufficient cumulative advantages to consolidate control of the enterprises in their families and their class ("class" in a sociological, not an economic, sense). This came about essentially because there were factors operating contrary to that of cumulative advantage, which Mills stresses so heavily. The main factor was the pressure to link executive responsibility with competence in such a way that the ascriptive rights of property ownership have tended to give way to the occupational functions of "professionals."

There are, above all, two ways in which Mills' treatment obscures the importance and nature of this shift. First, he continues to speak of power *within* the economy as based on property. To a considerable degree, of course, this is legally true, since the legal control of enterprise rests with stockholders. But, as Berle and Means first made abundantly clear, very generally it is not substantively true. In the old-style family enterprise, still predominant in the small-business sector of the economy, the functions of management and ownership are fused in the same people. In the larger enterprise they have by and large become differentiated. The fact that executives receive large salaries and bonuses is not to be twisted into an assumption that they control, so far as they do, through their property rights. Paradoxical as it may seem, a relatively backward industrial economy like that of France is far more *prop-*

71

erty-based than is the case with the United States. In general, property holdings have not, of course, been expropriated, except for their diminution through inheritance and income taxes, which are not as negligible as Mills maintains. What has happened is that their relation to the *power* structure of the economy has been greatly altered. Mills almost entirely passes over this change.

The second problem concerns the process of recruitment in the higher occupational reaches of the economy. It is entirely clear that the process operates in the higher reaches overwhelmingly by appointment, i.e., the decisions of superiors as individuals or in small groups as to who should occupy certain positions. It is also true that the process is relatively unformalized—e.g., there are no competitive examinations and few, if any, formal qualifications of training. But from these facts Mills concludes, and again and again reiterates, that executive competence has very little, if anything, to do with the selection, that it is an overwhelmingly arbitrary process of choosing those who are congenial to the selectors, presumably because they can be counted upon to be "yes men." At the very least this contention is unproved, and I seriously doubt its correctness. There are certainly many difficulties and imperfections in the selection process. But I think it almost certain that higher levels of competence are selected than would on the average be the case through kinship ascription, and that, as such processes go, the levels selected are relatively high.

One final point in this field. It does seem probable that the factor of cumulative advantage has a good deal to do with the high levels of financial remuneration of the higher executive groups and with the discrepancies between their incomes and those of governmental and professional people on comparable levels of competence and responsibility. But this is very far from the great fortune level of the founding entrepreneur type, and the evidence seems to be that the discrepancy has not been cumulatively increasing to an appreciable degree, particularly relative to wages at the labor levels; cases like that of the academic profession are somewhat special.

So far I have been speaking about the nature and power position of the elite *within* the economy. The general tenor of my argument has been that, given the nature of an industrial society, a relatively well-defined elite or leadership group should be expected to develop in the business world; it is out of the question that power should be diffused equally among an indefinite number of very small units, as the ideal of pure competition and a good deal of the ideology of business itself would have it. But first I question whether the position of power of the business leadership groups is such that a heavy operation of the factor of cumulative advantage must be invoked to account for it. Secondly, I must stress that the business elite is no longer primarily an elite of *property*-owners, but that its center of gravity has shifted to occupationally professional executives or managers. Differential advantages of family origin, etc., are about the same for admission to this group as to other groups requiring educational and other qualifications. Again the evidence is that the proportion of its members recruited from the upper economic and social groups is and remains relatively high, but it has not, in recent times, been increasing, as the theory of cumulative advantage would lead us to expect.

The problem of an elite within the economy must, however, be clearly distinguished from that of an elite in the society as a whole and the power position occupied by such an elite. There are two main orders of questions bearing on the transition from one to the other. Though a thorough consideration of this transition would lead into very far-reaching questions, for present purposes one can be treated rather briefly.

Mills gives us the impression that "eliteness" in any society, including our own, is overwhelmingly a question of the power that an individual or a group can command. By this, he means (I shall further discuss his concept of power presently) influence on the "big" decisions directly affecting what happens in the society in the short run. But there are many elements in the society which are relatively powerless in this sense, but nevertheless of the greatest functional importance. Our society has almost divested kinship units as such of important power in this sense. But this does not mean at all that the family has ceased to be important. Closely linked with this is the question of the feminine role. Women qua women by and large do not have a position of power comparable to that of men; but this is not to say that they are unimportant—otherwise how can we account for the extent of our national preoccupations with questions of sexuality? Finally, there is a *distinct* difference between the rank-order of occupations—which, relative to other role-types, are closely involved with decision-making in a society like ours —by power and by prestige. The most striking case is the relatively high position of the professions relative to executive roles in business, as revealed by the famous North-Hatt data. Physicians as a group do not exercise great power, but there is no reason to question their very high prestige, which has been demonstrated in study after study.

The second main context, however, directly concerns the question of power. In a complex society the primary locus of power lies in the political system. There are many subtle analytical problems involved in the delineation of this system and its functions in the society which cannot be gone into here; this formula will have to suffice. Two questions are, however, primary for our purposes: the degree of differentiation of the political system from other systems; and its own internal structure. These two problems, it will be noted, parallel those raised with reference to the economy.

For historical reasons, it seems clear that the development of the American political system, since the breakdown of the first synthesis associated with the "founders of the Republic," has lagged behind that of the economy. This is a function primarily of the two factors already noted—the economic emphasis inherent in our system of values, and the relative lack of urgency of certain political problems because of our especially protected and favored national position. Relative to the economic structure, which had by that time grown enormously, the political was at its weakest in the period from the Civil War to the end of the century; this situation is sketched by Mills in broadly correct terms. Since then, both internal exigencies and the exigencies of our international position have been stimuli for major changes.

Internally, beyond the more elementary provisions for law and order and essential minimum services—much of this, of course, on a local basis—the main focus of the development of our political system has been *control* of economic organization and processes, and coping with some of the social consequences of economic growth and industrialization. The process started well before the turn of the century with the Interstate Commerce legislation and the Anti-Trust Act and continued through the New Deal era, not steadily but with waves of new measures and levels of political control.

A major problem in relation to Mills' analysis is whether this is "genuine" control. His view seems to be that at times it has been, but that on balance it is the business power-holders who control government, not vice versa; the above quotation about the outcome of the New Deal puts it succinctly. In my opinion this is a misinterpretation. If genuine, and, in some sense, effective controls had not been imposed, I find it impossible to understand the bitter and continuing opposition on the part of business to the measures which have been taken. Even some of those most completely taken for granted now, like the Federal Reserve system, were bitterly fought at the time. It therefore seems to me to be the sounder interpretation that there has been a genuine growth of autonomous governmental power—apart from the military aspect, which will be discussed presently—and that one major aspect of this has been relatively effective control of the business system. This control and the growth of "big government" have been generally accepted in the society as a whole. The participation of big-business men in governmental processes is by no means to be interpreted as a simple index of their power to dominate government in their own interests, as Mills often seems to maintain.

To me, another indication of Mills' biased view of the governmental situation is his almost complete failure even to mention the political parties, or to analyze their differences. It seems to me broadly true that the Republican party, though a coalition, is more than any other single thing the party of the bigger sector of business. Four years of a Republican administration—two of them without control of Congress—is certainly not enough to indicate that big business, through its favorite party organ, controls the government on a long-run basis. So Mills is practically forced to the view that the alleged control operates above and beyond the party system. This seems to be connected with his relegation of the legislative branch to the "middle level" of power. I have strong reservations about this, but also it must not be forgotten that the presidency is the biggest prize of all in party politics, and it is its importance which forms the primary integrating focus of our particular type of party system. Surely the presidency is not simply the football of an inner clique which manipulates the executive branch independently of the party.

Mills, of course, recognizes that the aftermath of two world wars, the rise of Communist power, and the relative decline of the older Western Great Powers provide the occasion for the increasing prominence of the military group in our governmental system. Before these changes—and, indeed, to a remarkable extent, as late as the 1930's—the military played a far smaller role in this country than in any other society of comparable scale and organizational and technological development. Part of the change may be interpreted as simply the redressing of a balance. But it seems to me correct to say that for the last ten years there has been a special situation attributable to the extremely unsettled condition of the world at large and to the difficulties entailed for the American system, given its background, in meeting the problem on its own terms. There is thus a sense in which it is true that the higher military officers have tended to fill a vacuum in the field of national decision-making. There are two main points to be made about Mills' treatment of the matter. First, more in this field than perhaps any other, Mills' discussion is marred by a hasty tendency to generalize from very recent short-run developments to the long-run prospects of the structure of the society. Even here he fails to mention that in certain crucial questions the recommendations of the military have been overruled by civilian authority, although the President is a former military man. Secondly, the tone of indictment, particularly evidenced by the quite unnecessary and, I think, inappropriate parading of the term "warlord," is stronger in his discussion of this area than in any other, except perhaps the "mass society."

Related to the position of the higher military officers is what Mills calls the "military metaphysic," meaning the definition of international problems in terms of the primacy of military force. That there has been such a tendency, and that it has gone beyond the objective requirements of the situation, seem to be unquestionable. But I very much doubt whether it is as absolute as many of Mills' statements make it appear, and a swing in another direction is discernible. This seems to be another case of Mills' tendency to make large generalizations about major trends from short-run experience.

Finally, let us say a word about what Mills calls the "political directorate"—that is, the nonmilitary component in the groups most influential in the affairs of government and politics. Again I think there is a certain correctness in his contention that a definite weakness exists here, and that the high participation both of business and of military elements in the exercise of power is related to this. But a difficulty arises in terms of the perspective on American society which I have been emphasizing throughout. Both the nonpolitical stress in American social structure and values generally, and the recency and intensity of the pressures to build up this aspect of our structure, would lead one to predict that it would be a major focus of strain. American society has not developed a well-integrated political-government elite, in the sense that it has developed a relatively well-integrated business-executive group. For this reason responsibility has been carried—imperfectly, of course—by a very miscellaneous group which includes members of the business and military groups, as would be expected, but also "politicians," in the usual sense of people making an at least partial career out of elective office and the influencing of elections; professional people, particularly lawyers but also economists, political scientists, and even natural scientists (e.g., John von Neumann as Atomic Energy Commissioner); journalists; and, a very important element, upperclass people in more than the purely economic sense that Mills employs, of whom Franklin Roosevelt was one and Adlai

Stevenson, though also a lawyer, is another. In my opinion, the structure of the American political leadership group is far from a settled thing. It certainly is not settled in terms of the long-run dominance of a business-military coalition.

Mills holds that the United States has no higher civil service at all, in the European sense, and seems to imply that we should have. There is relative truth in his empirical contention, though I think he tends to underestimate the real influence of "nonpolitical" government officials on longer-run policy. Good examples are the Department of Agriculture and the Reclamation Service of the Department of the Interior—and now, increasingly, the Public Health Service. I think that this is even true of the Foreign Service, and that Mills here, as in so many other connections, seriously exaggerates the probable long-run consequences of the McCarthyites' intervention in the affairs of the State Department.

At least it seems highly probable that, in the nature of the case, the tendency will be toward a strengthening of the element of professional governmental officials who are essentially independent both of short-run "politics" and of elements extraneous to the structure of government and its responsibilities. In fact, the military officer is a special case of this type, and though his role is not stabilized, it presumably must come to be more important than it traditionally has been. However, it is questionable how far the specific models of civil service organization either of Britain or of Continental Europe—particularly, certain of their special connections with the class structure and the educational system—are appropriate to American conditions. Such connections in the American case would accentuate rather than mitigate the prominence of the Ivy League element to which Mills so seriously objects. I think it correct to say that five years of Labour government in Britain, far from lessening the prominence of Oxford and

Cambridge educations as qualifications for the civil service, in fact increased their relative importance, by increasing the national importance of the civil service itself.

Above all, I do not think that Mills has made a convincing case for his contention that the power structure impinging directly on American government is in process of crystallizing into a top business-military coalition with a much weaker political "junior partner" whose main function presumably is, by manipulation of the mass media and the political process in the narrower sense, to keep the great majority of Americans from protesting too loudly or even from awakening to what allegedly is "really" going on. On a number of counts which have been reviewed, there is a case on a short-run basis for part of his interpretation. But I think that the kinds of factors brought out in the previous discussion make it extremely dubious that even the partial correctness of his interpretation of a current situation will prove to be a sound indicator of what is to be expected over such longer periods as a generation or more.

My conviction on this point is strengthened by a variety of other considerations which, for reasons of space, cannot be discussed here, but may be mentioned. First, I am extremely skeptical of Mills' interpretation of what he calls the "mass society," which includes the structural position of the great majority of the American population. In this he ignores both kinship and friendship, and the whole mass of associational activities and relationships. One example is the spread of church membership—which I suppose Mills would dismiss as simply an escape from the boredom of white-collar life, but in my opinion is of considerable positive significance.

Another very important complex which Mills either treats cavalierly or ignores completely involves education at the various levels, and with it the enormous development, over a century, of science and learning and the professions resting upon them. It is true that the people rooted in these areas of the social structure are not prominent in the power elite, and are even subject to some conflicts with it; but they would not be expected to be prominent in this way—their functions in the society are different. Nonetheless, they must be taken very seriously into account in a diagnosis of what has been happening to the society as a whole. One of the most important sets of facts concerns the ways in which the services of technical professional groups have come to penetrate the structures both of business and of government, a circumstance which over a period of time has greatly enhanced the role of the universities as custodians of learning and sources of trained personnel.

Finally, there is one special case of a professional group whose role Mills treats with serious inadequacy—namely, lawyers. First, he dismisses the judicial branch of government as just "trailing along," with the implication that with a slight lag it simply does the bidding of the "real" holders of power. This seems to be a most biased appraisal of the role of the courts. Not to speak of the longer-run record, the initiative taken by the courts in the matter of racial segregation and in the reassertion of civil liberties after the miasma of McCarthyism does not appear to me to be compatible with Mills' views. Similar considerations seem to apply to various aspects of the role of the private legal profession, notably with respect to the *control* of processes in the business world. Mills tends to assume that the relation between law and business is an overwhelmingly one-way relation; lawyers are there to serve the interests of businessmen and essentially have no independent influence. This, I think, is an illusion stemming largely from Mills' preoccupation with a certain kind of power. His implicit reasoning seems to be that since lawyers have less power than businessmen, they do not really "count."

III

The last problem I wish to raise, therefore, concerns Mills' conception of power and its use as a category of social analysis. Unfortunately, the concept of power is not a settled one in the social sciences, either in political science or in sociology. Mills, however, adopts one main version of the concept without attempting to justify it. This is what may be called the "zero-sum" concept; power, that is to say, is power *over* others. The power A has in a system is, necessarily and by definition, at the expense of B. This conception of power then is generalized to the whole conception of the political process when Mills says that "Politics is a struggle for power."

Within limits, every student of social affairs is free to define important concepts the way he prefers; there is no canonically "correct" definition. But choosing one alternative will have consequences which differ from those implied in another, and this is the case with Mills' conception of power. The essential point at present is that, to Mills, power is not a facility for the performance of function in, and on behalf of, the society as a system, but is interpreted exclusively as a facility for getting what one group, the holders of power, wants by preventing another group, the "outs," from getting what it wants.

What this conception does is to elevate a secondary and derived aspect of a total phenomenon into the central place. A comparison may help to make this clear. There is obviously a distributive aspect of wealth and it is in a sense true that the wealth of one person or group by definition cannot also be possessed by another group. Thus the *distribution* of wealth is, in the nature of the case, a focus of conflicts of interest in a society. But what of the positive functions of wealth and of the conditions of its production? It has become fully established that the wealth available for distribution can only come about through the processes of production, and that these processes require the "co-operation" or integration of a variety of different agencies—what economists call the "factors of production." Wealth, in turn, is a generalized class of facilities available to units of the society—individuals and various types and levels of collectivities—for whatever uses may be important to them. But even apart from the question of what share each gets, the fact that there should be wealth to divide, and how much, cannot be taken for granted as given except within a very limited context.

Very similar things can be said about power in a political sense. Power is a generalized facility or resource in the society. It has to be divided or allocated, but it also has to be produced and it has collective as well as distributive functions. It is the capacity to mobilize the resources of the society for the attainment of goals for which a general "public" commitment has been made, or may be made. It is mobilization, above all, of the action of persons and groups, which is binding on them by virtue of their position in the society. Thus within a much larger complex Mills concentrates almost exclusively on the distributive aspect of power. He is interested only in *who* has power and what *sectoral* interests he is serving with his power, not in how power comes to be generated or in what communal rather than sectoral interests are served.

The result is a highly selective treatment of the whole complex of the power problem. There is, in the first place, a tendency to exaggerate the empirical importance of power by alleging that it is only power which "really" determines what happens in a society. Against this, I would place the view that power is only one of several cognate factors in the determination of social events. This bias of Mills' is particularly evident in his tendency to foreshorten social processes and emphasize overwhelmingly short-run factors. There is, secondly, the tendency to think of power as presumptively illegitimate; if people exercise considerable power, it must be because they have somehow usurped it where they had no right and they intend to use it to the detriment of others. This comes out most conspicuously in Mills' imputation of irresponsibility to his "power elite" and the allegation, vaguely conceived and presented with very little evidence, that they are characterized by a "higher immorality." It is notable that as he approaches the climax indicated by the title of his final chapter the tone of indictment becomes shriller and shriller and the atmosphere of objective analysis recedes.

Back of all this lies, I am sure, an only partly manifest "metaphysical" position which Mills shares with Veblen and a long line of indicters of modern industrial society. I would call it a utopian conception of an ideal society in which power does not play a part at all.

This is a philosophical and ethical background which is common both to utopian liberalism and socialism in our society and to a good deal of "capitalist" ideology. They have in common an underlying "individualism" of a certain type. This is not primarily individualism in the sense that the welfare and rights of the individual constitute fundamental moral values, but rather that *both* individual and collective rights are alleged to be promoted only by *minimizing* the positive organization of social groups. Social organization as such is presumptively bad because, on a limited, short-run basis, it always and necessarily limits the freedom of the individual to do exactly what he may happen to want. The question of the deeper and longer-run dependence of the goals and capacities of individuals themselves on social organization is simply shoved into the background. From this point of view, both power in the individual enterprise and power in the larger society are presumptively evil in themselves, because they represent the primary visible focus of the capacity of somebody to see to it that somebody else acts or does not act in certain ways, whether at the moment he wants to or not.

There are, in contemporary society, three main versions of this individualistic utopianism, which may be called "liberal" and "capitalist" and "socialist"—I place all three terms in quotation marks deliberately. The liberal version is mainly "humanistically" oriented to the *total* welfare of the individual as a person, and in American terms it is very likely to assume a Jeffersonian cast, to hold up the vision of a simpler and hence almost by definition "better" society against the inhumanities and impersonalities of large-scale modern industrialism and all its concomitants.

The capitalist version is, with all the qualifications which such an assertion must occasion, *primarily* production-oriented. Essentially it says that, whatever the cost to individuals —including even businessmen themselves, or especially so— production must be achieved, carried on, and so far as possible increased. This is the focus of what has been called the "business creed." Understandably it has been highly sensitive to "interferences" on both fronts, from liberal sources which would sacrifice productivity to humanistic values, and from governmentalist sources which would "interfere" with the businessman's primary responsibility for production. Social organization beyond the level of the firm is thus presumptively a limitation of its freedom.

The socialist version has been a secondary theme in American ideology largely because of the apolitical character of American society, which, as I have noted, has been prominent historically. The opposition to capitalism has centered on two fronts, the control of the economy in the interests of preventing abuses of power and the steering of the benefits of productivity in the humanistic direction of "welfare." But the socialist

85

questions whether *control* of the abuses of private enterprise is possible at all; to him, for the state to take over production directly is the only way. From this perspective, furthermore, the "Jeffersonian" version of romantic utopianism seems particularly unrealistic and unacceptable.

From one point of view, the socialist romanticizes the state and the political process. Whereas he distrusts private interests almost totally and feels that they cannot be entrusted with any responsibility, he romantically believes that if public authority alone is entrusted with all responsibilities, all will be well— because some mystical "popular will" or "public interest" controls it—forgetting that public authority, like other forms of social organization, is administered by human beings. And that he does not fundamentally trust even public authority is evidenced by his ultimate ideal that the state should "wither away" and the spontaneous cooperation of institutionally unorganized human beings should take over. The socialist has been put in a particularly difficult position in the contemporary world by the development of Communism which, while still paying lip service to the eventual withering-away of the state, carries the enforcement of its predominance over all private interests, including the liberties of its citizens, to the totalitarian extreme.

Mills does not make his own position explicit in this book. As noted, at times he speaks like a nostalgic Jeffersonian liberal. I understand, however, that he professes to be a socialist —non-Communist, of course. But a basic strain of his thinking is consistent with both wings of the liberal-socialist dilemma on the basically *individualistic* premises that I have outlined: either that social organization beyond the level of the family and the local community is a bad thing *in toto,* or that it is instrumentally justified only to get society over a particular hump, the threat of the capitalist evil.

Mills seems to be suggesting that the development of the power elite is bringing that capitalist evil to a climax, to a situation which is intolerable to liberals and socialists alike. I suggest an alternative view: that, though of course accompanied by a whole range of "abuses," the main lines of social development in America are essentially acceptable to a humanistic ethic which in my case is closer to the liberal than to either of the other two outlined here. But it differs in not being in the older sense an individualistic liberalism. If the individualistic assumptions are modified in favor of a set which not only admit the necessity but assert the desirability of positive social organization, much of the ideological conflict between the three positions as total "systems" evaporates. Above all, it can be positively asserted that power, while of course subject to abuses and in need of many controls, is an essential and desirable component of a highly organized society. This position, in asserting and justifying the increased importance of government, thus grants that there is a grain of truth in the "socialist" theme. There is, however, also some justification for the existence of "capitalism," if by that is meant the institutionalization of responsibility for the larger part of economic production in the hands of a variety of private, nongovernmental agencies. To my mind, there is no more reason why all important economic production should be controlled by government than why all scientific research should be.

Hence, in my opinion, many of the difficulties of Mills' analysis of a crucial problem in American society arise from his failure to transcend the dilemmas inherent in much of the individualistic tradition in American and, more broadly, in Western thought. It seems to me that he is clearly and, in the degree to which he pushes this position, unjustifiably anti-capitalist. He is partly pro-liberal and probably even more pro-socialist. But in the American scene a choice between these old alternatives of ideological orientation is no longer enough. It is necessary not only to criticize existing conditions from the older philosophical or ideological points of view, but to take serious stock of the ideological assumptions underlying the bulk of American political discussion of such problems as power.

Power in America

BY DENNIS H. WRONG

Like Professor Mills' earlier books, *The Power Elite* is an uneven blend of journalism, sociology, and moral indignation. Having previously examined labor leaders and white-collar workers, Mills here turns his attention to the topside of American society: the old families enshrined in the *Social Register,* the celebrities of the mass media, the corporation executives, the generals and admirals, and the major politicians. But he does a good deal more than merely buttress a series of descriptive accounts of these august circles with the conventional apparatus of sociological research; his chief concern is with developing a theory of where the decisive power lies in American society, how it got there, and how it is exercised.

Mills maintains that the United States is run by a "power elite" of corporation executives, military men, and politicians

Dennis Wrong teaches sociology at New York University. He is the author of American and Canadian Viewpoints *and* Population and Society. *This review appeared in* Commentary, September, 1956.

whose interests converge or coincide, and who "are in a position to make decisions with terrible consequences for the underlying populations of the world." This theory is introduced in the opening chapter. The middle chapters, dealing with the various American upper classes, old and new, constitute an attempt to document and illustrate the central thesis, which is then elaborated in the final section of the book, where Mills examines and rejects alternative views. He closes with a ringing indictment of American society as immoral, politically irresponsible, and led by the "second-rate mind."

The early chapters of the book contain the best writing and some of the most incisive analysis. They trace the decline in the autonomy of the small town and its self-contained social world, the development of fashionable society and of a stylized upper-class way of life in the metropolitan centers of the East, and, finally, the replacement of the society lady and the debutante by the movie star, with the emergence of a nationwide celebrity system created and sustained by the mass media. No one, to my knowledge, has written with greater insight into the larger significance of cafe society, where the stars of all fields of endeavor mingle in the spotlight of publicity. And Mills' criticism of Veblen's conception of the leisure class is as acute as any I have seen. "He was," Mills writes, "not quite serious enough about status because he did not see its full and intricate importance to power"—an omission by Veblen which Mills more than makes good.

Moving from the theme of status and wealth to that of power, Mills describes the executives, the military, and, much more briefly, the politicians—the three groups he sees as an "interlocking directorate" at the apex of the American power hierarchy. He provides a lot of information about each of them, some of it based on original research and some of it merely taken from the Luce publications and business magazines. In trying to persuade us that there is really an "interlocking directorate" at work in America, he makes much of the degree to which careers in the corporate, military, and government bureaucracies are becoming interchangeable, listing the generals who have been appointed directors of large corporations or participated actively in politics, and the businessmen who have accepted government posts. Most of this data is drawn from the record of the past four years, and one may perhaps be pardoned for hesitating to join Mills in regarding the Eisenhower administration as the goal and culmination of long-term trends in American politics.

Mills completes his picture of the power structure by identifying a "middle level" of power where Congress, state political machines, and regional economic interest groups are located, and where the conception (advanced by David Riesman, John K. Galbraith and others) of a relative equilibrium between competing groups has rough applicability. He argues, however, that the Riesman-Galbraith restatements of the traditional liberal theory of a balanced society confuse the part with the whole and the desirable with the actual. (Here Mills is a polemicist and at his best, without the tone of tough-guy knowingness about the facts of power that pervades much of the book.)

Below the elite and the "middle level" lie the powerless masses, pulverized by metropolitan living and rapid industrial growth, manipulated by the power elite, and distracted from any serious concern with politics by the commercial machinery of amusement. Clearly, in Mills' vision of them, they no longer bear much resemblance to the classic "public" of democratic theory.

Except for this almost eschatological view of the passive, violated masses, Mills' account of who holds the power in American society is, it seems to me, broadly acceptable. The fundamental weakness in his whole analysis lies in his failure to tell us clearly *what* the elite does with its power, or *why* it does some things and not others—for power is not an absolute: there is only power to do particular things. What exactly does Mills' power elite do that leads him to think it plays so crucial a role? It makes "decisions having at least national consequences." The decisions he uses as examples are the most obvious ones conceivable: the chain of events leading up to American entrance into World War II, the dropping of the bomb on Hiroshima (referred to repeatedly), the commitment of troops to Europe under NATO, the Korean war, the decision to defend Formosa. Congress wasn't consulted about these decisions, says Mills (sounding for all the world like an Old Guard Republican), nor were you and I.

And so we weren't, but decisions bearing on war and peace —the only kind Mills mentions—are rarely submitted to plebiscites. Most modern governments give their executive branches unusual prerogatives to deal with situations considered relevant to national security. Lincoln was in effect a military dictator during the Civil War, often neglecting to consult even his own Cabinet, and this was in a period when, Mills himself informs us, the power elite had yet to achieve its ascendancy. Wars and cold wars have vastly increased the emergency powers of the Executive and it may be that too many vital policy decisions are being concealed from Congress, the press, and the public. A lot of people have been saying as much for some time. But Mills' anguished cry against the awesome power of the elite adds up in the end to little more than reiteration of these fairly familiar complaints, which hardly justify his view of America as virtually a totalitarian country.

But it is not only Mills' inadequately defined notion of power that is open to question; there is also the fact that he never specifies precisely what are the interests on the basis of which the power elite decides policy. They are not, he says, the profit motives of a capitalist "ruling class" in the traditional Marxist sense, but represent a "coincidence of interest among economic, political, and military organizations." Businessmen, he reminds us, have captured control of the New Deal Federal agencies that were created to control them, while corporations profit from orders placed by the Pentagon. Yet Mills makes it clear that he has in mind a more comprehensive unity of interests than that implied by these familiar occurrences which involve only a few industries and areas of government activity. American capitalism, he argues, is no longer a mere "scatter of special interests": it began to produce industry-wide spokesmen like Owen D. Young in the twenties, and today the heads of the great corporations have moved "from the industrial point of interest and outlook to the interest and outlook of the class of all big corporate property as a whole."

Do the shared interests of the members of the elite arise, then, from the fact that they know one another personally and have common social origins and a common style of life? This is not the whole story either, according to Mills, for to see the elite as no more than a clique of like-minded men would be to succumb to a "simple-minded biographical theory of society and history." Mills is after something more solidly rooted in history than this: he wants to identify "objective interests" that have been created by long-run "structural trends" in American institutions. Economic men, he tells us repeatedly, were dominant from the end of the Civil War until the depression, politicians acquired greater power in the New Deal era, military men became important during World War II, and all three have made common cause under the Eisenhower administration. But his account of these undeniable historical developments does not succeed in enlightening us as to what exactly are the "coincident interests" of the three groups making up the power elite.

What Mills fails to state outright, but is, I think hinting at, is that big business has joined with the big politicians and the generals and admirals to maintain a "permanent war economy" for the purpose of averting an otherwise inevitable economic depression. The hydra-headed elite, according to this view, has a clear interest in perpetuating the present situation because, if the threat of war were removed, the military leaders would lose their positions of power and prestige, while another depression would perhaps spell the extinction of capitalism. Although it is needed to cap his argument, Mills neglects to make this extravagant theory explicit, possibly because he can't really bring himself to believe that his power elite is so far-seeing and Machiavellian.

I find the theory incredible. Are we to conclude that the armed belligerency of Germany, Japan, and Russia made only a secondary contribution to the new role of the military in American life? Is Soviet armed might today simply a bogey conjured up by the power elite to justify its position? Mills doesn't say as much, but he refers in a most oblique way to the fact that America is now "in a military neighborhood" and mentions the Soviet Union only once, remarking that the United States is not yet *that* totalitarian! The fact is that his sense of an irresistible determinism in events commits him to a strange brand of isolationism that sees changes in American society as being virtually self-generated by the "internal dynamics" of institutions.

Mills is alive to the fact that he might be charged with advancing a new "conspiracy theory of history." He insists that the power elite is not a band of plotters, but has come into being only because men have availed themselves of oppor-

93

tunities created by "institutional forces." Recently I asked an adherent of Mills' views whether or not he thought that important changes in American foreign policy would result if the Democrats won the 1956 election and chose as Secretary of State George Kennan, who is far from being an intellectual mediocrity and has sharply criticized what he regards as the excessive militarization of American policy. "Certainly," was the quick response, "but the power elite would never let Kennan have the job." Mills, of course, is not responsible for what others make of his views, but they clearly lend themselves to the idea of an organized clique secretly manipulating events. He himself finally half-recognizes this, and quotes Richard Hofstader to the effect that identifying conspiracies in history is not the same thing as arguing that history is a conspiracy. Granted, but I do not think that Mills' new key fits the lock of history any better than those of earlier Populist and Marxist writers.

Are the Blind Leading the Blind?

BY A. A. BERLE, JR.

The American "power elite," C. Wright Mills tells us, is that group of men who command the major organizations in our society: "They rule the big corporations. They run the machinery of the state and claim the prerogatives. They direct the military establishment. They occupy the strategic command posts of the social structure in which are now centered the effective means of the power and the wealth and the celebrity which they enjoy."

He makes a case for that claim. Then, with restrained bitterness, he tears into the resulting structure. Political scientist Harold Lasswell has expounded the idea that all society is a pyramid; at its apex a small "elite" holds top directing positions; below are subordinate directing groups, connected by organization to the mass.

Mr. Mills, associate professor of sociology at Columbia, author of *White Collar* and other books, presents our "power elite" as a merger of three interlocked groups with interchangeable members: (1) "big rich" combined with "corporate rich" —company executives; (2) military and naval men ruling the Pentagon and its works; (3) high political figures in government. Mills maintains all are products of a more or less common environment. Unlike Marx, he thinks the "big economic man" is no longer controlling alone; he has merged with "war

A. A. Berle, Jr., is a corporation lawyer and adviser to Democratic presidents on Latin American Affairs. He is well known for his The American Economic Republic, Power Without Property, *and* The Modern Corporation and Private Property (*with Gardner Means*). *This review appeared in* The New York Times Book Review, *April 22, 1956.*

95

lords" and "selected politicians." Organization and mass media do the rest. This elite has no dogma, accepts no standards, works in a system of "organized irresponsibility," in a frame of "higher immorality."

More impressive is the author's analysis of the underlying "mass society." There he has a point. American increase in population and the rise of large organizations did, without doubt, shatter the individual communities in which men lived in town meeting days. Big organizations do push their leading figures so far from the bottom millions that communication is hard, or perhaps lost.

Contemporaneously came problems that do not yield to popular discussion. The man in the street knows he does not understand nuclear engineering, intricate financing, economics, or complex international problems. He can only give confidence to men he thinks do understand. Increasingly he is in the hands of experts or representatives. His only recourse—if he has any—is to fire them when results are bad.

Information and appraisal he must get through "mass media," which, Mills suggests, are oftener instruments for manipulating than for informing the public. Educational institutions which should help to produce disciplined and informed minds, "bold and sensible individuals who cannot be overwhelmed by mass life," translating "troubles into issues, and issues into terms of their human meaning," aim rather at "life adjustments," encouraging happy acceptance of mass ways rather than struggle for individual or public ascendancy. This hurts. It has a considerable content of truth.

There are no values. The "conservative mood" has no basis in ideas, merely maxims straight out of Horatio Alger. "Liberalism" skirts mindlessness, enshrines a set of administrative routines and defends rather than exercises civil liberties. Freedom (Mills quotes Archibald MacLeish) is no longer something you use, it has become something you "save," something you protect like your other possessions. Liberalism, now "painless to the rich and powerful," no longer defines issues or proposes policies.

In sum, Mills concludes we have arrived at a "higher immorality"—a mindless vacuum with no elaborated justification of ideas and values. Elite members are not the product of virtue or ability, of a sensitive civil service, of responsible national parties, nor are they held in check by a plurality of voluntary associations. "Commanders of power unequaled in human history, they have succeeded within the American system of organized irresponsibility."

So there! An Army lieutenant who survived the war in the Pacific once read Norman Mailer's *The Naked and the Dead.* "If that book is a picture of the Army," asked he, "how come we won the war?" If the American command is as accidental, mindless, amoral, undogmatic, irresponsible, disconnected with the mass as all that, how come it hangs together and, despite defects, provides people with the highest content of economic, esthetic, and intellectual opportunity yet offered a population block of 165 million?

There is, nevertheless, an uncomfortable degree of truth in Mills' attack. It is not the whole truth. It is weakened by semantic slant. American business executives are not "corporate commissars"; American high officers are not fairly described as "war lords"; American high government officers are politicians but to be good they must be something more. Some "big rich," corporate executives, and Army officers do act as Mills records. Others run museums of modern art, foreign aid programs, civic services, *ad infinitum.* Mills' portrait is an angry cartoon, not a serious picture.

There are also errors of fact. He is wrong in asserting a general "coincidence of interests between military and corporate needs as defined by war lords and corporate rich"; and corporate capitalism is not a "military capitalism," save in a few specialized fields. Nor does the social system move in an intellectual vacuum; Einstein and Oppenheimer could match the "power elite" and defeat it. But the need of a solid value system is great, as Walter Lippmann and the late Russell Davenport have recently pointed out.

The author insists the characteristic member of higher circles today is an "intellectual mediocrity"—perhaps conscientious but still mediocre. Probably. So were most top groups in history. Perhaps not in Pericles' Athens, or at the founding of the American republic; but social structures are usually run by second-rate men with mixed motives doing the best they can. Probably one test of a society is whether it can carry on with mediocrities. If it depends on quantity production of first-raters, it is precarious indeed.

Mr. Mills rejects a suggestion made by the reviewer that corporations are gradually developing standards of conduct amounting to a "corporate conscience." Not convincing, he says; corporations live up to standards only because this makes "good public relations." Fair enough: St. Peter will settle whether the creditable things we did were motivated altruistically or by self-interest. Social students must be content with results. If the Pentagon, corporations, and political parties do good because they think it good policy, good policy has to serve.

This book is so carefully documented, it deals with such real problems, it hits so many sore spots that it deserves to be read—also to be supplemented. The indictment of the power elite by Mr. Mills is, for lack of a system of values, in need of a guiding philosophy. But that requires the accuser to posit some value system as a takeoff point. To indict for social anarchy assumes some form of social law. "Higher immorality" predicates some moral order. Objectively the American structure is not a failure. You cannot condemn it as a "bad society" unless you at least conceive a "good society."

Actually, the last half-century increased America's population by nearly eight million. It lifted her production and her standard of living beyond dreams. It brought her into direct military contact with a warring world from which the sea had previously isolated her. Organization of production in big units pushed into national power men trained only for the less dangerous decisions of business. Old structures crumbled; the new forms are barely evident.

Intellectually, the five decades lifted many millions from drudgery to a degree of contact with books, news, music, art, even though mass culture has not attained heights achieved by past smaller groups. Educational institutions too often have had to settle for half a job on thousands to the detriment of first-rate work on a few. We grope in an age of unparalleled expansion.

But it is not true to say that men who reach the top are more unthinking or less moral than usual because they do not spell out intellectual credos. If he believes what he writes, Mr. Mills has cut out his next job. He must tackle the problem of elaborating the values and the institutional forms that can lead to the society he believes to be good.

PART III

Radical Critics of THE POWER ELITE

Radical critics applauded The Power Elite, *although they were not without their criticisms. They liked it for its colorful language, for its subject matter, and for its critical stance. In short, they shared Mills' moral judgments and therefore enjoyed his attacks on liberalism.*

If the radicals shared Mills' critical stance, they were not satisfied with his theoretical framework. Most of all, they took exception to the footnote in chapter 12 into which Mills crowded his rejection of the notion "ruling class."[1] *Radicals are usually distrustful of "elites" and "institutions" in a social analysis because these concepts were used by Pareto, Weber,*

[1] The footnote reads as follows:
"Ruling class" is a badly loaded phrase. "Class" is an economic term; "rule" a political one. The phrase, "ruling class," thus contains the theory that an economic class rules politically. That short-cut theory may or may not at times be true, but we do not want to carry that one rather simple theory about in the terms that we use to define our problems; we wish to state the theories explicitly, using terms of more precise and unilateral meaning. Specifically, the phrase "ruling class," in its common political connotations, does not allow enough autonomy to the political order and its agents, and it says nothing about the military as such. It should be clear to the reader by now that we do not accept as adequate the simple view that high economic men unilaterally make all decisions of national consequence. We hold that such a simple view of "economic determinism" must be elaborated by "political determinism" and "military determinism"; that the higher agents of each of these three domains now often have a noticeable degree of autonomy; and that only in the often intricate ways of coalition do they make up and carry through the most important decisions. Those are the major reasons we prefer "power elite" to "ruling class" as a characterizing phrase for the higher circles when we consider them in terms of power.

and others to refute the claims of socialism and because elite theories often counterpose a powerless mass to the powerful elite.

The radicals understood that Mills was a fellow radical, but they had an uneasy fear of a theory which took its concepts from an enemy camp, especially in the hands of a theorist who was later to characterize the orthodox radical hope in the working class as a "labor metaphysic."

Power in the United States

BY ROBERT S. LYND

Power, Tawney remarks, is the most obvious characteristic of organized society; but it is also, he adds, the most ambiguous. Professor Galbraith suggests a reason for this ambiguity: "Power obviously presents awkward problems for a community which abhors its existence, disavows its possession, but values its exercise." This awkwardness, markedly characteristic of a capitalist society that professes democracy, has grown in the present century as specialization and the resulting heightened interdependence of social and institutional parts has made it clear that industrial society, like it or not, is a collective society. For collective interdependence requires institutional compatibility and agreement regarding objectives.

On the democratic side of the marriage of capitalism and democracy, our Constitution grants the government no authority over the "general welfare," and the courts have held that every power is a delegated power. Therefore the liberal state has been held back from developing a positive interpretation and open use of power as a resource for broadening and deepening the democractic character of our society. What political democracy intends, and would progressively become if it were not thus blocked off, was well stated by the late Franz Neumann in the *Columbia Law Review*. Discussing "the growing antagonism between the potentialities of our historical situation and their actual utilization," he stressed that "democracy

Robert S. Lynd teaches sociology at Columbia University. He is author of Knowledge for What? *and co-author of* Midd'etown *and* Middletown in Transition. *This review appeared in* The Nation, *May 12, 1956.*

is not simply a political system like any other; its essence consists in the execution of large-scale social changes maximizing the freedom of men."

Under such a conception the people and their development, not institutions, come first. But since the liberal democratic state has been largely prevented from placing the people first, some other agency must instate its version of collective coherence and purpose as the society's. For the one indubitable requirement—in an age that knows Keynes, the collective benefits of full employment as well as the collective losses of depressions, and the requirements of total war—is some version of integrated action. Largely—and by no means accidentally—it has devolved upon our capitalist economy to provide the statement of our national collective purpose and the methods of realizing it.

Central to the awkwardness in power today is, therefore, the fact that the conception of "democratic welfare" has become an incidental adjunct to "business welfare": our national purpose is business prosperity measured in dollars and volume of production of those things it is profitable to private business to produce. The unstated assumptions are (1) that private business enterprise produces the things that people need; and (2) that if people earn enough they will know how to turn their dollars into *human* welfare. The unstated realities are (1) that private business is not interested in such collective needs as better schools and well-paid public-school teachers, in socially adequate housing for the mass of the population, in the qualitative *human* adequacy and balance of the things involved in a richly diverse development of persons and families; and (2) that an increasingly pressure-sold—the new word is "pre-sold"—population is accordingly encouraged to lose sight of those collective and personal values, important in the development of democratic society, that are not advertised and capable of yielding visible and instant popular status.

The need is to view contemporary power not piecemeal but as a whole, in its full setting, and when one writes about detailed aspects of power to do so in this perspective. To say this is not an academic counsel of perfection, but a sober conclusion from considerable evidence of the obstruction to clear thinking about power that results from analyses that deal only in immediate terms of personality, or of whether monopoly is or is not efficient, or of bureaucracy, or other isolated aspects. The most characteristic feature of power in society is that separate powers, however based, tend to flow together in working arrangements and so to become a structure of power coterminous with the society: and this means that attempts to deal fragmentarily with power and the problems it raises are largely frustrated.

In the temper of our times bold and candid writing about power is a most direct form of putting one's head into the lion's mouth. The writer's greatest temptation is to be so circumspect that he can be reasonably sure in advance that the lion won't really bite. Within limits, power is a salable topic. It has a secret fascination, particularly for those who fancy they are, or are about to become, members of the powerful. A book can sell if it is forthright enough to arouse talk, and yet smooth enough to leave no deep grudge with the reader. Power may even be personalized so long as many persons in many spheres are named. But the writer on power much more surely invites the lion's jaws if he forsakes discursive talk about the powerful and lays it on the line that good and bad persons—including even leaders—are incidental, and that it is the whole structure of society and its institutions, which strong men like to think of themselves as serving and ornamenting, that is at

105

fault. It was doubtless good salesmanship for the American publishers of Tawney's *The Sickness of an Acquisitive Society* to soften and blur the title of the American edition to *The Acquisitive Society*. For who would doubt that we live in an acquisitive society—but that it is "sick"!

It is not surprising, therefore, that our literature dealing directly and analytically with power is meager. One may cite such comparatively recent books as Bertrand Russell's ambling *Power;* Robert Brady's important *Business as a System of Power;* books with a prevailingly psychological or logical-deductive focus by Lasswell; de Jouvenel's *On Power* with its religious, semi-authoritarian bent; and Hans Morgenthau's *Scientific Man vs. Power Politics,* with its bitter emphasis upon the irrational, whereby "The very act of acting destroys our moral integrity."

To this list is now added *The Power Elite* by Professor C. Wright Mills, whom many will identify from his *The New Men of Power,* on American labor leaders, and from his *White Collar,* which deals with the middle class. *The Power Elite* should be one of the widely discussed books of the year. Much of the picture of power is here, and interestingly presented. Mills is a sophisticated man who writes with a muscular vitality that never allows the reader's attention to flag; and his forty-nine pages of footnotes, many of them elaborations of the text, indicate the breadth of the materials from which he draws. Such a book invites the application of the criteria for writing about organized power set forth above.

The substantial core of the book, following the opening chapter in which the author defines what he means by "elite" ("a set of higher circles whose members . . . command the [different] institutional hierarchies of modern society"), comprises chapters five through eleven on the Very Rich, Corporation Executives and the Corporate Rich, the Warlords and the

Military Ascendancy, the Political Directorate, and an excellent chapter on the fallacy of imputing a "satisfactory or even good" balance to the *status quo* of conflicting interests in our society. The remaining seven chapters, on Local Society, Metropolitan 400, Celebrities, Mass Society, The Conservative Mood, and The Higher Immorality, depend unevenly from the hard core of the book. The architecture of the book leads up rather gently and discursively to the hard-biting middle group of chapters, and then glides down again so as to deposit the reader on familiar ground in scarcely more ruffled mood than he might experience after reading one of the occasional critical articles on American institutions in *Harper's*.

This point on the book's overall structure is relevant because it explains the reader's growing uneasiness over the possibility that perhaps the analysis—all this significant documentation and good thinking—was not intended to get anywhere. Whether a book cumulates in meaning towards the point of joining its several strands in an interlocked body of conclusions, however tentative, is a matter of choice for the author. But not to do so in a book of such weight and potential importance on this subject seems peculiarly unfortunate.

Mills' failure to deal with the meanings for democracy of the impressive power trends he analyzes is the colossal loose-end of *The Power Elite*. He simply fades out on the expectation his pages encourage that this crucial arc in the analysis will be closed before the book ends. The book's opening paragraph stresses the central importance of this problem: " 'Great changes' . . . from every side . . . now press upon the men and women of the mass society, who . . . feel that they are without purpose in an epoch in which they are without power." This invites the hope that the pages to follow will provide a confrontation between the purposes of the powers-that-be and the efforts of men in democracy to affirm other purposes for which democracy stands. But, curiously, the potentially crucial chapter on The Mass Society is deferred until the third from the end, when the book is already tapering off, and then contents itself with describing what mass societies are and how they happen. Mills tells us that "The United States today is not altogether a mass society"; but he describes a movement towards a mass society that is in full tide, and the power setting of the rest of the book implies that it is to continue unchecked. If Marxism encourages distortion through viewing society from the bottom up, it may be the characteristic distortion of elite analysis that it looks from the top down, and not very far down at that.

This leaves one wondering whether the great bulk of modern society is to Mills but fodder for his elite. If so, he may be correct; but, if so, this becomes the most momentous unstated and unexamined conclusion of his book. If this is what things add up to, then reading about the who's and why's of elites is for us like reading about the scurry of ants zigzagging under the feet of a herd of elephants. Again, this may be correct for our generation. But such a conclusion simply repeats the bankrupt scarcity theory of power: that some people have it, and because they have it none is available for the rest of us. And, over longer time, does what the democratic idea intends provide nothing for man to fight for, and with?

The book has a hit-and-glide quality which derives, I think, from its central effort to instate elites as the master key in the analysis of power. Elite analysis is popular among sociologists nowadays. Its popularity derives, I believe, quite as much from the things it enables an analyst to avoid, as from the things it enables him to do. Most important, it provides a glittering focus above common, troublesome things like capitalism and the class structure of a capitalist society.

108

Let's look at Mills' book in terms of what the approach to power through elites does to his analysis.

Power is a factor, unconscious or conscious, in all relations between people. It takes many forms, ranging from affection and spontaneous persuasion at one extreme to organized force at the other. One observes it in action in persons, in small groups and large organizations, in classes, in institutions, in whole societies. Mills sees power as basically in institutions, and the elite in terms of "institutional position," with "position" referring to the horizontal stratifications of people in institutions. He selects three institutions as the Big Three: the economic, the political, and the military. From each of these, men emerge at the top. These are, respectively, the economic elite, the political elite, and the military elite; and, together, they comprise "the American elite." In their persons, in informal and formal interaction, understandings are reached and crucial policies that control the country are launched into effective action. Roughly, this is all right, as far as it goes.

But it leaves important questions unanswered. Mills correctly stresses the need to bring the diversity represented by the several elites together, to see the resulting American elite as a whole. The simplest unity may be seen in the fact that, though they come up from different institutions, these diverse members of the elite do arrive at concrete, agreed-upon policies. This poses the question: what is responsible for the readiness of these top persons to agree? I see three possible answers: (1) Men who rise that high in society may be counted on to be seasoned administrators who by long experience recognize the need, through adjustment and compromise, to reach some workable agreement about things to be done. This answer, correct as far as it goes, bases the tendency to agree upon nothing more substantial than influence and expedient bargaining among individuals. (2) Elites from different institutions act together and reach common agreements because one institution represented in the total American elite has power and rewards enough to force other institutions and their respective elites to act in the main in ways compatible with its interests. If this is the answer—as it is in part—Mills would need to assess and to identify the relative weights of his three institutions. This he does not do. (3) Elites from different institutions act together because the same influential class in society spreads across all institutions and controls them in a common general direction. This answer—which includes the relevant parts of the two preceding—provides much the broadest and soundest basis for the analysis of power in American society.

By locating the cohering factor in the elite superstructure, Mills leaves other weighty factors unlashed-in and flapping like loose sails. He does not hold steadily in focus the massive continuities involved in the fact that ours is a capitalist society; the factor of class is belittled; the relative weights of his three institutions in a capitalist society go unassessed; and an unwarranted autonomy is imputed to the several institutions.

Capitalism appears intermittently in the analysis. The author knows that we live in a capitalist society; and I am sure he is aware of how important it is in our system of power. At certain points he makes this explicit:

> The corporations are the organized centers of the private property system. . . . [The] corporate revolution . . . has transformed property from a tool of the workman into an elaborate instrument by which his work is controlled and a profit extracted from it.

> Now the corporate seats of the rich contain all the powers and privileges inherent in the institutions of private property.

The trouble is not that the author fails to deal with capitalist power. He does so explicitly in the chapters on the very rich and on corporate big business. But he reserves property as a basis of power for one discrete set within the elite, and makes no solid effort to appraise the relative weight and the diffused spread of the power of property throughout all institutions under capitalism. He holds back on such unifying tendencies in order to reserve this dramatic role for his elites.

Mills is correct in insisting that power does not inhere in persons, and that it is not prevailingly a conspiracy. To analyze power under capitalism as a conspiracy of persons, rather than the weighted movement of circumstances in a given society, belittles the realities of power. But can one escape facing the reality that, historically, capitalism means and has always meant that the whole institutional system has become weighted so that, like loaded dice, events tend to roll with a bias that favors property?

There is a similar in-and-out vagueness about class in the book. Through most of the pages one tends to assume that the author takes the presence of classes for granted. He is explicit about it, for instance, when he says that "to have power requires access to major institutions, for the institutional positions men occupy determine in large part their chances to have and to hold . . . valued experience"; or when, in discussing the role of big business executives, he says they have reorganized "the property class . . . into the broader economic and political interests of a more genuinely class type"; or when he says that the elite "derive in substantial proportion from the upper classes. . . . The bulk of [them] derive from, at most, the upper third of the income and occupational pyramid." He even refers to "the elite as a social class." But three-quarters of the way through the book it turns out that he does not really mean "class," as class is historically identified. By confining the term to the economic sphere (" 'Class' is an economic term."), and by forcing the term class into the extreme meaning of economic determinism, he limits the involvement of class so defined in the totality of his elite to the immediate representatives from the strictly economic sphere. This enables him to reserve for the elite as a whole the spreading, unifying tendency long identified with class as it operates across the institutions of a capitalist society. But then he must qualify his reference to "the elite as a social class" by differentiating it from a "ruling class." If " 'Class' is an economic term; 'rule,' " he says, is "a political one." So he prefers to identify the imputedly non-class character of his "elite as a social class" simply as a "power elite." If the reader has difficulty in following these sophistications, so did I.

Since when has the concept "class" been only "an economic term" and ceased to refer to social aggregates? Along with Mills, I, too, dislike the term "ruling class." But if we dislike its over-inclusive implications, surely we may not overlook the fact that the essence of power under capitalism is ability to exercise continuing influence, to the point of control where that is deemed necessary, over major decisions. Does one dispose of such upper-class power under capitalism by fleeing to the term "power elite"? "Who or what," Mills asks, "do these [elite] men at the top represent?" He wrestles to explain why it is that the elite exhibit such unity of interest and direction of policy, why they tend to have "codes and criteria in common." And he forsakes the social and institutional level and resorts to the psychological level in such explanations as that "There is a kind of reciprocal attraction among the successful." Agreed. But what is it in our society that gives such emphasis to "success"?

All of this confusion stems from Mills' effort to give to his elite an independence and a diversity in outlook uncomplicated by the solid realities generally associated with class membership and interest and with the desire of those marginal to economic power to get under its tent. If Mills' reasoning does not appeal to historically oriented social scientists, it should permit members of the American "power elite" to sleep better nights.

If Mills does, by main strength and awkwardness, hold his elite somewhat apart from our society's upper class, he has more trouble in keeping institutions apart. Of course he does not intend or imply that institutions are actually sharply separated; the issue is, rather, are institutions and the elites that represent them sufficiently autonomous under capitalism so that, for instance, the economic elite may be expected to have interests and commitments markedly different from the elites representing other institutions? Of corporate business and government he says: "We should . . . be quite mistaken to believe that the political apparatus is merely an extension of the corporate world, or that it has been taken over by the representatives of the corporate rich." Of course. His saving word here is "merely." But the question he repeatedly avoids: how much big business control is enough to give it preponderant control? He does say:

> . . . today the successful economic man, either as propertied manager or manager of property, must influence or control those positions in the state in which decisions of consequence to his corporate activities are made.

> The long-time tendency of business and government to become more intricately and deeply involved with each other has [since the 1930's] reached a new point of explicitness. The two cannot now be seen clearly as two distinct worlds. . . . As of World War II [the corporate business chieftains] have come to dominate [the political directorate].

> . . . today [corporations] are, of course, as much political as economic. As political institutions, they are of course totalitarian and dictatorial, although externally they display much public relations and liberal rhetoric.

113

[Speaking of "decisions responsibly made in the interests of the feudal-like world of private property and income"] Not the politicians of the visible government, but the chief executives who sit in the political directorate, by fact and by proxy, hold the power and the means of defending the privileges of their corporate world. If they do not reign, they do govern at many of the vital points of everyday life in America, and no powers effectively countervail against them, nor have they as corporate-made men developed any effectively restraining conscience.

Selected statements like these seem to march straight toward an important conclusion—so much so that they appear to refute my strictures on the inconclusiveness of the book's analysis. The questions that all but ask themselves from these assembled excerpts are: If the contemporary trends in corporate business power and its influence in government are as here suggested, why pretend that government and business are any longer importantly apart? Do such statements imply, when taken with the present increasing dependence of the political sphere upon business prosperity, that big business is increasingly in the position to dominate political democracy? Is the increasingly mass character of our society prevailingly traceable to the serviceability of a mass society to capitalist mass production?

These are weighty questions, and one has no right to insist that a man who writes a book shall answer them. But if that man sees warrant for making such judgments as the above quoted passages imply in a book devoted to the appraisal of power, is one justified in asking that he go on to ask the questions that then become unavoidable, to attempt to answer them, and that his answers—however guarded and tentative—be made the explicit basis for whatever else he thinks is relevant enough to the problem of power to be discussed in his book?

I am indebted to Professor Mills for much that he says in his book, particularly for his straightforward documentation at a number of points. But the basis of my criticism, as the above suggests, runs deep. The book reads as though it were written by two people: one with a relatively sure grasp of the realities of a capitalist society, and the other bewitched by the plausible appeal of a book on elites; and that the two never got together, but the man at work on elites succeeded in blurring and impairing what the other had to say.

So, to conclude: This book demonstrates the need to return to a more full-bodied approach to the problem of organized power in society than elite theory provides.

Power Elite or Ruling Class?

BY PAUL M. SWEEZY

There is a sort of contrived bloodlessness about American academic social science today. Its practitioners are much better trained than they used to be, but the consequence is not only technical competence. No less striking is the way they all fit into a few neat molds, like the models of an automobile com-

Paul M. Sweezy is an economist who has taught at Harvard, Stanford, and Cornell. He is co-editor of the Monthly Review. *His books include* The Present as History, Cuba: Anatomy of a Revolution (*with Leo Huberman*), *and* Monopoly Capital (*with Paul Baran*). *The present review appeared in* Monthly Review, *September, 1956.*

ing off the factory assembly lines. They talk alike, deal in the same brand of trivialities, and take each other enormously seriously. Above all, there is a kind of tacit conspiracy to banish all really interesting and important issues from the universe of "scientific" discourse.

Against this background, C. Wright Mills, associate professor of sociology at Columbia University, stands out as a man of courage and imagination, an iconoclast who cares little for the sacred cows of university administrators and foundation trustees, an innovator who wants to get along with the important business of understanding the United States of America in the middle of the twentieth century. In *White Collar: The American Middle Classes,* he explored the emotional and cultural wastelands of American society. Now, in *The Power Elite,* he goes a step farther and asks who really runs the show and what makes them tick. The result is an absorbing book that has the added fascination which always attaches to forbidden topics.

The plan of Mills' book is as follows: He opens with a chapter ("The Higher Circles") which gives a general sketch of the theme of the work as a whole. There then follow nine chapters devoted to analyzing the Higher Circles from various angles and by various breakdowns: Local Society, Metropolitan 400, The Celebrities, The Very Rich, The Chief Executives, The Corporate Rich, The Warlords, The Military Ascendancy, and The Political Directorate. Finally come five chapters of interpretation and argumentation: The Theory of Balance, The Power Elite, The Mass Society, The Conservative Mood, and The Higher Immorality. There is no compelling logic to the organization of the material, and rigor and elegance are not among Mills' outstanding virtues as a writer. The result is that the book contains not a few asides and excursions, much repetition, and considerable excess verbiage. The whole work would have benefited from a severe editing, and its impact on the reader would, I think, have been sharpened and intensified if it had been cut by, say, a quarter to a third.

Perhaps the greatest merit of *The Power Elite* is that it boldly breaks the tabu which respectable intellectual society has imposed on any serious discussion of how and by whom America is ruled. Those of us who inhabit what may be called the radical underworld have, of course, never been constrained by this particular tabu, but it must be admitted that radicals have produced very little of scientific value in recent years, and even work that does meet minimum standards of competence has been pretty effectively smothered. In contrast, *The Power Elite,* written by a professor at a respectable university and brought out by a properly conservative publishing house, has already been widely reviewed in such media as *Time* and *The Saturday Review of Literature,* and seems certain to provoke controversy among Mills' professional colleagues. For the first time in a long while, the literate public has been exposed to a serious discussion of social power and stratification at the na-tional—as distinct from the local—level, and currently fash-ionable theories of the dispersal of power among many groups and interests have been bluntly challenged as flimsy apolo-getics. This is all to the good, and we may hope that Mills' ex-ample will be not only heeded but also emulated by other academic authors and established publishers.[1]

[1] Let me take this occasion to express a subsidiary hope that writers like Mills will become even bolder in challenging the tabus of respectability. Ever since it was founded in 1949, *Monthly Review* has consistently sought to analyze and clarify the problems of *national* power in American society —not, I hope, without throwing out some useful and interesting suggestions. Mills makes generous reference in his notes to our analysis of "The Roots and Prospects of McCarthyism" (*MR,* January 1954) but otherwise fails to note, even in a bibliographical way, any of the numerous articles and edito-rials which have dealt with one or more aspects of his chosen subject. Of course, it is possible that Mills may not be familiar with this material or may consider it of no value. A more likely explanation of his ignoring it, I

117

The fact that it raises crucially important issues is by no means the only merit of *The Power Elite*. Indeed, a reviewer cannot pretend even to list all the book's many excellencies: to appreciate them, one must read and study it with the care it deserves. But I do want to call attention to certain features which struck at least one reader as particularly noteworthy:

(1) There are numerous flashes of insight and happy formulations which not only enliven the narrative but, more important, help us to understand difficult or obscure problems. It would be hard to find a juster or more damning description of our postwar intellectuals than "those who have abandoned criticism for the new American celebration" (25). It is more than merely salutary to be reminded that "class consciousness is not equally characteristic of all levels of American society: it is most apparent in the upper class" (30). Much of the restless movement of the United States today is illuminated by the statement: "To succeed is to leave local society behind—although certification by it may be needed in order to be selected for national cliques" (39). How vividly the connection between wealth and social standing comes out in this remark: "All families would seem to be rather 'old,' but not all of them have possessed wealth for at least two but preferably three or four generations" (49). And how very apt and accurate is the designation of our present-day corporate system as an "apparatus of appropriation" (107) which showers on its beneficiaries all kinds of blessings in addition to their take-home pay. (Mills is right to emphasize this theme in several different contexts: my only criticism is that he doesn't emphasize it

---

think, is a (perhaps unconscious) fear of what might be called "guilt by citation." At any rate this fear is certainly common enough in academic circles nowadays, whether or not it was operative in Mills' case. From the point of view of the "power elite," it serves the useful purpose of helping to isolate radicals and censor radical thought. From the point of view of scientific discussion and advance, needless to say, its effects are wholly negative.

enough.) These are but a few random samples, taken from the first quarter of *The Power Elite,* of what I mean by "flashes of insight and happy formulations." They are among the real pleasures and rewards of the book.

(2) Equally impressive is the factual material which Mills has assembled and analyzed in support or illustration of his arguments. He has made good use of the specialized work of social scientists—for example, H. B. Hollingshead's *Elmtown's Youth* and Dixon Wecter's *The Saga of American Society*— but for the most part he relies on original research in the current press and biographical sources. In this connection, he presents a number of statistical and semi-statistical studies which are important contributions in their own right and which should go far toward exploding some of the more popular and persistent myths about the rich and the powerful in America today. Chapter 5 on "The Very Rich" is essentially such a study, and there are others of a somewhat less ambitious nature in most of the chapters which undertake to categorize and describe "the power elite." Mills is well aware that an individual researcher, even with considerable help from friends, students, and assistants, can hardly hope to do more than scratch the surface of the vast amount of relevant material which exists in this country: he was, in fact, frequently obliged to put drastic limits on the scope of his efforts. Nevertheless, his factual statements are for the most part solidly, if not exhaustively, supported; and in a field which is not likely to benefit from the generosity (or curiosity) of the well-heeled foundations, we shall probably have to remain content with the contributions of individual researchers. One could only wish that they were all as careful, competent, and imaginative as Mills.

(3) It seems to me that Mills speaks with the voice of an authentic American radicalism. He is highly critical of the American system and frequently lays about him with strong

119

adjectives, heavy sarcasm, and biting invective. But he doesn't *hate* "the American way of life" and turn his back on it, as so many of our foreign critics do; and he isn't overawed by foreign authority, as so many of our native radicals have always been. One gets the impression that Mills not only understands but to a considerable extent even shares the predominant values of the American "mass society." He indulges in none of the currently fashionable deprecation of "materialism," and his attitude toward wealth is well indicated in a passage which is worth quoting at some length:

> The idea that the millionaire finds nothing but a sad, empty place at the top of society; the idea that the rich do not know what to do with their money; the idea that the successful become filled up with futility, and that those born successful are poor and little as well as rich—the idea, in short, of the disconsolateness of the rich—is, in the main, merely a way by which those who are not rich reconcile themselves to the fact. Wealth in America is directly gratifying and directly leads to many further gratifications.

> To be truly rich is to possess the means of realizing in big ways one's little whims and fantasies and sicknesses. "Wealth has great privileges," Balzac once remarked, "and the most enviable of them all is the power of carrying out thoughts and feelings to the uttermost; of quickening sensibility by fulfilling its myriad caprices." The rich, like other men, are perhaps more simply human than otherwise. But their toys are bigger; they have more of them; they have more of them all at once (163–164).

The same idea is more simply summed up in a statement quoted from Sophie Tucker (without either approval or disapproval in the context): "I've been rich and I've been poor, and believe me, rich is best" (346). For a radical, the corollary of this attitude is that it is not wealth that is wrong with

America but poverty, and that what is reprehensible about the rich is not that they enjoy the good things of life but that they use their power to maintain a system which needlessly denies the same advantages to others. Mills, to be sure, doesn't spell this out, but I think it is undeniably implicit in his whole position.

It is easy to criticize this point of view, and indeed much of what Mills himself says about the irresponsibility, mindlessness, and immorality of "the power elite" would furnish the basis of a damning indictment of wealth in a context of exploitation, an indictment which Mills conspicuously fails to elaborate in any thorough or systematic way. But I think that Mills' weaknesses in this connection are characteristically American and that for this reason they have much to teach us about the possibility and requirements of an effective American radical propaganda. Denunciations of wealth as such, in the earlier tradition of radical thought, are likely to fall on deaf ears in this country today; rightly or wrongly, most Americans approve of it and want more for themselves. A successful radical movement must convince them that it really has more of it to offer the great majority of them than has the present system of waste and plunder.

(4) Mills performs a very valuable service in insisting, emphatically and at times even dogmatically, that what happens in the United States today depends crucially on the will and decision of a relatively very small group which is essentially self-perpetuating and responsible to no one but its own membership. And in upholding this position, he earns our gratitude by a forthright attack on the social harmonics of our latter-day Bastiats such as J. K. Galbraith and David Riesman. Galbraith and Riesman are able social scientists and keen observers of the American scene, but their overall "theories," for which they have received so much praise and fame, are childishly

pretentious and superficial. It is high time that a reputable member of the academic community should say so. Some day American social scientists will acknowledge the debt they owe to Mills for having been the first among them to proclaim in no uncertain terms that the king is naked.

I do not mean to imply by this any blanket endorsement of Mills' theoretical contributions. As I hope to show immediately, Mills' theory is open to serious criticism. But he has the very great merit of bringing the real issues into the open and discussing them in a way that anyone can understand; and he refuses to condone the kind of slick cover-up job that so many of his academic colleagues have been helping to put over on the American and foreign publics in the years of the "American celebration."

It is not easy to criticize *The Power Elite* from a theoretical standpoint for the simple reason that the author often states or implies more than one theory on a given topic or range of topics. Sometimes, I think, this arises from haste in composition and a certain intellectual sloppiness or impatience which seems to characterize much of Mills' work. Sometimes it seems to result from acceptance of the substance as well as the terminology of a kind of "elitist" doctrine which is basically antithetical to the general trend of his thought. And sometimes, no doubt, it arises from the fact that Mills, like most of the rest of us, has not made up his mind about all the problems of American social structure and finds himself with conflicting ideas rattling around in his head. In the brief space available here, I cannot attempt to untangle these confusions and contradictions, nor can I presume to say which of various possible interpretations most accurately reflects Mills' true meaning. Rather, I shall concentrate on trying to show what's wrong with certain ideas, adding in advance an invitation to Mills to correct me to the extent that I am wrong in attributing them to him or to make any other rejoinder he may think called for.

Mills starts off with a concept of the power elite which is disarmingly simple. Those who occupy the "command posts" of our major economic, military, and political institutions constitute the power elite—the big shareholders and executives of the corporate system, the generals and admirals of the Pentagon, and the elected and appointed officials who occupy political positions of national significance. But this of course tells us nothing about the men who stand at these posts—how they got there, their attitudes and values, their relations with each other and with the rest of society, and so on—nor does it provide any but an admittedly misleading clue to these questions: Mills himself repeatedly rejects the notion that the power elite in his sense constitutes some sort of natural aristocracy of ability and intelligence, in spite of the common connotation of the term "elite."

Having in effect defined the power elite as composed of the big shots of industry and government, Mills' next task is to devise a theoretical scheme within which to locate them and to guide his empirical investigations into their characteristics and habits. Two general approaches readily suggest themselves, and Mills follows them both without ever clearly distinguishing them, without asking how far and in what respects they may be in conflict, and without any systematic attempt to reconcile their divergent results. The first approach is via social class: the hypothesis can be put forward and tested that those who occupy the command posts do so as representatives or agents of a national ruling class which trains them, shapes their thought patterns, and selects them for their positions of high responsibility. The second approach is via what Mills variously calls the "major institutional orders" (e.g., 269), the "major hierarchies" (287), the "big three domains" (288), and other more or less synonymous terms. This assumes that there are distinct spheres of social life—the economic, the military, and the political—each with its own institutional structure, that each of these spheres throws up its own leading cadres, and that the top men of all three come together to form the power elite.

Now there may be societies, past or present, in which this idea of more or less autonomous orders, hierarchies, or domains has enough relevance to make it a fruitful approach to problems of social structure and power. But it seems perfectly clear to me that the United States is not and never has been such a society. Moreover, the cumulative effects of the empirical data presented by Mills is decisively against any such interpretation of the American system. He adduces a wealth of material on our class system, showing how the local units of the upper class are made up of propertied families and how these local units are welded together into a wholly self-conscious national class. He shows how the "power elite" is overwhelmingly (and increasingly) recruited from the upper levels of the class system, how the same families contribute indifferently to the economic, military, and political "elites," and how the same individuals move easily and almost imperceptibly back and forth from one to another of these "elites." When it comes to "The Political Directorate" (Chapter 10), he demonstrates that the notion of a specifically political elite is in reality a myth, that the crucial positions in government and politics are increasingly held by what he calls "political outsiders," and that these outsiders are in fact members or errand boys of the corporate rich.

This demonstration in effect reduces "the big three" to "the big two"—the corporate and the military domains. There is no doubt at all about the decisive importance of the former, and Mills makes some of his most useful and interesting contributions in discussing the wealth, power, and other characteristics of the corporate rich.[2] But the evidence for an autonomous, or even semi-autonomous, military domain of comparable importance is so weak that it can be said to be almost nonexistent. Historically, to be sure, the military has normally been somewhat separated from the mainstream of American life, and in this sense one could perhaps speak of a military domain. But it has been small and completely subject to civilian control, quite impotent in terms of the national decision-making which is the special function of Mills' power elite. In wartime, of course, the military has swelled enormously in size and power, but it is precisely then that it has ceased to be a separate domain. The civilian higher circles have moved into commanding military positions, and the top brass has been accepted into the higher circles. What happens in such times is that the "power elite" becomes militarized in the sense that it has to concern itself with military problems, it requires military skills, and it must inculcate in the underlying population greater respect for military virtues and personnel.

All this has nothing in common with the rise to power of a military order headed by an elite of "warlords," though it is in these terms that Mills describes what has been happening in the United States since the beginning of World War II, and indeed *must* describe it or else abandon the whole theory of a composite power elite made of separate "domainal" elites; for on his own showing the "political directorate" is merely an emanation of the corporate rich. To support the theory of "The Warlords" (Chapter 8) and "The Military Ascendancy" (Chapter 9), Mills brings forth little evidence beyond the

[2] The three chapters entitled "The Very Rich," "The Chief Executives," and "The Corporate Rich" are not really about different groups. They are simply about differently constructed but widely overlapping samplings of what is essentially a homogeneous social stratum which can be aptly designated as "the corporate rich."

125

well-known facts that the military trade has traditionally required a specialized training and code of conduct, and that the Pentagon is an important center of power in American life. But these facts require no such fancy interpretation and are perfectly compatible with a more prosaic theory of the locus of power in mid-twentieth-century United States.

But Mills really relies much less on facts than on a sort of unstated syllogism to back up his warlord-military ascendancy theory. The syllogism might be formulated as follows: the major outlines of American policy, both foreign and domestic, are drawn in terms of a "military definition of world reality" which has been accepted by the power elite as a whole; this military definition of reality (also referred to as "military metaphysics") must be the product of the professional military mind ("the warlords"); *ergo* the warlords now occupy a decisive position within the power elite ("the military ascendancy"). This may look impressive and convincing at a first glance, but a moment's reflection will show that it explains nothing and constitutes no support whatever for Mills' theory. Professional military people naturally think in military terms and have doubtless always tried to persuade others to see things their way. Throughout most of United States history, they have succeeded, if at all, only in wartime. The real problem is to understand why it is that since World War II the whole "power elite" has come to think increasingly in military terms and hence to accord a place of greater honor and power to the military. Without an answer to this, all the facts that seem to Mills to add up to the "military ascendancy" of the "warlords" remain quite unexplained.

Now Mills himself never faces up to this question, and the only relevant answer I can find is that the United States now, unlike in the past, lives in a "military neighborhood" (the phrase is used on a number of occasions), which presumably means that the country is under constant threat (or potential threat) of attack and military defeat. This is more sophisticated than saying that we live in mortal danger of red aggression, but its explanatory value is exactly the same: in either case the increasing militarization of American life is the result of external forces. The rise of the warlords, then, is seen as the outcome of a world historical process for which the United States has no responsibility and over which it has no control, and not, as Mills clearly wants to prove, as the outcome of *internal* forces operating in the military domain.

Thus, while Mills appears to have little in common with the cold-war liberals, and in fact rather generally holds them in contempt, his theory of the role of the military leads to very much the same conclusions. I believe that this is no accident. "Elitist" thinking *inevitably* diverts attention from problems of social structure and process and leads to a search for external causes of social phenomena. Simon-pure elitists like Pareto and his followers frankly adopt this method and find what they are looking for in the alleged natural qualities of their elites. Semi-elitists like Mills—people who think they can adopt the terminology without any of the basic ideas of elitist theory— tend to get bogged down in confusion from which the only escape is to borrow the most banal ideas of their opponents.

It is too bad that Mills gets into this kind of a mess, because, as I indicated above, his work is strongly influenced by a straightforward class theory which, if he had stuck to it and consistently explored its implications, would have enabled him to avoid completely the superficialities and pitfalls of elitist thinking. The uppermost class in the United States is, and long has been, made up of the corporate rich who directly pull the economic levers. Prior to the Great Depression and World War II, the corporate rich left political and military matters largely (though by no means exclusively) in the control of

127

hired hands and trusted agents; but since the highly dangerous economic breakdown of the thirties, the Big Boys have increasingly taken over the key positions themselves. Their unwillingness to solve the economic problems of capitalism through a really massive welfare-state program meant that they welcomed the war as the salvation of their system. Since the end of World War II, they have accepted, nay created and sold through all the media of mass communications, a "military definition of reality" as the ideological-political underpinning of the war-preparations economy, which remains crucial to the whole profit-making mechanism on which their wealth and power rest. For this purpose, they have lavishly subsidized and encouraged the military, which in turn has not only grown vastly in size but also has been enormously flattered and has become the most loyal defender and promoter of the "free enterprise" system. The picture of "warlords" exercising a "military ascendancy" is fanciful: *our* warlords have no fundamental values or purposes different from those of their corporate colleagues; many of them perform virtually indistinguishable jobs; and the crowning achievement of a military career today is the board chairmanship of a billion-dollar corporation.[3] At the same time, we have nothing even approaching a unified military order or caste seeking to impose its "military metaphysics" on the nation. The most famous of our "warlords," President Eisenhower, is now the most peaceful of our influential politicians; while our most strident "militarists" are civilian Sena-

[3] On this whole range of topics, see the fascinating article entitled "They're Masters of Buying By the Billion" in *Business Week* for June 23, 1956. "They" are Generals C. S. Irvine and E. W. Rawlings, in charge of procurement and supply for the Air Force. Mr. Dudley C. Sharp, civilian Assistant Secretary of the Air Force, is quoted as saying: "These two could run any business in the world. They're absolutely the finest executives I've ever met." Chances are, too, that they will end up running one or more of the world's biggest businesses!

tors Symington and Jackson whose closest affiliations would seem to be with the multi-billion-dollar aircraft industry.

No, the facts simply won't fit Mills' theory of three (or two) sectional elites coming together to form an overall power elite. What we have in the United States is a *ruling class* with its roots deeply sunk in the "apparatus of appropriation" which is the corporate system. To understand this ruling class—its metaphysics, its purposes, and its morals—we need to study, not certain "domains" of American life, however defined, but the whole system of monopoly capitalism.

A large part of Mills' theory and most of his facts support this view. This, indeed, is why his book, for all its weaknesses, is such a vital and powerful document. Let us hope that in the future he will drop *all* the elitist nonsense and make the contribution he is capable of making to deepening our theory and understanding of the American class system.[4]

In conclusion, I should like to comment very briefly on four of the many issues which would merit detailed discussion in a full-dress review of *The Power Elite*.

(1) Because he blurs the whole problem of class and class relations, Mills fails to throw any but incidental light on the dynamics of the class system—how people lose high-class

[4] Mills' reasons for rejecting the ruling class concept are stated in a footnote (277) which deserves no more than a footnote in reply. "Ruling class," he says, is a "badly loaded" phrase in the sense that it contains the theory that "an economic class rules politically." What of it? The question is whether the theory is applicable to the United States today, and if investigation shows that it is, then the only "loading" is on the side of truth. As I have argued above, most of Mills' factual material supports the ruling class theory to the hilt—provided only that one doesn't insist on interpreting the words "economic" and "class" in an impossibly narrow and tortured way. For the rest, I have already said enough about Mills' alternative theory, repeated in the footnote in question, that a "coalition" of the "higher agents" of the "three domains" constitutes a power elite. (There is, of course, no loading at all in the phrase "power elite"!)

status, how new members of the ruling class are co-opted, and so on. In this connection, he completely fails to understand the role of the preparatory schools and colleges as recruiters for the ruling class, sucking upwards the ablest elements of the lower classes and thus performing the double function of infusing new brains into the ruling class and weakening the potential leadership of the working class. It is this aspect of the American educational system, involving as it does fairly generous scholarships and other forms of assistance for the bright poor, which is most often and least deservedly praised as democratic.

(2) While Mills' chapter on "The Celebrities" is informative and amusing, it is a hopeless muddle from the theoretical point of view. The celebrities—of screen, TV, radio, stage, sport—are not an integral part of the ruling class or the power elite, and in general they do not compete in prestige with the rich and the powerful. On the contrary, the rich and the powerful have every interest in building up the celebrities, partly because it is good business and partly to divert the attention of the underlying population from more serious matters. This is all part of what Mills elsewhere calls, in a memorable phrase, "the grim trivialization of American life." Mills' confusion on these questions—which of course does not prevent him from saying many true and penetrating things about them—stems in large part from the lack of any clear or usable theory of prestige. He treats prestige as a pure magnitude and quite misses the point that there are different kinds as well as quantities of prestige and that they have different bases and perform different functions in the social structure.

(3) I pointed out above (p. 121) that Mills strongly insists, quite rightly in my view, that major national decisions in this country are made by a relatively small group of people at the top of the social pyramid. But in his concern to drive this

point home, it seems to me that he goes much too far in the direction of what I may call "historical voluntarism." On page 24 of *The Power Elite,* Mills makes the following statement:

> It is . . . true that if most men and women take whatever roles are permitted to them and enact them as they are expected to by virtue of their position, this is precisely what the elite need *not* do, and often do not do. They may call into question the structure, their position within it, or the way they are to enact that position.

If this were really true, our only hope of understanding the behavior of the top group would be through psychoanalysis: the objectively discoverable pressures and compulsions of the social order which operate on the rest of us would be irrelevant to these august Olympians. But of course it is not true, and I make so bold as to say that most of the time Mills himself knows it perfectly well. What corporation executive can afford to order his behavior without regard to his company's profit-and-loss statement? What American politician today can flout the interests of the corporate rich who put him in office? What military man can say that the Soviet Union is no menace and the United States should set the world an example of unilateral disarmament? To be sure, each one of these gentlemen can behave in the indicated fashion, provided he is prepared to lose his job and with it his power. But this is precisely the point: like everyone else, the "elite" have roles to perform, and for the most part they are exacting ones: failure means loss of position and power.

What Mills could and should have argued in this connection is that the roles are *not* like those of a theatrical performance, completely mapped out and rigidly determined in advance. The actors have a *range of choice* which is set by the nature and laws of the social structure under which they live, and this range may even include such fateful alternatives as that which faced Harry Truman in August of 1945, whether or not to drop a bomb that would in a single flash snuff out the lives of a quarter of a million human beings. "Men make their own history," Marx wrote in the *Eighteenth Brumaire,* "but they do not make it under circumstances chosen by themselves, but under circumstances directly found, given and transmitted from the past." That is the simple truth, confirmed by mountains of historical and personal experience alike. Why can't social scientists as reasonable and sensible as C. Wright Mills take it *and hold onto it?*

(4) Finally, a word about a matter which has undoubtedly disturbed some left-wing readers of *The Power Elite.* Mills, they say, explodes many myths about the United States today. He shows that the country is run by a tiny irresponsible minority, and that in crucial respects the consequence is a drift from bad to worse. But he says nothing at all about what can or should be done about it.

For my part, I see no valid ground for criticism here. We should be grateful for such a good book, and we can draw our own conclusions about what to do about the situation it reveals. We can even go farther and commend Mills for his restraint: we know from his association with the magazine *Dissent* that Mills considers himself a socialist, and we can be pretty sure that under present circumstances *The Power Elite* with explicitly stated socialist conclusions would never have been published, reviewed, and read as it has been without the conclusions.

For the rest, it is no violation of principle not to set down everything in your mind every time you put pen to paper. What *is* a violation of principle is to set down a lot of things that aren't true or you don't believe, and on this score, so far as I am able to judge, Mills deserves a clean bill of health.

Power in America

BY HERBERT APTHEKER

The central theme of *The Power Elite* is well conveyed in its title. It is that there *is* an elite who dominate the American social order; this power complex, Mills holds, is made up of three related but fairly autonomous forces—the masters of the private corporative economy, the rulers of the governmental apparatus, and the commanders of the colossal military machine.

The volume undertakes to demonstrate the validity of this analysis by describing the sources, nature, habits, and conduct of each of these three strands, and by arguing against the major differing estimates of the contemporary American scene.

Mills' conclusions deserve to be read in his own words. In searching for those paragraphs which would do this with fullest justice—within reasonable space limitations—I have chosen two:

> The shape and meaning of the power elite today can be understood only when these three sets of structural trends [identified above—H.A.] are seen at their point of coincidence: the military capitalism of private corporations exists in a weakened and formal democratic system containing a military

Herbert Aptheker received his Ph.D. in history from Columbia University and has written numerous articles and books on American Negro history, including American Negro Slave Revolts. *He is editor of* Political Affairs, *the director of the American Institute for Marxist Studies, and a member of the National Committee of the U. S. Communist Party. The present review appeared first in* Mainstream, *September, 1956, and then in a slightly revised form as a chapter in his* The World of C. Wright Mills (*New York: Marzani and Munsell, 1960*), *from which this version is reprinted.*

order already quite political in outlook and demeanor. Accordingly, at the top of this structure, the power elite has been shaped by the coincidence of interest between those who control the major means of production and those who control the newly enlarged means of violence; from the decline of the professional politician and the rise to explicit political command of the corporate chieftains and the professional war lords; from the absence of any genuine civil service of skill and integrity, independent of vested interests (276).

And, to fill in other fundamental features of his estimate, the paragraph ending the volume:

> The men of the higher circles are not representative men; their high position is not a result of moral virtue; their fabulous success is not firmly connected with meritorious ability. Those who sit in the seats of the high and the mighty are selected and formed by the means of power, the sources of wealth, the mechanics of celebrity, which prevail in their society. They are not men selected and formed by a civil service that is linked with the world of knowledge and sensibility. They are not men shaped by nationally responsible parties that debate openly and clearly the issues this nation now so unintelligently confronts. They are not men held in responsible check by a plurality of voluntary associations which connect debating publics with the pinnacles of decision. Commanders of power unequaled in human history, they have succeeded within the American system of organized irresponsibility.

Mills sees in the United States a trinity-like, immoral elite, dominating for purposes of aggrandizement and perpetuation. He combats with a high degree of effectiveness the views of those who, through various systems, present an idyllic United States; he combats these views as features, in one form or another, of the "New Conservatism." Thus, he refutes the thesis of those who, like Louis Hartz, see nothing but a "middle class" among the propertied interests here and explain their vision on the basis of an absence of feudalism in American history. Mills would have been more effective had he pointed out that there was a relative, not an absolute, absence of feudal forms and institutions here—they were, for example, important in upstate New York and in Maryland—and that there was a prefeudal form in our history, chattel slavery, which played a decisive role in American development through the Civil War, just as some of its survivals exert so decisive an influence upon present-day American life. These failings, and especially the latter, which is but one instance of Mills' consistent ignoring of the Negro question in all his writings, seriously diluted the sharpness of his analysis.

Mills does, however, offer the essential refutation of those who would develop an American "exceptionalism" out of the (relative) absence of feudalism here. For while he agrees that this was "of decisive importance to the nature of the American elite, as well as to American society as a whole," nevertheless, he continues, "this does not mean that there are no upper strata in the United States. That they emerged from a 'middle class' that had no recognized aristocratic superiors does not mean that they remained middle class when enormous increases in wealth made their own superiority possible."

Related to historians who see only a "middle-class" history —David Potter, Daniel J. Boorstin, and Robert E. Brown are other examples—are sociologists who see only a "middle-class" society. Mills labels this the nonsense it is: a fairy tale that "Once upon a time in America there were the fabulously rich; now that time is past and everyone is only middle class." Mills does this in a chapter entitled "The Very Rich," which is, of course, crucial for his argument of a power elite. The chapter is, from one approach, an effective refutation of the "middle-class" school, for it demonstrates what is the fact: the existence of an infinitesimal fraction of the population which owns and controls a decisively significant portion of the nation's wealth.

Once again, however, Mills' argument would have been enhanced if he had attacked the "middle-class" school not only from the viewpoint of the existence of a "very rich" but also from the viewpoint of the existence of a "poor" and a "very poor." Data were available when Mills wrote his *Power Elite* showing that as of 1954 there were *seventeen million people* living in United States families with a total annual money income, *before* taxes, of under $1,000, not to speak of the *majority of families* with under $4,000 annual income, before taxes!

The accuracy of the picture of the United States ruled by a power elite, as presented by Mills, is seriously marred by his failure to consider this aspect of its life; it is related to Mills' rejection of the mass line in political analysis and program projection.

Connected with the idea of an all-middle-class United States is the idea that while some rich remain they are only a vestigial phenomenon—antedating the present "confiscatory" tax system—whose days are quite limited. To the contrary, Mills shows the historical continuity of the very rich, and demonstrates that with each passing generation the fraction among them who are "self-made" men—who pushed their way out of a "lower" class into the highest circle—declines. The very rich of 1925, he shows were the lineal descendants, generally, of the very rich of 1900, and "the 1950 very rich are very much a continuation of the very rich of 1925."

Concerning the legend of a confiscatory tax system so far as the very rich are concerned Mills has a detailed exposure substantiating his conclusion: "For virtually every law taxing big money, there is a way those with big money can avoid it or minimize it."

Another myth of the "New Conservatism" basic to the State Department's "People's Capitalism" is the notion that the ownership of the American corporate system is widely dispersed. "The idea of a really wide distribution of economic ownership is a cultivated illusion," writes Mills. "At the very most 0.2 or 0.3 percent of the adult population own the bulk, the pay-off shares of the corporate world." Such figures are enough where the concentration is on the power elite alone, but once again such a focus, if unrelieved, gives rise to one-sidedness. Thus, it is important in examining the question of dispersal of corporate ownership not only to see that a fraction of 1 percent owns "the bulk, the pay-off shares" but to see that a total of about 7 percent of the population owns some corporation stock—about the same percentage as in the 1930's. It is important also to see that dispersal of ownership—such as there is—actually assists monopolization, for it cuts the percentage of ownership required for effective control.

At the same time, Mills would have avoided a certain appearance of special pleading if he had noticed this 7 percent of stock owners, for that amounts to over 11 million people—no insignificant base, surely, in purely numerical terms, for the building of illusions about a "People's Capitalism" and similar petty-bourgeois visions.

Mills also refutes the idea of an "income revolution" in the United States put forth by Simon Kuznets and Arthur E. Burns among others, and intimately connected with the "People's Capitalism" propaganda. In doing this, Mills again would have strengthened his case had he referred to, or known, the excellent critique of this idea by Victor Perlo.[1] He also effec-

[1] *The Income "Revolution,"* by V. Perlo (New York, 1954). Professor Mills never refers to or cites American Marxist writers, though their work

tively combats Galbraith's widely heralded theory of "counter-vailing power" and A. A. Berle's transparently demagogic dependence on a "corporate conscience"—both devices for washing away the unpleasant reality of monopolization. Char-acteristically witty and well-turned is Mills' concluding dismissal of Berle's hypothesis: "Mr. Berle, in brief, mistakes expedient public relations for a 'corporate soul.' "

The Nevins-Hacker effort to make "creative personalities" and folk heroes out of the voracious robber barons is deftly handled by Mills, though he attributes contrary evaluations only to the muckraking school of Gustavus Myers. Actually, the original study entitled *The Robber Barons,* by Matthew Josephson (published in 1934) is a good deal more profound than muckraking and is in no way deepened by Mr. Mills himself.

Various "harmony-of-interests" schools and Riesman's theory of infinite power sources—all efforts at displacing a class-struggle concept condemned in 1959 as "thoroughly un-American" by no less a scholar than Dwight D. Eisenhower—are found to be inadequate by Mills. His arguments are directed against these ideas in terms of vindicating his own theme of a power elite, and they are effective, for his own theme is so much closer to social reality. Again, however, Mills views the arguments rather narrowly, from his own special vantage point, and does not offer an alternative general theory of historic and social dynamics. The nearest he comes to this is in another sec-tion—sixty pages away from his polemic with the Riesman and "harmony" ideas—where, commenting upon earlier epochs, he

---

anticipates and expands much of his own. This is true of Anna Rochester's studies of monopoly, of the Labor Research Association's studies of the economy, of Louis Fleischer's critique of A. A. Berle, in *Political Affairs* (June, 1955) and of my own critiques of David Riesman and Allan Nevins, in *Laureates of Imperialism* (New York, 1954) and *History and Reality* (New York, 1955), and of other instances.

138

writes, as an aside, of "the Marxian doctrine of class struggle, which surely was then, and certainly is now, closer to reality than any assumed harmony of interests."

Unfortunately, this appears in the thirteenth chapter of a fifteen-chapter volume and receives neither demonstration nor evaluation. Since Mills gave an entire chapter (242–268) to the harmony-of-interests school it is unfortunate that he saw fit to consign "the Marxian doctrine of class struggle" to only part of one sentence, especially since he says that that idea is "closer to reality." It would be splendid to get a volume from Mills devoted directly to testing the validity of that Marxian concept for the present United States scene. It has not come in his *Sociological Imagination,* for there, in a footnote, he remarks that "Marx was quite right about much of the structural change [in modern capitalism]; he was mistaken and inadequate about its psychological consequences"; while further on he reports both John Stuart Mill and Marx—that is, both liberalism and Marxism—to be inadequate for an analysis of the modern world. Yet, again, there are no more than these bare and very brief allusions.

Perhaps in a future work Mills will yet face up fully to the challenge of Marxism by testing its propositions against American reality as he sees it today.[2] Should he do so, he will need a more developed comprehension of the Marxian outlook than any of his writings show him to have, and in the course of this work we shall refer to inadequacies in this regard. Above all, Mills will have to master Lenin, whose contributions to the application and development of Marxism, for the twentieth century, have completely escaped Mr. Mills' attention—at least so far as his published works show.[3]

[2] Ed. note: Mills did this in *The Marxists* (Dell, 1962), his last book.
[3] In avoiding Lenin, Mills is, of course, characteristic of American sociologists. Thus, a fifty-year index to the *American Journal of Sociology,*

C. WRIGHT MILLS AND *THE POWER ELITE*

Mills' rejection of the various conservative apologies is philosophically grounded. In his *Power Elite* he directly attacks the eclecticism so prevalent in the teaching of social science in United States colleges and insists that value judgments and interpretive generalizations are a vital part of the scholar's effort. Social scientists, he holds, must "go beyond a mere enumeration of all the facts that might conceivably be involved and weight each of them in such a way as to understand how they fit together, how they form a model of what it is you are trying to understand."

He does not accept the idea—also quite prevalent in U.S. academic circles—of history as chaos or "blind drift," and sees its existence, somewhat invidiously, I thought, as "largely a fatalist projection of one's own feeling of impotence and perhaps, if one has ever been active politically in a principled way, a salve of one's guilt." The attribution of motives arising out of feelings of impotence or guilt is unfortunate; surely it does not help in understanding the hold of such ideas upon a man like Charles A. Beard. It tends, too, to ignore the more fundamental social and historic, the structural, sources for such ideas, and to depend upon a psychologizing against which Mills himself argues effectively in another of his books, the *Sociological Imagination.*

Overall, in *The Power Elite,* Mills takes an unequivocal and generally well-argued—and much needed—stand against the New Conservatism. He overstates matters, I think, when he declares that "In America, there has not been and there can be no conservative ideology of the classic type." This is an error stemming from Mills' complete ignoring of Southern life and history and the realities of a kind of industrial feudalism in U.S. development; it is an error that leads him, in this in-

---

covering the years 1895–1947, shows three listings under Marx, and Marxism, and no listing under Lenin or Leninism.

stance, to insist that there exists in the United States, in the present period, only a "conservative mood." Still, his description of this "mood," which is really very much more profound and more consequential than a "mood," is sensitive, and exemplifies Mills' thought-provoking abilities and his vibrant style:

> It is a mood quite appropriate to men living in a material boom, a nationalist celebration, a political vacuum. At its heart there is knowledge of powerlessness without poignancy, and a feeling of pseudo-power based on mere smugness. By its softening of the political will, this mood enables men to accept public depravity without any private sense of outrage, and to give up the central goal of western humanism: the presumptuous control by reason of man's fate.

Professor Mills certainly retains a splendid dedication to humanism—though I am not so certain as he that the West alone may claim it—and his healthy sense of outrage has not been dulled. His *Power Elite* is filled with unequivocal writing in defense of civil liberty, of rationalism, of dedication to learning as in itself a noble pursuit; it is filled also with burning attacks—as passionate but not as muted as that of his mentor, Veblen—upon the social and personal immorality of the rich, their coarseness, cruelty, hypocrisy, greed, and lustfulness.

He finds that the vulgar accoutrements of the elite—their white Cadillacs with gold-plated dashboards, their homes with faucets pouring out Scotch, bourbon, champagne, or beer, their ladies using lipsticks that cost $300, their gentlemen sending shirts from California to New York by air-express so that Sulka may launder them—are merely the manifestations of deeper moral decay, "the higher immorality," as he calls it.

Where in American literature is there so acute and devastating a paragraph on *Fortune's* ideal executive as this one:

141

C. WRIGHT MILLS AND *THE POWER ELITE*

Speak in the rich, round voice, and do not confuse your superiors with details. Know where to draw the line. Execute the ceremony of forming a judgment. Delay recognizing the choice you have already made, so as to make the truism sound like the deeply pondered notion. Speak like the quiet competent man of affairs and never personally say No. Hire the No-man as well as the Yes-man. Be the tolerant Maybe-man and they will cluster around you, filled with hopefulness. Practice softening the facts into the optimistic, practical, forward-looking, cordial, brisk view. Speak to the well-blunted point. Have weight, be stable; caricature what you are supposed to be but never become aware of it much less amused by it. And never let your brain show.

One wants to go on and on with examples of superb prose-pictures of the elite and their lackeys, as of the "expense-account executives" and their purchased "All-American Girls." I can't resist sharing his lines on that which is "the American danger." He does not see it in the "barbarous irrationality of dour political primitives"—whose significance, I must say, he generally underestimates—but rather in "the respected judgments of the Secretaries of State, the earnest platitudes of Presidents, the fearful self-righteousness of sincere young American politicians from California." He continues:

Such men as these are crackpot realists; in the name of realism they have constructed a paranoid reality of their own; in the name of practicality they have projected a utopian image of capitalism. They have replaced the responsible interpretation of events with the disguise of events by a maze of public relations; respect for public debate with unshrewd notions of psychological warfare; intellectual ability with agility of the sound, mediocre judgment; the capacity to elaborate alternatives and gauge their consequences with the executive stance.

Mills cogently criticizes the American schools today as being at best adjusters rather than inspirers; he offers telling

142

estimates of the mass media which "often encroach upon the small-scale discussion, and destroy the chance for the reasonable and leisurely and human interchange of opinion"; he makes stimulating references to the problems of metropolitan living in the United States: the fragmenting and depersonalizing of people, their dehumanization, even, in certain respects, and the difficulties of maintaining full, time-tested, mature friendships. In this connection I would emphasize very much more than does Mills the relationship between the planlessness and the exploitative essence of capitalism and the anti-human features of urbanization; after all, it is not urbanization per se that he is examining, but rather capitalist urbanization.

Mills has a way of seeming to toss off a paragraph—but it has not been tossed off, you may be sure—that has enough in it for hours of thought. As an example, at one point he refers to the instrumentalizing of knowledge so that now in the United States it is a question of what knowledge will *do* for you, or how much prestige it will bring for one's own side: "Knowledge is no longer widely felt as an ideal; it is seen as an instrument. In a society of power and wealth, knowledge is valued as an instrument of power and wealth, and also, of course, as an ornament in conversation."

More significantly, I would add, and here Mills would agree, knowledge sanctifies authority, a use to which it was put openly and without shame in the medieval period. Closed systems, systems approaching or at senility, and systems that are exploitative prostitute knowledge as the handmaiden of sheer authority; thence derive, fundamentally, the tendency toward the instrumentalization of knowledge, as also the drives toward conformity and obscurantism.

Mills' ideal is knowledge which tells one what he is and so frees him, and defines a social order and so helps free its inhabitants. But is the separation of knowledge in itself and

143

knowledge as instrument a real one, or rather only a mental construction? Does the immutable usefulness of knowledge necessarily make less elevated the passion to know, the search for truth because of the beauty and excitement of the search and the unutterable fulfillment of success? Is the human usefulness of knowledge incompatible with the holding of knowledge as an ideal? I would suggest a certain snobbishness as adhering to such a view, akin to the contempt with which human exertion is viewed by aristocrats where such exertion has a useful and/or practical end.

I think Mills has confused what Tawney called *The Sinfulness of an Acquisitive Society* (retitled simply *The Acquisitive Society* for the American market!) which corrupts everything it touches with what knowledge must be or become in a socialist society.

I have three main areas of disagreement with Mills' *Power Elite*. In my opinion, he tends at times to identify the characteristics of the elite with those of the American people as a whole; he depicts the power elite as, in fact and despite some qualification, all-powerful and so makes the masses of people generally powerless; his projection of the concept of a triangular power elite, which he explicitly offers in preference to that of a ruling class, is based on a misconception of "ruling class." Moreover, in his tripartite division of the wielders of control he avoids comparing the relative weight of each of the three and tends to ignore the central depository of power—the financial overlords.

We turn to a consideration of these points of difference.

The confusing of the elite with the general American population and a certain excessiveness of expression that goes beyond the permissible bounds of even heated debate appear in such passages as this:

144

For all the possible values of human society, one and only one is a truly sovereign, truly universal, truly sound, truly and completely acceptable goal of man in America. That goal is money, and let there be no sour grapes about it from the losers.

That Mills is not expatiating here on what the elite think but rather he is presenting what he thinks the elite have succeeded in imposing upon the morality of all Americans is clear from the whole context of the *Power Elite* volume. He makes this plain, repeatedly, in his work. Thus:

The moral uneasiness of our time results from the fact that older values and codes of uprightness no longer grip the men and women of the corporate era, nor have they been replaced by new values and codes which would lend moral meaning and sanction to the corporate routines they must follow.

And:

Money is the one unambiguous criterion of success, and such success is still the sovereign American value.

Mills is wrong, I think, in the success he attributes to the elite's effort to make all Americans morally as corrupt as the elite themselves are. Surely there is moral corruption, but there is good reason to doubt that the mass of Americans are corrupt or as fully corrupt as Mills asserts. Most of them, for instance, are not "making money"; they are, rather, making, or trying to make, a living. And most of them seek this—as man historically has always sought it—as part of a collective unit, and in the face of difficulties shared with many others. This has developed in the past, and develops now, everywhere, including in our own country, at least among many working people, a sense of comradeship, fraternity, and helpfulness. This is especially marked among the most exploited, especially the "darker" peoples—Negroes, Puerto Ricans, Mexican-Americans—who, though ignored in Mills' work, do number about twenty-five millions.

Further, it is a fact that, despite all monopoly capitalism has been able to do, there persists among many productive and creative people in the United States a sense of social responsibility. I shall never forget the remark made to me by the great pioneer in Negro historiography, the late Dr. Carter G. Woodson, who said, apropos of other comments: "I have never deliberately set out to make money in my life."

Dr. Woodson was nearly alone in the eminence he reached, but he was not alone in his moral dignity; and had he been, there would have been no possibility for accomplishment even for him. We find Mills' own writing filled with splendid passion for learning and decency; with profound concern for the welfare of others as well as with every mark of the pride of craftsmanship. And in his acknowledgments, at the conclusion of *Power Elite,* Mills names thirteen fellow scholars "who have generously given me the benefit of their advice" and thanks many other colleagues at several institutions of learning for their help. Furthermore, he writes:

> Several individuals who know at first hand the Federal government, the military, or large corporations have helped me enormously. Without their help this book would be much the poorer, which makes all the more onerous to me the fact that at their request I cannot acknowledge their help by name.

Surely that a professor at Columbia University finds it necessary in a scholarly work to withhold the names of some of those who have helped him is a shattering commentary on the degree of success which the elite have had in their campaign of intimidation and repression waged against the intelligentsia; but that they have not fully succeeded in intimidating, let alone corrupting, even there, is confirmed by Mills himself.

I find it hard to believe that Mills has not seen hundreds and perhaps thousands of examples of creativity, sacrifice, unselfish struggle, and steadfastness. These qualities are all about us and, notwithstanding Nixon and Eastland, they are firmly imbedded in many American people. My own view is that this is present in most American people, but I am aware that this is something I could not prove. Still, Mills cannot prove the opposite, but the point is that he writes as though the opposite were proven or were so true as not to need proof. In this sense, at least, his wholesale condemnation is excessive, and is related, as we shall try to show, to failures of an analytical and programmatic nature.

It is noteworthy that in Mills' analysis of the sources of corruption in our country today his choosing of an elitist conception rather than a class conception militates against his achieving fullest depth in analysis. The structural quality of corruption in a monopoly-capitalist society—its organic presence in the nature of capitalism, which, being exploitative and parasitic, must be immoral, though least so when young—is missed by Mills; it is missed, I think, because he rejects the Marxian analysis of society. From this analysis, too, arises an awareness of the intensifying decay of capitalist society, especially manifested in the moral area, with the aging of capitalism itself. This also is missed by Mills, so that he leaves unexplained the deterioration of "older values and codes of uprightness" as he leaves unexplained their existence in the first place.

Racism, which has had special relationship to and impact upon the development of American capitalism, is a particular source of immorality in our own country; it has had and continues to have a profoundly corrupting influence on the ethics of white America, with class lines in this instance not being very effective distinguishing features. In Mills' discussion of immorality in the United States, and the impact of corruption, his blind spot concerning the whole matter of the Negro, which impairs his analysis generally, is especially glaring.

Related to Mills' idea that the elite has succeeded in corrupting the whole of American society is the fact that he tends to attribute omnipotence to that elite and helplessness to the masses of people. At one point, laboring to deny the conspiracy theory of history—and Mills overworks himself on this, fearing, with some reason, that his thesis lends itself to this kind of concept—he writes that such a theory "is a hurried projection from the difficult effort to understand how shifts in the structure of society open opportunities to various elites and how various elites take advantage or fail to take advantage of them."

It is the limitation of Mills' confining his vision to the elite —which actually distorts the elite, too—that leads him to focus on how various elites react to "shifts in the structure of society." But what shall the social scientist say of those shifts in society's structure; are these not very much more significant, more deep-seated, than the resulting maneuverings of the elite?

And if the problem Mills has set himself is how an elite reacts to the structural shift, can he simultaneously hold the elite to be omnipotent within that society whose shifts induce such reactions? The fact is that the power-elite theory, being generally devoid of real conflict, is a theory that cannot explain the dynamics of society; but since change is continual and certain, its explanation is basic to science even if one wants to understand only what *is,* let alone if one wants to understand what is *to become.*

Mills makes quite plain his feeling that only the top of United States society operates meaningfully and effectively, for: "The middle levels are a drifting set of stalemated, balancing forces; the middle does not link the bottom with the top.

The bottom of this society is politically fragmented, and even as a passive fact, increasingly powerless. . . ." That this is deep-seated in Mills appears from the fact that it also runs through his volume *White Collar,* published in 1951. Most Americans, he there wrote, "are not radical, not liberal, not conservative, not reactionary; they are inactionary; they are out of it. If we accept the Greeks' definition of the idiot as the privatized man, then we must conclude that the U.S. citizenry is now largely composed of idiots."

This particular image is a favorite one with Mills. It reappears, in almost identical prose, in his *Causes of World War III* and *Sociological Imagination.* But quite aside from Mills' deliberately shocking prose, which is a literary mannerism, this idea of the masses of people as "powerless," as, politically speaking, idiotic, is not true. That it is adhered to by Mills is a basic source of his programmatic approach, developed at particular length in his *Causes,* where he deliberately rules out of consideration the masses of the population and chooses to confine himself to an appeal to the intelligentsia as the last possible source of effective opposition to the elite. Let us consider whether or not Mills' description of the masses in the United States coincides with reality.

It is true that the elite have succeeded, through their domination and prostitution (to a large degree) of the mass media, in spreading much cynicism and corruption. It is true that the active repression of dissidence and nonconformity has taken its toll. It is true that the mistakes and failings of the nonconformists themselves—not least, those among us who are Marxists—have hurt. It is true that a decade of capitalist prosperity and of Cold War have had their morally corroding effects.

But, in the first place, it is also true that a partial explanation of what appears to be inaction is a searching for effective alternatives; that some elements, at least, of what appears to be apathy may be, and often are, a conscious withdrawal having deep moral and political motivations; passivity too, I believe, often is a shrewd judgment on a prearranged frame-up, of which the abstainer wants no part.

In the second place, it is also true that despite everything there is profound interest in politics among broad areas of the American population; despite everything, this interest does find expression in organized forms and does have profound effect upon the course of history and upon the course of action open to and taken by the power elite.

Between the will of that elite and its capabilities of implementing that will stands public opinion, including American public opinion. This public opinion is not simply shaped by the elite, and this public opinion does affect what the elite tries to do and what it does and how it does what it does. Moreover, in whole areas of life—as in wages and working conditions, housing and education, the battle against Jim Crow and against war—the desires and the power of the masses do exert great influence, manifested in buses that stop running and in atomic bombs that, though loaded aboard planes that are alerted to take off, never are dropped in war.

Let us be somewhat more specific by examining the two actual instances cited by Mills in his *Elite* to demonstrate the elite's decisive power.

In a chapter entitled "The Military Ascendancy" Mills writes of Admiral Radford, chairman of the U.S. Joint Chiefs of Staff, who felt "that Red China had to be destroyed even if it required a fifty-year war" and who argued "for the use of 500 planes to drop tactical A-bombs on Vietminh troops before the fall of Dienbienphu" in 1954. Certainly that Admiral Radford, with such views, holds the position he does reflects the power of the elite, of which he is an eminent member. But what of the fact that there has been no war with People's China? What of the fact that the United States did not use A-bombs in the Indochinese liberation struggle and, in fact, did not actively intervene therein with its own troops or personnel at all?

Certainly it is true that the growing might of People's China, already apparent by 1954, played no small part in undoing Radford's plans; and most certainly the fact that the Soviet Union several times informed whoever might be interested that she had a firm alliance with People's China and would consider any attack upon that country as an attack upon herself and would reply to such attack with every force at her command, this too, undoubtedly, was a consideration of no little weight upon the deliberations of the U.S. Joint Chiefs of Staff.

But, in addition, is there no relationship between the unpopularity of the Korean War in the United States and the failure of Admiral Radford to start his fifty-year crusade against China? It may be that Professor Mills was not aware of a ground swell of popular opposition to our becoming involved in an endless slaughter where American troops would be battling hundreds of millions in the spaces of China, but it is certain that such a ground swell existed and it is highly probable that this was noticed by the Joint Chiefs of Staff.

Let us turn to the Dienbienphu incident itself. On April 3, 1954, Secretary of State Dulles held a confidential meeting with Senator Knowland, then Majority leader, Senator Johnson, then Minority leader, and Joseph Martin, then Speaker of the House. Present, in addition, were the Secretary of the Navy, the Under-Secretary for Defense, and our old friend, Admiral Radford. The gentlemen were told by Mr. Dulles that the meeting was being held at the President's request. They

151

were told that the President wanted a joint resolution from Congress permitting him to use air and naval power against the "rebels" besieging Dienbienphu.

The National Security Council—correctly described by the man giving the fullest report of this extraordinary meeting as "the inner core of the government, where our most vital decisions are worked out"—had approved, of course, of this line of action. Admiral Radford then spoke to the members of Congress and told them that 200 planes aboard two carriers in the South China Sea, and hundreds of other planes in bases in the Philippines, were loaded and ready to strike at a moment's notice. "Some of those at the meeting," wrote Chalmers M. Roberts, "came away with the feeling that if they agreed that Saturday to the resolution, planes would have been winging toward Dienbienphu without waiting for a vote of Congress— or without a word in advance to the American people."

But this was not done, and even Vice President Nixon's carefully prepared and well-publicized speech to the newspaper editors' convention on April 16—"If the United States could not prevent the loss of Indochina, then the Administration must face the situation and send troops"—did not force it to be done. On the contrary, that speech brought a deluge of mail from the "idiots," as the State Department and the Vice President ruefully admitted, demanding that peace be preserved; and world public opinion (manifested in desperate diplomatic action by England and France) not only blocked Dulles and Radford and the rest of the elite but resulted in the first Geneva Conference of April 26, 1954. There, despite Dulles' boycott, peace, not war, came to Indochina.

Most recently, in January, 1960, the serial publication of Sir Anthony Eden's *Memoirs,* in the London *Times,* has offered confirmation of the validity of this account, as first published by Mr. Roberts, in *The Reporter* (September 14,

1954). And now that Eden's *Memoirs* has appeared, other evidence is being made public. Thus, Joseph Barry, the Paris correspondent for the New York *Post* (January 21, 1960), tells of "the day, early in June, 1954, when Mendes-France mounted the tribune," of the French Parliament, pointed at a weak and fading Foreign Minister Georges Bidault, and said:

> You had a plan revealed at the beginning of May for the large-scale intervention of the American Air Force at the risk of provoking Chinese intervention and starting a general war. . . .

> The American intervention plan had been prepared, and was about to come into action—at your request. The attack was to be launched on April 28, and the ships with the aircraft and the atom bombs were on the way. President Eisenhower was going to ask Congress on April 26, for the necessary authority. The French parliament was going to be faced with a *fait accompli*. . . .

> Fortunately, the plan was rejected by Britain *and by public opinion in the United States*. (Italics added—H.A.)

Of course, in this, American public opinion was not alone; world public opinion and splits among the imperialist partners, and divisions in the opinions of the American elite (the last something completely ignored by Mills, in part because he denies the class approach), were also potent forces. But all of these were related to American public opinion and it is an indubitable fact that that opinion was very powerful in staying the hand of Mills' "Military Ascendancy."

Mills' other specific reference to the "powerlessness" of those not of the elite is the 1954 Congressional elections. Of those elections he writes as follows:

> Slogans and personal attacks on character, personality defects, and counter charges and suspicions were all that the electorate

could see or hear, and, as usual, many paid no attention at all. Each candidate tried to dishonor his opponent, who in turn tried to dishonor him. The outraged candidates seemed to make themselves the issue, and on that issue virtually all of them lost. The electorate saw no issues at all, and they too lost, although they did not know it.

I think there is a good deal of truth in this analysis. Much of the campaigning, though not all of it, was and is on the abysmally low level Mills describes. It is true that many of the electorate seemed—perhaps in self-defense—to "pay no attention at all," and it is true that in 1954, as compared with 1952, there was a decline of 32 percent in the number of voters, but I suggest that some of this was the result not of inattention, but of close attention and deliberate decision to abstain.

But when Mills writes "the electorate saw no issues at all" he is wrong, and the results of the 1954 election show it. For the electorate saw issues—whatever Mills or anyone else may think of its vision—and voted accordingly, giving the Republicans, despite President Eisenhower's strong appeals, a serious setback in Congress. The Republicans suffered a net loss of eighteen seats and became the minority party in Congress. Quite striking was the defeat of particularly right-wing McCarthyite candidates, as Clardy and Ferguson in Michigan, Kersten in Wisconsin, Graham in Pennsylvania, Meek, Vail, and Busbey in Illinois, and Shepard in New Jersey. I do not want to go into a lengthy analysis of that election, and there was much quite partial and obscure in its results, but enough has been said to serve my main purpose: to demonstrate the grossly excessive and substantively wrong estimate of the 1954 elections by Mills, who in particular ignored the participation of 42,000,000 Americans. To say that this "electorate saw no issues at all" is to fly in the face of the facts.

In dealing with Mills' *Elite* volume, we confine our remarks to the 1954 elections; but since Mills, in books published in 1958 and 1959, takes on this matter substantially the same view, it is proper to point out that the elections of 1956 and particularly 1958 even more strongly negate his position. The electorate rejected the Eisenhower-Dulles policies in the November, 1958, elections—despite an overwhelmingly pro-Republican press—and in many areas throughout the country on matters both foreign and domestic, the issues were significant and the results clear-cut. The gap between the expression of the electorate's will and the implementation of that will by Congress is another matter and tends to demonstrate the essentially class character of the state itself. Even in this, however, to describe that gap as establishing the "powerlessness" of the masses is wrong. Despite the deceptions and dishonesties and demagogy of bourgeois politics, these elections show that Mills is wrong when he dismisses the majority of American adults today as "idiots" in a political sense.

The main point is that the elite are by no means omnipotent, and the masses of people in our country are neither powerless nor apathetic. It is worth remembering that despite the nearly unanimous desire of the press owned by the elite Franklin Delano Roosevelt was three times reelected President. And the voting percentages for F.D.R., taking 1936, 1940, and 1944 together, were: bourgeoisie, 38.8 percent; professionals, 52.6; workers, 69.6.

Mills' position, expressed particularly in his *Causes* volume, is to insist upon a complete discontinuity in contemporary history and that the modern world represents an absolutely new phenomenon; this is of special importance when he develops his opinions on foreign affairs. But here, in domestic matters, Mills may feel that the data on F.D.R. are irrelevant as marking an era without substantive connection to an allegedly altogether unique present. But in that view he is wrong, I think. A decisive fact in the politics of the United States is that the Rooseveltian "revolution" is by no means played out and that in important respects political developments of the late forties and the fifties reflect not a discontinuity but a significant continuity.

Samuel Lubell, a quite conservative political analyst and statistician, in his *Revolt of the Moderates,* published in 1956, observed:

> The most heavily Democratic districts in the North are becoming those which are poorest economically and which have the largest Negro population—two characteristics which tend to pull the representatives of these districts back to the old appeals of the New Deal.

The results of 1958 offer further substantiation of this analysis.

We are not here arguing the limitations of the two-party system, or the deep reality of political demagoguery which permeates that system. We are arguing that the two major parties must and do react, in varying degrees, to public opinion, which does in fact exist; we are arguing that public opinion is articulate, does have power, and has demonstrated that power, in spite of the two-party system, throughout United States history.

If the masses are viewed as helpless then all concern with political activity in any really democratic form is, of course, illusory. But they are not helpless. When this is established one can argue about the best methods and forms and programs for political action, and I am urging Professor Mills to join in this effort because it is not illusory; it is worthwhile and it is, in fact, the only way toward significant social advance. I am not insisting on this in contradistinction to Mills' eloquent calls, especially in his *Causes* and *Imagination* volumes, for political

156

involvement by intellectuals, artists, and scholars. I am stating that Mills' concentration upon *only* these elements because he feels that only these elements have the potential today of resisting the elite is wrong in analysis and harmful in direction.

In one section of his *Elite,* Mills feels called upon to argue against thinkers like Le Bon, Lederer, and Ortega y Gasset, who have raised the "fear" that the masses are all-powerful and, describing the masses as unthinking brutes, have warned that their alleged omnipotence threatens "civilization." Mills is effective in his challenge of the anti-democratic uses to which these men put their theories of the masses, but he is wrong, I think, in denying the power of the masses and in ignoring the great new political fact in modern history—the idea of the people's sovereignty. It is, indeed, the effort to implement that idea and the resistance thereto which make up the body of world politics in modern history.

Necker, Minister of Finance for the last Louis before the great French Revolution, saw this then new force, ". . . that invisible power which, without treasure, without guards, and without arms, imposes its laws on the city, on the court, and even in the palaces of kings."

There is much to be done before that will is imposed everywhere, and fully, but its existence is a central social fact, and its growing ascendancy is plain in history. Our own era will not see its demise; rather, I think, it is seeing its rise and will see its triumph.

I have tried to show, in the preceding pages, some of the limitations of Mills' power-elite concept as compared with the Marxian one of class struggle. Mills states that he is avoiding "simple Marxism" and "vulgar Marxism" because he thinks it does not do justice, in its concept of the ruling class, to the complexities of the modern power structure. But there is a

Marxism which is neither simple nor vulgar; and it is certainly not the economic determinism that Mills equates with Marxism.

In this he is following Max Weber, the German sociologist whose influence on Mills has been so great; Weber held that Marxism was faulty in that it insisted that economics was the sole factor in social causation. He attempted to stress the plurality and interdependence of causes. But Weber was wrong in equating Marxism with economic determinism. Where one does this he has a "simple Marxism" and a "vulgar Marxism" —which is to say he does not have Marxism at all. Marxism does not deny plurality of causation; it focuses upon what it holds to be primary causation, ultimately decisive, and holds the material foundations of any social order to be the relationships of production. This emphasis is not one denying significance to noneconomic or nonmaterial matters; it is one which emphasizes the *originating* quality of the material foundations. In doing this it does not seek to deny or to diminish the significance of other forces and factors. And Marxism, being dialectical, insists upon the interpenetrating quality of phenomena, so that this element in Weber is not only not original with him but is fundamental to the Marxist outlook, though often pointed to as "overlooked" by Marxism.

Though, as we have seen, Mills insisted upon the need, in social studies, of going "beyond mere enumeration" and of "weighing" descriptive data "in such a way as to understand how they fit together," in his own trinity—economic, military, political—he does not do this. He seems to fear that doing it may, in this case, blur distinctions or play down autonomous and interacting features. It is on this ground, among others, that he rejects "simple Marxism."

Mills made his position on this matter especially clear in a paper, "The Power Elite: Military, Economic, and Political," which he delivered in 1955 at Wayne State University in Detroit.[4] There he declared:

> But we must always be historically specific and we must always be open to complexities: (1) the simple Marxian view makes the big economic man the real holder of power; (2) the simple liberal view makes the big political man the chief of the power system; and (3) there are some who would view the warlords as virtual dictators. These are each an over-simplified view. And it is to avoid them that we use the term "power elite" rather than, for example, "ruling class."

And further along, in the same paper:

> Neither the idea of a "ruling class" nor of a simple monolithic rise of "bureaucratic politicians" nor of a "military clique" is the correct view. The power elite today involves the often uneasy coincidence of economic, military and political power.

Marxism is dialectical, not "simple" in the way Mills uses that word. Mills makes a tripartite power base but his composite is mechanical rather than dialectical. Hence he offers no analysis of priorities either in terms of origin or in terms of impact. Marxism, in its emphasis upon the "economic," is not referring to the "big economic man"; it is referring to the property relationships characterizing the social order and is insisting that upon that base is reared, with interpenetration, the rest of the juridical, political, ideological, and cultural features of the society.

Marxism does not deny the weight of the military or political—or psychological and cultural, one may add. It seeks rather to pinpoint the basic, the fundamental, the source. It holds that *ultimately* the economic relationships are determinative, not that other relations are insignificant or without great

[4] Arthur Kornhauser (ed.), *Problems of Power in American Democracy* (Detroit: Wayne State University Press, 1957), pp. 165, 166.

159

impact—including impact upon the economic relations. In assigning relative weight, and in determining the basic, in distinguishing between origin and significance, Marxism offers an illuminating structural critique; at the same time Marxism in this way serves to place in proper perspective those features of the social order which are not fundamental but are rather derivative.

Noah Webster asked, in 1787, "In what, then, does *real* power consist? The answer is short, plain—in *property.*" That is, in property ownership and property relationships, and I think the answer *is* short, plain, and basically true. Similarly, despite Mills' three-point elite, his own work, in its descriptive passages, shows not only that the economic and political and military are interdependent but also that the economic is ultimately decisive and fundamentally controlling.

Mills sees that "the top of American society is increasingly unified"; he knows that " 'interlocking directorate' is no mere phrase" and that it is basic to "the community of interest . . . that prevails among the propertied class." As he writes, "there is an ever-increasing interlocking of economic, military and political structures." Yes, and that interlocking comes together at the point of, and is dominated by control over, the productive plant. As Mills writes: "Money provides power and power provides freedom."

The whole matter is summed up by a witness devoted to capitalism and quite friendly to big business, in this way:

> In terms of power, without regard to asset positions, not only do 500 corporations control two-thirds of the non-farm economy, but within each of that 500, a still smaller group has the ultimate decision-making power. This is, I think, *the highest concentration of economic power in recorded history.*

These are the words of A. A. Berle, Jr., former Under-Secretary of State and an authority on the nature of the modern corporation, as stated in his recent pamphlet, *Economic Power and the Free Society* (Fund for the Republic, N.Y.). They serve to substantiate the characterization of the socio-economic structure of the United States as a monopoly capitalist one; this characterization derives from, as it confirms, the Marxist critique of capitalism, particularly as that critique was extended into the era of imperialism by Lenin. In this there is neither simplification nor vulgarization; there is illumination. With the class-defined nature of power in the United States one has a more truthful, and therefore more useful, analysis than that provided by the power-elite picture offered by Mills. And far from being "simple," it is more complex than is that of Mills, for it is more profound and more evaluative.

I think Mills errs, too, in assigning to financiers "middlemen" roles in terms of the domination of the great corporative structure. He is here, of course, following those economists who see in the accumulation of great capital backlogs by industrial giants a force freeing them from the credit and money control of the financial titans. The facts point rather, in the recent period, to an intensification of the domination of the sinews of capitalism by the banking colossi and to the mounting merger movement among the banks themselves. "The end result," said former Senator Herbert H. Lehman, himself a banker, speaking at City College in New York,

> is not only a decreased number of banks and less competition, but a more highly centralized control of the nation's financial system, with mounting danger to the entire national economy if a relatively few individuals should decide, for whatever reason, to misuse *their control over the life-blood of our economy.* (*New York Times,* April 3, 1957, italics added.)

161

C. WRIGHT MILLS AND *THE POWER ELITE*

Since Mr. Lehman's warning, the process of financial merging has accelerated. In 1958 alone there were such spectacular mergers as those of J. P. Morgan and the Guaranty Trust Company; of the Firstamerican Corporation of California (assets over three billion) with the California Bank of Los Angeles (assets over a billion); of two of the largest banks in New Jersey, National State Bank and Federal Trust; of two of the largest banks in Pennsylvania, Fidelity Trust and Potter Bank and Trust, etc.

The increasing domination "over the life-blood of our economy" by the enormous investment trusts also confirms the analysis that Lenin made of the epoch of imperialism, and once again the fact that Mills ignores Lenin militates against the accuracy of his analysis. This is as good a place as any to remark that while Mills accurately "told off" Mr. Robert Lekachman by reminding him that a knowledge of Marx was a prerequisite for any well-educated person, it is only somewhat slightly less true, I think, that a knowledge of Lenin also is a prerequisite for any well-educated person today, especially if such a person seeks to understand the economics and politics of the twentieth century.[5] It is not necessary, of course, in achieving the status of "well-educated" that one agree with Lenin; it is necessary, however, that one come to grips with Lenin and if he rejects him to say so and why.

[5] Ed. note: Aptheker is referring to Lekachman's claim in the March, 1957, issue of *Commentary* that there were Marxist overtones to Mills' work. Here is Mills' reply to the editor of *Commentary*:

It is less important that your writer imputes to me opinions I do not hold than that he obscures serious problems by such fashionable superficiality. Let me say explicitly: I happen never to have been what is called "a Marxist," but I believe Karl Marx one of the most astute students of society modern civilization has produced; his work is now essential equipment of any adequately trained social scientist as well as of any properly educated person. Those who say they hear Marxian echoes in my work are saying that I have trained myself well. That they do not intend this testifies to their own lack of proper education.

A study of the facts of the U.S. economy demonstrates[6] the controlling power of the nine conglomerates of financial power in our country. This is the apex of power today in the United States, and its absence from Mills' *Power Elite* seriously hurts the book's validity from the viewpoint of sheer description as well as basic definition.

A striking omission in Mills' work—also traceable, I should think, to the neglect of Lenin—is the lack of any reference to or consideration of the imperialist character of the U.S. power elite. That is, in Mills' stout volume no mention is made of U.S. hegemony over the "Free World" and of the meaning of this in terms of the U.S. economy or its politics, and directly in terms of the interests, investments, careers, psychologies of the elite.

I am not here demanding that Mills include in his *Elite* volume a study of foreign policy—which his *Causes of World War Three* is; I am saying that a study of the character of the ruling forces in the United States today that omits its overseas connections and interests and its external sources of strength and embarrassment is exceedingly partial. I have particularly in mind the need for Mills to give some indication that he understands the phenomenon indicated in these opening lines of a recent *New Statesman* editorial (January 2, 1960):

> Few tears will be shed for the Fifties. Cynical, materialistic, selfish, the decade made the rich richer, the poor poorer. To the advanced countries of the West, it brought unprecedented

[6] Among works available to Mills at the time he was writing *The Power Elite,* that by Victor Perlo—*American Imperialism* (New York: 1950), especially Chapter 3—is most persuasive. There relevant literature is cited. Also available before the publication of the *Elite* were later government studies, especially: *Bank Mergers and Concentration of Banking Facilities,* House Comm. on Judiciary, Staff Report No. 5 (1952), and *Interim Report of the Antitrust Subcommittee on Corporate and Bank Mergers,* House Comm. on Judiciary (1955). For material since Mills' *Elite,* see Perlo's *The Empire of High Finance* (New York, 1957).

prosperity, *achieved largely at the expense of the vast and growing proletariats of Asia and Africa.* (Italics added.)

Or that he has pondered the consequence of the condition indicated in this sentence in the autobiography of Frederick Jesup Stimson, a former U.S. Ambassador to several Latin-American countries, "But we Nordics are all living on the cheap labor of the tropics—we whites by the sweat of the brow of the blacks." (*My United States,* Scribner's, New York, 1931, p. 203.)

The omission of this dimension damages the depth of Mills' analysis of the American elite; it even more seriously detracts from his later work on foreign affairs.

In this respect, as in Mills' omission of the reality of poverty in the United States, of intraclass differences and conflicts, of the Negro people, and his general demeaning of the awareness of the American people, one has important evidence of his simplification of the United States scene. It is somewhat ironic that simplification should be the result of neglecting those areas which, had Mills employed the Marxist-Leninist outlook—or, at any rate, taken its critique more seriously—he never could have overlooked.

There remain, however, the solid values in Mills' study: an incisive, if limited, critique of the anti-democratic values and results of the oligarchic rule that exists in the United States. This, spelled out in detail in each of several important areas of life, illuminated throughout by keen insights, conveyed in sparkling prose, and permeated by a quite unfashionable humanistic passion, made the work when it appeared a breath of fresh air, and repays the most careful study today.

PART IV

Highbrow Critics of THE POWER ELITE

The highbrows were more concerned with The Power Elite *as an "event" than as a theory. They were concerned with its appeal, tone, mood, and intent. For example, one of the highbrows believed that the use of "ambiguous" terms by Mills "reinforces a sense of helplessness and belies the resources of a free society." Another pointed out that "some men hunger for theory as for salt; and those who do and yet see the inadequacies of Marxism will find in Millsism a doctrine that satisfies many of their yearnings."*

Even the highbrow who went furthest in accepting the substance and ethos of The Power Elite *nonetheless accused Mills of "posturing," offering a mood of "vague resentment," and failing to provide "a single saving myth." Moreover, said this critic, Mills seems to assume that social criticism still has some reforming value, when it has in fact become but another sparkling commodity in a consumption-hungry mass society.*

To classify these reviews by their tone and attitude, however, is not to say that they are without substantive commentary.

Socialism and Sociology

BY PHILIP RIEFF

To the ironic critics of the age, the militancy of C. Wright Mills is suspect. Annoyed, as by a gadfly who insists on landing somewhere, Mills' fellow critics have fixed on the exaggerations to which his militancy has led—the partisan use of evidence, the unrelieved gloom. In American social letters, Mills is bracketed as a naif, a pure dissenter in an agreeable time. If this were all, if Mills were accused of nothing worse than being naive, of remaining narrowly negative in a period of ideological as well as material abundance, the charges should of course be dismissed. He is, however, vulnerable to the more serious charge of posturing. As Christianity, following the death of Christian belief, multiplied its armchair apologists in the universities, so Socialism has its professional and passionate academics, transforming their socialism into sociology. Mills must be ranked as one of these caretakers of the socialist polemical tradition. He incites without hope; he offers not a single saving myth—no hope from the proletariat; nor from the engineers; and certainly not from a cultivated and responsible upper class, that fantasy-compliment of the conservative critics to themselves. Further, it is hard to see what group of readers Mills can hope to move. Literate *and* committed audiences are as scarce these days as salvation-bearing social classes. Mills' sympathetic reader is, I suppose, that stable *Partisan Review* type, culturally rather than politically com-

Philip Rieff is a sociologist at the University of Pennsylvania. He is the author of Freud: The Mind of the Moralist *and* The Triumph of the Therapeutic. *This review appeared in* Partisan Review, *Summer, 1956.*

167

mitted—the literary son of socialist fathers, who takes over the tatters of liberal belief and becomes the moralizing man in an immoral society.

What confutes the militancy of C. Wright Mills is his marginal relation to both the academy and the doctrinal vacuum of American politics surrounding it. From inside the academy Mills looks like a political man, a polemicist; from outside his commitments look academic. Just this double jeopardy makes it likely that his criticism, despite its genuine cutting edge, will gain public favor. Criticism is part of the largess of American culture, and the critic who bestows it may hope for generous receipts. Even Mills, the angry man of American social letters, may ultimately expect to hitch a ride on the American gravy train, against his personal will, as one of its most celebrated critics. For criticism too is a salable commodity, as long as it remains professional and sharpens no movement of protest. If Veblen, to whom Mills is often compared when he is being rated favorably, can be canonized by *Fortune,* Mills may expect no less, and probably within his own lifetime. *Time* could render his face iconic for a week. This means no insult to Mills. The mass society which is rapidly overtaking our inherited liberal one has no explicit faith, and its implicit faith is so diffuse that it can digest any virtuoso heretic striking blindly at where dogma used to be.

The dogma at which Mills strikes has become so shadowy that he never locates it explicitly as his target. Briefly, it is the classical liberal thesis that the institutions of government are distinct from the institutions of property. Mills' antithesis, also not stated explicitly in this book, is the classical socialist denial: power is not separate from property; corporate property cannot be realistically or legitimately considered private. By submitting the present American situation to an essentially socialist analysis, Mills demonstrates (successfully, I think) how irrelevant to American reality liberalism has become. Property, and the hidden privileges and flow of opportunity that go with it, does not exist antecedently to government. Indeed, in our present social arrangement, the major institutions of government and the major institutions of property tend openly to merge. The primitive stuff of institutions are the humans who staff them, and Mills goes about the theoretically simple but polemically complex task of spotting the men who circulate among the merging institutions, therefore occupying what he calls the "command posts" atop American society.

Mills perhaps credits the old liberal dogma of separate and balancing institutions with too much life, so that he fatigues the reader with lengthy parades of tycoons in Washington, generals at ease in executive suites, and the new hybrid politicians, with business hearts and military heads. But the book is no mere exposé of money lords, or of the vested interests of our military economy. Indeed, Mills says too little of the movement of funds that is sapping the economic potential of America, and talks mainly about the movement of men that is sapping our civic potential. For this alliance, between the high officers of executive government and the chief managers of corporate property, Mills finds a new name: the power elite. Despite the fact that such an alliance is the staple of socialist theory, Mills holds that this new name for it is necessary. For a third institution, the armed services, has become the mortar holding the two familiar old institutions of rule together, and has come to personify for a politically illiterate public the idea of political and economic stability: a permanent war economy based on a negative ideology of an absolute enemy.

Mills has written as fine an obituary notice on liberal society as any lover of the genre could hope to read. Chapters 11 and 12, in particular, survey our liberal inheritance and exhibit its bankruptcy both as political theory (Chapter 11: "The

Theory of Balance") and political fact (Chapter 12: "The Power Elite"). The liberal principles of a government instituted and operated separately from property, against which the propertied classes had rights and toward which the powers of government were limited—these principles have been quietly abrogated. Even granting that the founding fathers, following Locke's *Second Treatise,* enacted a government charged with protecting the natural rights of property, nevertheless according to classical liberalism political institutions were something superimposed upon economic ones and different from them. By gradual extension, the liberal principle retracted the absolute guarantee of property inserted into the very definition of the liberal State. Thus extended, liberalism operated occasionally to check the in any case fragmented interests of the propertied classes. And in the regime of FDR the liberal principle of an autonomous political order was turned to check the increasingly unified interests of the executive class that had come to be the representative men of property. Having slowly learned the lessons that the New Deal had to teach it, the executive class simply took over the administration of the bureaucratic welfare state and merged its personnel and purposes with it. Thus, when the historical carriers of liberalism were no longer served by it, the liberal principle of autonomous and mutually limiting political and economic orders was scuttled. In America the scuttling is so recent that Mills takes almost all of his examples of it from the Eisenhower years, though of course it began in the Roosevelt war-preparedness period.

To explain why there has been so little serious opposition to the scuttling of American liberalism, Mills resorts to the obvious tautology that American society is, anyway, in process of transition from liberal to mass form. And, as a result of this trend, the classes and the masses grow together. If anything, I should say that the elites Mills studies are farther along toward

the psychology characteristic of a mass society than large segments of the population. The elites are incapable of contem-
plating serious questions steadily; they have a few fixed ideas
and no fixed morality. This much Mills confirms. But the intellectual and moral condition of the many is scarcely better than
that of the ruling few; Chapter 13, "The Mass Society," makes
this clear. Being so unsentimental as to label the "people" of
nineteenth-century liberalism and socialism alike as a "mass,"
Mills is at a loss to find a sharp angle from which to criticize
the higher immorality of the elite. Unwittingly, he demonstrates
that the powerless mass and the power elite complement each
other perfectly. The lower immorality differs only in size and
import from the higher. Such essential agreement creates a
major problem of approach for Mills. As a serious critic, who
will allow neither his socialism nor his respect for the liberal
civilization of an earlier America to bemuse his vision of the
present, Mills is unable to moor the repugnant facts of American public life against the pier of American values. In a manner
no critic has yet adequately described, the pier has somehow
torn loose and floats around like another fact on the calm, oily
surface of American life.

Of course to defend is to be conservative, as Mills points
out. But just at its best, as an attack, Mills' performance is
purely negative. Against the conservative mood of the liberals,
Mills offers a mood of vague resentment. He has looked into
the faces of the American elite and realized with dramatic
pleasure that they are blank. It is the misfortune of the socialist critic in our time, equipped with better social psychology
than his forebears, to look into the faces of the mass and see
that these too are irremediably blank. Masses are merely the
poorer relations of elites. For all Mills' middle-western devo-
tion to the idea that American power is won on the playing
fields of Exeter, and other such eastern places, the fact is that

171

the elites are quite as mindless as the mass and share a similarly empty inner life. False consciousness is here to stay; it is the happy psychic condition of a mature and still dynamic industrial civilization that has worked back through a religion of transcendence to a religion of immanence based on a supra-primitive fetishism of infinitely variable commodities. Criticism, when it serves no religion of transcendence, not even a secular one, such as socialism, becomes another bright and shiny thing, to be admired and consumed. All the same, even if blame can be bought like praise nowadays, he who blames is still to be preferred to he who praises.

The Interlocking Overlappers

BY RICHARD ROVERE

C. Wright Mills is a distinguished American sociologist who finds American society as presently organized an inferior piece of work. In *The Power Elite,* he says that our political life is managed by "crackpot realists" who have "constructed a paranoid reality all their own." What these men do, at home and abroad, is crazy. Almost nothing about our civilization, a term he would find unwarranted, seems admirable to him. American

Richard Rovere is a staff writer for the New Yorker *who has reported on the Washington, D.C., scene for many years. His books include* Senator Joe McCarthy *and* The Eisenhower Years. *This review first appeared in* The Progressive, *June, 1956, and was then reprinted in a collection of his essays,* The American Establishment *(New York: Harcourt, Brace, and World, 1962), from which this version is reprinted.*

democracy is form without substance. American culture is jejune, inane. American education? Nothing more or less than a racket to train, and/or condition, people for industry, commerce, or the state at public expense. He will not even praise our technology—he says they make better things in Germany and England. From bottom to top, as Mills sees it, American life is pretty much of a fraud. The American public is rapidly turning into a jellied American "mass." The people nowadays exist only to be manipulated. Mills is certain he knows who does the manipulating, and how, and why. The "power elite" runs the country. It is "an interlocking directorate" drawn from among the leading figures in three spheres: the corporate, the political, and the military. It is "an intricate set of overlapping cliques [who] share decisions having at least national consequences. In so far as national events are decided, the power elite are those who decide them." He is persuaded that all the really important "events" are "decided."

As a sociologist, Mills is scornful of ideology, which he regards as a minor function of "position" and "interest." He insists that he is not constructing an ideological system of his own but merely a method of analysis. Nevertheless, he may be thought of, at least in terms of one of his own functions, as a reviser of Marxism. Some men hunger for theory as for salt, and those who do and yet see the inadequacies of Marxism will find in Millsism a doctrine that satisfies many of their yearnings. Although Mills offers it not as an explanation of all historical reality but merely of the present reality in the United States, it imposes order on seeming chaos; it provides a key to the mysteries, a plot for the story, a dramatis personae. He nourishes the precious sense of victimization. His world, like Marx's, is riven. It consists of the shearers and the shorn, the exploiters and the exploited, those who have and those who are

173

had. The slaves are pretty much the same, but the masters are different—or, at any rate, more varied in function and origin. Mills thinks the Marxist term "ruling class" won't do for our time. " 'Class' is an economic term; 'rule' a political one. The phrase . . . thus contains the theory that an economic class rules politically." He thinks the contained theory is two-thirds wrong for the United States at the present time. It leaves out the political and military orders, which are of roughly equal importance. Anyway, the members of his "interlocking directorate" are "commanders of power unequaled in human history."

Millsism offers no comforting dialectic. It offers explanation but no remedy, even through bloody revolution. Unlike Marx, Mills perceives no significant amount of social tension. If there ever was a "struggle," it is all over now. He thinks that the "mass" is intuitively and quite cynically aware of "the power situation," but it is not greatly troubled by its awareness. It is not in revolt. The conservative fears of de Tocqueville and Ortega y Gasset were unfounded. "The bottom of this society," he says, "is politically fragmented . . . and increasingly powerless. . . . [The] masses in their full development are sovereign only in some plebiscitarian moment of adulation to an elite as authoritative celebrity." I think that by this last sentence he means that the people are given the illusion of sovereignty by being allowed to vote for President Eisenhower every four years and by being kept up to date on the doings of Rita Hayworth and Grace Kelly. All this is demoralizing.

I believe that Mills' book is at its core mistaken. I also believe it is symptomatic and important. It has some solid merits, and these must be acknowledged. By far the greater part of *The Power Elite* is descriptive. There is, as Daniel Bell has pointed out, a Balzacian texture in Mills' accounts of the lives of representative Americans. When Mills is not choked with indignation and disgust, he commands a strong and vivid satirical style. Moreover, I think he is fairly close to being right in his judgments of where the power centers of our society are. He is on solid ground in arguing that there is an almost autonomous political directorate in this country today. It is not as unified as he seems to think, but on what he calls the "big decisions," the big men of rival factions hammer out agreements that give continuity to major foreign and domestic policies. (Less hostile critics sometimes point to this fact as a reflection of the "stability" of American society, an expression of "consensus.") I am not so sure that the military can be set apart from either the corporate or political elements as easily as Mills thinks they can, but there is no doubt that in the postwar years, the military establishment has played a huge and at least semiautonomous role in American life and government. I believe that the power elite has some important members Mills does not recognize—drawn in part from the "public" he believes has disappeared, in part from the intelligentsia he regards as powerless, in part from the technological and managerial classes. Still and all, Mills' view of the basic elements in the power structure is, I think, reasonably sound. What seem to me to be absurd and destructive are his assumptions and conclusions about what power is and how it is wielded. He devotes relatively little space to this, but it is a central matter, and when he does deal with it he is forthright. His view is summed up in this passage:

> The course of events in our time depends more on a series of human decisions than on any inevitable fate. . . . As the circle of those who decide is narrowed, as the means of decision are centralized, and the consequences of decisions become enormous, then the course of great events often rests upon the decisions of determinable circles. . . . [The] pivotal moment does arrive, and at that moment small circles do decide or fail to decide. In either case, they are an elite of power. The drop-

175

ping of A-bombs over Japan was such a moment; the decision on Korea was such a moment; the confusion about Quemoy and Matsu, as well as before Dienbienphu were such moments; the sequence of maneuvers which involved the United States in World War II was such a "moment." Is it not true that the history of our times is composed of such moments?

It is indeed true that the history of our time is quite largely composed of such "moments." They are not the whole story, of course; history is also the passage of time, the accumulation of knowledge and anxieties, the development of creeds and institutions, and everlasting change—some of it planned and intended and more or less directed, some of it wholly unforeseen and probably wholly unforeseeable. But the moments Mills mentions (all of them, interestingly, having to do with war) were important and they were pivotal. Is it reasonable, though, to believe, as Mills does, that "the warlords, the corporate chieftains, and [the] political directorate" determined the American responses? I think it is demonstrably unreasonable—except just possibly in the case of our entry into World War II, an "event" made of such an "uncountable totality" of other events (to use a phrase of Sir Isaiah Berlin's) that it would be as difficult to demonstrate that the "decision" was not made by a particular group as to determine that it was. The other instances reveal, I think, the essential inadequacy of Mills' doctrine, and I shall attempt to show how they do so:[1]

[1] The literature of these events has, of course, grown enormously in the five years since this piece was published in *The Progressive*. In the late fall of 1961, for example, we have had yet another account of the decision to use the atomic bomb—Robert C. Batchelder's *The Irreversible Decision*. A few months back, Sherman Adams' *First-Hand Report* appeared with some new material on Quemoy and Matsu and Dienbienphu. I have not read everything in the field, but I have read quite a bit, and I have come upon nothing that would cause me to alter the substance of my original comments on Mills' four "moments." In the passages dealing with them, I have not used any of the new material—either to qualify what I wrote in 1956 or to amplify it by documentation. For my purposes here, the original

Hiroshima and Nagasaki: In the first place, very few members of the power elite knew there was any atomic bomb to be dropped or not dropped. Harry Truman has taken full personal as well as Constitutional responsibility for the decision. Though it must have been about as solitary an act of mind and will as any in history, we can acknowledge that no man ever acts wholly on his own—wholly unaffected, that is, by his immediate environment and by all that has gone into the making of the human being he is. In this case, Truman received a certain amount of advice from an *ad hoc* committee organized by Henry L. Stimson, a certifiable member of the power elite. (Stimson was an "overlapping clique" within his own person, being part of the corporate power of the nation, part of the political directorate, and, as Secretary of War and a former officer, a high figure in the military command.) Also, Winston Churchill and Joseph Stalin, a pair of foreigners, were consulted and ratified the decision in advance. (It is not clear that Stalin knew what he was ratifying, though if we are to believe Senator McCarthy, he knew at least as much about the atomic bomb as Harry Truman.) Truman, however, reports in his memoirs that he was decisively influenced by the opinions of the nuclear physicists whom he consulted or who were consulted in his behalf by the Secretary of War. According to Mills, physicists as intellectuals are powerless in our society and physicists as technicians are mere servants of the corporations and the military establishment. It is possible, to be sure, that Truman is no more accurate an appraiser of the origins of his own behavior than Mills is. But he is surely a bit closer

---

text suffices. The paragraph on Hiroshima and Nagasaki is based on my reading of the written history available at the time I wrote. In discussing the other events, I have drawn mainly on information I acquired as a reporter in Washington when the "events" (I recoil from the word but use it for want of a better) occurred.

to the source, and in the absence of compelling evidence to the contrary, one must, it seems to me, accept his account. At all odds, the first atomic bombs were dropped on the authority of one man who was the beneficiary of very sketchy advice from a handful of other men, most of whom were not, in Mills' terms, "commanders of power." In the nature of the case, it was quite impossible for any "intricate set of overlapping cliques" to have had much to do with this huge decision.

Korea: The decision to intervene was made in the course of a few hours by a very few men, hastily assembled to meet an unanticipated crisis. Earlier, some of the same men had determined that the national interest did *not* call for the defense of Korea. Some of those involved in both decisions could be regarded as important agents of the power elite. (There were no representatives of corporate power whose advice was asked or who proffered it unasked.) Those members of the government[2] who met with President Truman on June 24, 1950, were not in the beginning agreed on what the American response should be. Some differences were overcome during the meeting, some were tabled. The President again exercised a good deal of independent judgment, which is what a President is paid to do. It is interesting to note that the "decision" could

[2] It is, I think, worth pointing out that they were agreed on the general framework of policy and strategy. The guidelines had been laid down in the late forties by the Policy Planning Commission, headed by George F. Kennan, whom Mills describes in *The Power Elite* as "a distinguished student of foreign affairs." Most members of Kennan's staff were public servants with highly acceptable credentials as intellectuals. They may, of course, have tailored their own thinking to that of the power elite. I am rather inclined to think that they, with the help of the President, forced their views upon the interlocking directorate. After General MacArthur's recall in 1951, there was a fearful brawl over the ends of American policy, and the power elite seemed split—and not split down the middle, for there was surely more corporate, political, and military power for General MacArthur than against him. He lost. The views developed by Kennan and his staff prevailed.

not really have been an effective one if it had not been for a circumstance which the power elite could not possibly have arranged—the providential boycott by the Soviet Union of the United Nations Security Council.

Quemoy and Matsu: Mills speaks of the "confusions" about Quemoy and Matsu as a "moment" of "decision." In another passage, he makes it clear that what he has in mind are the feeble commitments the Eisenhower administration made to the Chinese Nationalists early in 1955—in our treaty with the Republic of China and in Public Law 4, a Congressional reso-lution that authorized the President to take certain actions in the Formosa Straits which he was already empowered to take by the Constitution. The situation, briefly, was this: to honor campaign pledges and to appease the Asia-firsters, the admin-istration had to put out some loud and lofty rhetoric affirming its undying solidarity with Chiang Kai-shek; to honor reason and to avoid outraging our allies, the rhetoric had be gutted, and it was. The treaty and the resolution committed the United States to the defense of Formosa, as the home and habitation of the Republic of China, and pledged the Republic of China not to attempt the reconquest of its former home and habita-tion on the mainland. (In the treaty, Chiang agreed to "refrain from the threat or use of force in any manner inconsistent with the purposes of the United Nations.") As for Quemoy and Matsu, they would be defended by the United States only in the event, according to Public Law 4, that an attack on them had been determined, by the President of the United States, to be preliminary to an attack on Formosa.

Many members of the power elite, including all but one of the Joint Chiefs of Staff, tried to argue the President into a more militant position. They failed. The reality is quite differ-ent from what Mills supposes it to be. The basic decision taken by this government was to make an act of disengagement sound like a declaration of engagement. Once again, it was, or seemed to most people at the time to be, a victory of the political arm of the power elite over its military and corporate arms.

Dienbienphu: Here is perhaps the oddest case of all. There is not much doubt that the power elite, to the extent that it had a single will and a single voice, wished the United States to intervene in Indochina, at the time of this critical battle.[3] At one time or another, the President, the Vice President, the Secretary of State, and again, all but one of the Joint Chiefs favored an effort to rescue the French. Among influential people generally, only a few were opposed, openly at any rate. Yet the decision that really counted was the one taken against the better judgment of the Washington representatives of the power elite—to stay out of the war.

"It was no historical necessity," Mills writes, "but an argument within a small circle of men that defeated Admiral [Arthur W.] Radford's proposal to bomb troops before Dienbienphu." "Historical necessity" is a term Mills constantly uses to cover any determinism or antideterminism that may be opposed to his own view. He uses it as a punching bag—the way certain materialist and positivist philosophers use "idealism" or "romanticism." In this context, I suppose he means that it was not historically inevitable that things turned out as they did and that an "argument" turning on calculations of power, logistics, the strengths and weaknesses of alliances, and strategic priorities settled the question. To those of us who tried to understand the decisions and indecisions of the time, however, it appeared that "public opinion," a force of negligible signifi-

---

[3] I am speaking here of the political and military branches. On matters of strategy the corporate branch often seems to lack a position. I doubt if it had one on Dienbienphu.

cance in the Millsian system, was of decisive importance. At the start of the controversy, not only the technicians of diplomacy and military power within the administration, but a Congressional majority seemed agreeable to the administration view. Some members supported it publicly; hardly any opposed it. Then John Foster Dulles went off to Europe to see what arrangements he could make with the British and the French. During his absence, something that can, for the purposes of the moment anyway, be described as "public opinion" began to take shape. The House of Representatives went into a brief recess. Congressmen returning from the provinces began to report that the people were anything but keen on saving Indochina from the Communists. Within a week or ten days, it became almost impossible to find a congressman who favored sending "American boys" to Indochina to smash Communism there. Admiral Radford was as much in favor of intervention as he had ever been, but now not even Senator William F. Knowland, of California, could be induced to declare flatly in favor of it. The affair began to take on some new dimensions as a result of the difficulties Dulles met with in London and Paris, but it is doubtful if these affected the basic American decision. What did affect it, so far as one could gather in Washington, was the attitude of what Mills describes as the "atomized and submissive" masses, who, Congressmen discovered while sniffing at the grass roots during the Easter holidays, were not at all well disposed to the idea of a shooting war in Indochina. It was recalled by shrewd Republican politicians that the Eisenhower administration's one great popular triumph had been in negotiating an end to the Korean war. The same administration would lose the political advantage thus gained if it led the country into another bloody jungle war. The masses, it seemed, were on this occasion sovereign.

Mills anticipates his critics and dismisses most of them as

obscurantists who see "the power situation . . . as a romantic confusion." Behind his use of "romantic," there seems to lie the implication that those who see "the power situation" as characterized by confusion rather want to see it that way and find history more entertaining and less demanding—intellectually and morally—when they can regard it as mysterious. He charges them with believing that "history goes on behind men's backs." For my own part, I find the power situation confusing but hardly romantic. It is confusing because it is obviously compounded of many elements which are difficult to isolate, classify, and weigh. I do not believe that history goes on behind men's backs—if "behind men's backs" means beyond their field of vision. History is the life of the community of men within the framework of time. It goes on all about us and among us, sometimes within our sight and comprehension, sometimes—especially when crucial "decisions" are being made by those with the power to make them—beyond them. The truth about it is not, I should think, undiscoverable. I believe with E. H. Carr that "human actions have causes which are in principle ascertainable." But I believe that the truth remains largely undiscovered, largely unascertained, and it seems to me no more obscurantist to say this than to say that the laws of the psyche continue to be somewhat mysterious. Whether they will remain that way forever or only for a short while longer is not the point. The point is that they are in large part mysterious today—and so is history, if for no other reason than that the causes of human action that "are in principle ascertainable" have yet to be fully ascertained.

It seems to me that it is the cocksure approach of people like Mills that is basically obscurantist and hostile to the spirit of objective inquiry and the traditions of the questing intellect. Mills takes a series of perceptions—some of them very sharp and useful—about American society and fashions them into a law of that society's operations. No attempt is made at an empirical testing of the law's soundness—of its value, that is to say, in accounting for observable developments. He does not examine the "decisions" he cites to show us how they reveal the decisive influence of the power elite. All that he tells us is that "a compact and powerful elite . . . does now prevail in America." If it "prevails," then, it follows, according to Mills' logic, that the "big decisions" are attributable to it. But of course it is by no means proved that it does "prevail" in this sense. The only possible way of determining whether it is what Mills says it is would be by examining the decisions themselves, which Mills never does. I would suppose that if a man working in any of the physical sciences offered a doctrine of cause and effect in this way, he would be hooted out of the academies.

Mills denies that he has come up with a "conspiracy theory," but I think that this is exactly what he has done. It is a more sophisticated conspiracy theory than most and has more elements of plausibility than most. Nevertheless, it begins as a search for the responsible, accountable parties in society (this only after Mills argues to his own satisfaction that in our time, if not in all others, "the course of events . . . depends on a series of human decisions"), and its mood is that of a highly intellectual lynching bee. It is interesting to note that practically all of the "events" and "decisions" Mills brings up in this book are ones of which he disapproves. Conspiracy theories are invariably the work of people concerned almost to the point of obsession with the "bad" developments in human history—those who seem to have, in Richard Hofstadter's words, "a commitment to hostility." So far as I know, no general theory of accountability has ever been developed to explain

183

the achievements of a civilization.[4] And none is the work of people who have much sense of being themselves implicated in history—as Mills would be, for example, if my analysis of Dienbienphu is reasonably sound. There is in their work no acknowledgment of the possibility that, as Dr. Bruno Bettelheim has put it, "maybe it [is] not society that created all these difficulties in man but rather the hidden, inner, contradictory nature of man that created these difficulties for society." I do not, of course, suggest that this is a viable doctrine for a sociologist or historian seeking to understand the "power situation" in the United States. I do, however, think that it is exceedingly difficult to write very helpfully about any aspect of the human comedy or the human tragedy if one regards oneself not as part of it but merely as a member of a small captive audience.

Mills repeatedly speaks of the "irresponsibility" of the people who decide. He does not mean that they are as individuals capricious or flip or reckless when they are dealing with matters of life or death. He means, if I understand him, that they exercise power with little of value in the way of tradition or philosophy to guide them. "It is not," he says, "the barbarous irrationality of dour political primitives that is the American danger; it is the respected judgments of Secretaries of State, the earnest platitudes of Presidents, the fearful self-righteousness of sincere young American politicians from Sunny Cali-

[4] Marxism may be regarded as an exception, but Marxism is not in any meaningful sense a conspiracy theory. Marx's "classes" do not "decide" or plot or plan or do anything, but behave as the pressures of history compel them to behave. It has been interesting to note that when Mills, some years after writing *The Power Elite,* became enthusiastic about Fidel Castro's Cuba, he tended to lapse into traditional Marxism. He saw no "interlocking directorates" or "overlapping cliques" bring Castro to power or maintain him there. He described the Castro revolution not as a plot but as a movement of restless, surging humanity struggling to fulfill its needs and aspirations. In fairness, though, he claimed no theoretical jurisdiction beyond the United States.

fornia. These men have replaced mind with platitude, and the dogmas by which they are legitimated are so widely accepted that no counterbalance of mind prevails against them. They have replaced the responsible interpretation of events with the disguise of events by a maze of public relations." He has John Foster Dulles, Dwight Eisenhower, and Richard M. Nixon clearly in mind, but he is as contemptuous of their immediate predecessors and would be as contemptuous of any imaginable successors.

Is he right in maintaining that they exercise their power within "the American system of organized irresponsibility"? I think he is very much in error. I believe that an examination of the crucial decisions reveals a high degree of responsibility in the "interpretation of events." I do not exclude the decision to drop the first atomic bombs. That act may be one for which the future, if it gets the chance, may damn Harry Truman and all the soldiers and scientists around him and all of us who were part of a society which was not thoroughly outraged. Still, I do not think the act was irresponsible. The President knew, in the first place, that he was making a decision of considerable moral significance. He could not have measured its significance as clearly as some of us now do, for the decision was taken in the last days of the preatomic age. He made the decision as a military commander, responsible for the lives of millions of young Americans summoned to risk death in the greatest war in history. As commander in chief, it was his duty to seek estimates of the probable saving of American lives and the probable loss of Japanese lives. As a human being, it was his duty to weigh values of a different sort—the effect of this act of war on the nature of the peace it might bring, the effect of a victory achieved this way on his country's standing in the world after victory, even the problem of whether it was right at all to see the problem in these terms.

185

Nothing that I have read about Harry Truman's decision suggests that he was heedless of these considerations. He approached his awful dilemma soberly, or as soberly as it was possible for a man like Harry Truman to be at a time when the world was awash with blood. He consulted others. In the nature of this peculiar case, he could not avail himself of all the wisdom in the country or the world. But he did, with proper humility, consult men whose judgment he regarded as in many respects superior to his own. Of their number, only a very few, perhaps five percent, counseled him not to use the bomb at all. A few suggested he give the Japanese a decent warning; others, however, thought that this might result in an even greater loss of life than an unannounced use of the weapon. In any case, he sought advice of this sort, and then he acted. I cannot see how he, or those around him, can be accused of "irresponsibility"—or of having constructed about themselves a "paranoid reality."

The Truman administration took us to war in Korea. The Eisenhower administration took us to "the brink of war" in the Formosa Straits and in Indochina and then withdrew. It happens to be my personal view that both administrations exercised sound and mature judgment in these three affairs. I think, in short, that the government was "right," and I set this down because I realize that a man who regards a judgment as a sound one could hardly be expected to regard it as irresponsible. But I think that I also understand the case against all these decisions, and I think the issue can be limited to responsibility alone. Those who decided to intervene in Korea believed that intervention, if it were successful, would prevent similar aggressions and that nonintervention would encourage them. A good deal of the confusion about the Korean war exists because the factor of *time* is not given enough weight. It was true that American policy, before June 22, 1950, held the

Republic of Korea to be outside our system of national security; that policy was abruptly reversed. But when the North Koreans attacked across the thirty-eighth parallel, it was the first aggression by a Communist army in the history of the cold war. Military pressure had been used before, as it was to be used again. Communist armies had fought non-Communist armies in wars of an essentially civil nature. Communist armies brought about the downfall of presumably sovereign governments by their mere presence as occupying forces. But this was the first assault against an international boundary. Thus, it was less Korea as a tract or even the Seoul government as the seat of a sovereign power to which policies and strategies did or did not apply—it was the Republic of Korea as the place where Communist power was seeking to determine whether it could succeed by armed conquest.

There were other considerations, to be sure. The "prestige" of the United Nations appeared to be involved. Though Korea was outside our "defense perimeter," the country was one for which we had shown a great deal of concern. I can well understand believing that none of those things justified our presence in Korea and that, in fact, it was not justified at all. Walter Lippmann is only one of the many estimable people who have taken this view. But again, I cannot see the decision to intervene as anything but one taken with a high degree of responsibility. Indeed, it seems to me that those members of the power elite who made the decision took a lofty and noble view of their responsibilities in this world. And a remarkably disinterested view as well. It is probable that on the night of June 22, 1950, they were not fully aware of the fact that they were leading the country into the most hated war in its history and that this might cost them and their party the control of the country. But all politicians and most statesmen know that all wars of even short duration are hated and that they were not marching down any highway to political success. If anything, their action was a bit too disinterested in this regard, for a large part of the case against the Korean war—seen from this perspective in time—was that it was so divisive and so productive of hatreds and bitterness that it might very well have been better never to have become involved in it. To a degree, these were the considerations that led to the Eisenhower administration's avoidance of commitments in Quemoy and Matsu and in Indochina. Other things were different as well: the Eisenhower administration, for all of Dulles' rhetoric, was more reluctant to assume initiatives of any sort than the Truman administration, and neither Formosa nor the French regime in Indochina could be regarded as having so clear a title to the disputed territories as the Seoul government, with its U.N. support, had in South Korea. But I am talking not about the problems but about the quality of responsibility in their eventual resolution. I am not an admirer of the general judgment of those in the Eisenhower administration who were charged with official responsibility in these matters, but I fail to see how they can be faulted for "irresponsible" decisions.

And, as a matter of fact, it seems to me that it is probably a general rule in our society—and perhaps in most societies—that what are thought of as the "big decisions"—those that are almost immediately crucial, those that involve the nation as a whole and are known to the world while they are being made or immediately afterward—are more often than not "responsible" and, within the limitations of the time and the men who seem to dominate the time, statesmanlike. There are exceptions, of course (Munich would come to mind and Eisenhower's determination of the adequacy of our scientific efforts), but if I were a C. Wright Mills and were seeking to show the unhappy influence of the interlocking directorate of corporate, political, and military leaders, I think I would look not to large decisions but to small ones and to the whole tone and temper of our society at the present time. But that is another story, and not the one his work compels us to deal with.

THE POWER ELITE *Reconsidered*

BY DANIEL BELL

Power is a difficult subject. Its effects are more observable than its causes; even the power-wielders often do not know what factors shaped their decisions. Its consequences are more re-fractory to control—and prediction—than any other form of human behavior. C. Wright Mills' *The Power Elite,* because it seeks to locate the sources of power in an identifiable constel-lation of elites, is one of those rare books in contemporary sociology that deal with the "world of causality" rather than mere description or methodological discussion. It is, in addi-tion, something else: a political book whose loose texture and power rhetoric have allowed different people to read their own emotions into it: for the young neo-Marxists in England (*vide* the group around the *Universities and Left Review*) and the old orthodox Marxists in Poland (*vide* the reception by Adam

Daniel Bell is a professor of sociology at Columbia University. He is the editor of The Radical Right and the author of The Reforming of General Education. This review first appeared in The American Journal of Sociology, November, 1958. It was then reprinted in his well-known The End of Ide-ology (New York: The Free Press, 1960), from which this version is taken.

Schaff, the Party's official philosopher), it has become a primer for the understanding of American policy and motives. This is curious, since Mills is not a Marxist, and if anything, his method and conclusions are anti-Marxist. But because it is tough-minded and "unmasks" the naive, populist illusions about power, it has won a ready response among radicals.

The Mood and the Intent

The mood that pervades Mills' book—and most of his work —provides some clue to the response. In writing about labor (*The New Men of Power*), the white-collar class, and now the power elite—the range of classes in society—Mills is modeling himself on Balzac and writing what Balzac called the *étude de moeurs,* the "comedy" of morals. Some of the Balzac method is there: Balzac sought to reconcile the discoveries of science with poetry and to build up visual effects by the massing of factual detail. Mills takes statistic after statistic and clothes them with angry metaphors.

But more than stylistic analogy is involved. Blazac lived at a time very much like ours: a time of upheaval, when old mores were called into question, a time of class change, when individual social mobility was becoming possible for the first time. Balzac's heroes, Louis Lambert, Rastignac, and most of all Vautrin (a collateral descendent of Macheath, of John Gay's *Beggar's Opera*), begin as mobile men, men seeking a place in society, but end by hating the bourgeois society they find. Their stance is that of the outsider, and their world (Vautrin's underworld is a *counter*-society to the upper world, as is Bertolt Brecht's underworld in *Threepenny Opera*) is built on the premise that the public morality, its manners and ideals, is all a fraud. It is interesting that Mills quotes with approval Balzac's dictum, "Behind every fortune is a crime," and sees it as a judgment which applies equally today. For Mills, too, is an outsider.

But whatever its initial emotional impulse, Mills' book is molded by more direct intellectual progenitors. These are: Veblen, from whom the rhetoric and irony are copied; Weber, for the picture of social structure, not, however, of classes, but of vertical orders, or *Standen;* and, most crucially, Pareto, but not for the definition of elite, which is much different from Mills', but the method. While the debts to Veblen and Weber are conscious, that to Pareto is probably not so. Yet there is the same scorn for ideas, and the denial that ideology has any operative meaning in the exercise of power. And by seeing power as an underlying "combination of orders," Mills parallels, in method, what Pareto was doing in seeing social groups as "combinations of residues." This leads, I think, despite the dynamism in the rhetoric, to a static, ahistorical approach.[1] For *The Power Elite* is not an empirical analysis of power in the United States, though many readers have mistaken its illustrations for such an analysis, but a *scheme* for the analysis of power; and a close reading of its argument will show, I think, how confusing and unsatisfactory this scheme is.

The Argument

One can examine Mills' book by an alternate scheme,[2] but

[1] My own masters, in this respect, are Dewey and Marx. Dewey, for his insistence on beginning not with structure (habit) but with problems: with the question of why something is called into question, why things are in change, and what people did; Marx, for the interplay of ideology and power: for the emphasis on history, on crises as transforming moments, on politics as an activity rooted in concrete interests and played out in determinable strategies.

[2] For one such alternate scheme, see Talcott Parsons' essay-review "The Distribution of Power in American Society" (pp. 60–88 of this volume). Parsons argues that Mills sees power as a secondary "distributive" concept in a zero-sum game, where the focus is on who has power. Parsons organizes his analysis on the functional, or integrative purpose of power in

C. WRIGHT MILLS AND *THE POWER ELITE*

as a prior necessity one must write a textual analysis: identify the key terms, see how consistently they are used, and relate evidence to propositions in order to test the coherence of the argument. This, then, is an exercise in hermeneutics.

The argument, as it unfolds in Mills' opening chapter (the others are largely uneven illustrations rather than development or demonstration of the thesis), shuttles perplexingly back and forth on the key problem of how power is wielded. One can show this only by some detailed quotation, a difficult but necessary burden for exposition.[3]

Within American society, says Mills, major national power "now resides in the economic, political and military domains."

> The way to understand the power of the American elite lies neither solely in recognizing the historical scale of events, nor in accepting the personal awareness reported by men of apparent decision. Behind such men and behind the events of history, linking the two, are the major institutions of modern society. These hierarchies of state and corporation and army constitute the means of power; as such, they are now of a consequence not before equalled in human history—and at their summits, there are now those command posts of modern society which offer us the sociological key to an understanding of the role of the higher circles in America (5).

Thus power, to be power, apparently means control over the *institutions* of power:

> By the powerful, we mean, of course, *those who are able to realize their will, even if others resist it.* No one, accordingly,

---

the ordering of society. Another view, which sees power as a positive force in securing social values for the benefit of society, is advanced by Robert S. Lynd in Arthur Kornhauser (ed.), *Problems of Power in American Democracy* (Detroit: Wayne State University Press, 1958).

[3] All italics, unless otherwise indicated, are mine. They are intended to underline key statements. All citations are from C. Wright Mills' *The Power Elite*, New York, Oxford University Press, 1956.

can be truly powerful unless he has access to the command of major institutions, for it is over these institutional means of power that the truly powerful are, in the first instance, powerful (9).

It is shared by only a few persons:

> By the power elite, we refer to those political and economic and military *circles* which as an intricate set of overlapping cliques *share decisions having at least national consequences. Insofar as national events are decided, the power elite are those who decide them* (18).

But although these people make the key decisions, they are not the "history-makers" of the time. The "power elite" is not, Mills says (20), a theory of history; history is a complex net of intended and unintended decisions.

> The idea of the power elite implies *nothing about the process of decision-making as such:* it is an attempt to delimit social areas within which that process, *whatever its character,* goes on. It is a conception of *who* is involved in the process (21).

But historical decisions are made:

> In our time the pivotal moment does arise, and at that moment small circles do decide or fail to decide. In either case, they are an elite of power . . . (22).

Does then the elite make history? Sometimes it is role-determined, sometimes role-determining (22–25). Mills is obviously wrestling with a contradictory position. For if the power elite are not the history makers, why worry much about them? If they are, it seems to lead to a simple-minded theory of history. Finally Mills resolves the problem:

> It was no "historical necessity," but a man named Truman who, with a few other men, decided to drop a bomb on Hiroshima. It was no historical necessity, but an argument within a

193

small circle of men that defeated Admiral Radford's proposal to send troops to Indochina before Dienbienphu fell (24).

If we extract a residue from all this backing and filing, it is that a smaller number of men than ever before holding top positions in government, economic life, and the military, have a set of responsibilities and decision-making powers that are more consequential than ever before in United States history —which, in itself, does not tell us very much.

But it is less the argument than the rhetoric which found an echo, and crucial to Mills' book are a set of operative terms —*institutions* (with which are interchanged freely, *domains, higher circles, top cliques*), *power, command posts,* and *big decisions*—the political use of which gives the book its persuasiveness. These are the key modifiers of the term "elite." What do they mean?

The Terms

(a) *Elite.* Throughout the book, the term elite is used in a variety of ways. Sometimes the term denotes "membership in clique-like sets of people," or "the morality of certain personality types," or "statistics of selected values" such as wealth, political position, etc. In only one place, in a long footnote on page 366, among the notes, Mills explicitly tries to straighten out the confusion created by the profuse interchange of terms. He says that he defines elites primarily on the basis of "institutional position." But what does this mean?

(b) *Institutions, Domains, etc.* Behind men and behind events, linking the two, says Mills, are the major institutions of society: The military, the political, and the economic. But, actually, the military, the economic, the political, as Mills uses these terms, are not institutions but sectors, or what Weber calls *orders,* or vertical hierarchies—each with their enclosed strata—in society. To say that this sector, or order, is more important than that—that in some societies, for example, the religious orders are more important than the political—is to give us large-scale boundaries of knowledge. But surely we want and need more than that.

Such usage as "the military," "the political directorate," etc., is extraordinarily loose. It would be hard to characterize these as institutions. Institutions derive from *particular, established* codes of conduct, which shape the behavior of *particular* groups of men who implicitly or otherwise have a loyalty to that code and are subject to certain controls (anxiety, guilt, shame, expulsion, etc.) if they violate the norms. If the important consideration of power is *where people draw their power from,* then we have to have more particularized ways of identifying the groupings than "institutionalized orders," "domains," "circles," etc.

(c) *Power.* Throughout the book, there is a curious lack of definition of the word power. Only twice, really, does one find a set of limits to the word:

> By the powerful we mean, of course, those who are able to realize their will, even if others resist it (9).

> *All* politics is a struggle for power: the ultimate kind of power is violence (171).

It is quite true that violence, as Weber has said, is the ultimate sanction of power, and in extreme situations (e.g., the Spanish Civil War, Iraq, etc.) control of the means of violence may be decisive in seizing or holding power. But power is not the inexorable, implacable, granite force that Mills and others make it to be. (Merriam once said: "Rape is not evidence of irresistible power, either in politics or sex.") And is it true to

195

say that *all* politics is a struggle for power? Are there not ideals as a goal? And if ideals are realizable through power—though not always—do they not temper the violence of politics?

Power in Mills' terms is domination. But we do not need an elaborate discussion to see that this view of power avoids more problems than it answers, and particularly once one moves away from the outer boundary of *power as violence to institutionalized power,* with which Mills is concerned. For in society, particularly constitutional regimes, and *within* associations, where violence is not the rule, we are in the realm of norms, values, traditions, legitimacy, consensus, leadership, and identification—all the models and mechanisms of command and authority, their acceptance or denial, which shape action in the day-to-day world, *without violence.* And these aspects of power Mills has eschewed.

(d) *The Command Posts.* It is rather striking, too, given Mills' image of power, and politics, as violence, that the metaphor to describe the people of power is a military one. We can take this as a clue to Mills' implicit scheme. But, being little more than a metaphor, it tells us almost nothing about *who* has the power. The men who hold power, he says, are those who run the *organizations* or *domains* which have power. But how do we know they have power, or what power they have? Mills simply takes as postulates: (1) the organization or institution has power; (2) *position in it gives power.* How do we know? Actually, we can only know if power exists by what people *do* with their power.

What powers people have, what decisions they make, how they make them, what factors they have to take into account in making them—all these enter into the question of whether position *can* be transferred into power. But Mills has said: "The idea of the power elite implies nothing about the process of decision-making as such—it is an attempt to delimit the social areas within which that process, *whatever its character,* goes on. It is a conception of who is involved in the process" (21). Thus, we find ourselves stymied. *Who* depends upon positions? But position, as I have argued, is only meaningful if one can define the character of the decisions made with such power. And this problem Mills eschews.[4]

Mills says, further, that he wants to avoid the problem of the self-awareness of the power holders, or the role of such self-awareness in decisions. ("The way to understand the power of the elite lies neither in recognizing the historic scale of events or the personal awareness reported by men of apparent decision behind the men and the institutions.") But if the power elite is *not* the history-maker (20), as Mills sometimes implies, *then what is the meaning of their position as members of the power elite?* Either they can make effective decisions or not. It is true that many men, like Chanticleer the Cock, crow and believe that they have caused the sun to rise, but if such power is only self-deception, that is an aspect, too, of the meaning of power.

(e) *The Big Decisions.* The power elite comes into its own on the "big decisions." In fact, this is an implicit definition of

---

[4] In his extraordinary story of policy conflicts between the Army, Air Force, and Navy on strategic concepts—policy issues such as reliance on heavy military bombers and all-out retaliation, against tactical nuclear weapons and conventional ground forces for limited wars, issues which deeply affect the balance of power within the military establishment—General James Gavin provides a striking example of the helplessness of some of the top Army brass against the entrenched bureaucracy within the Defense Department. "With the establishment of the Department of Defense in 1947," he writes, "an additional layer of civilian management was placed above the services. Furthermore, by the law, military officers were forbidden to hold executive positions in the Department of Defense. As a result the Assistant Secretaries of Defense relied heavily on hundreds of civil service employees, who probably have more impact on decision-making in the Department of Defense than any other group of individuals, military or civilian." From *War and Peace in the Space Age* (Harper and Brothers), reprinted in *Life,* August 4, 1958, pp. 81–82.

the power of the elite: only they can effect the "big decisions." Those who talk of a new social balance, or pluralism, or the rise of labor, are talking, if at all correctly, says Mills, about the "middle levels" of power. They fail to see the big decisions.

But, curiously, except in a few instances, Mills fails to specify what the big decisions are. The few, never analyzed with regard to how the decisions were actually made or who made them, are five in number: the steps leading to intervention in World War II; the decision to drop the atom bomb over Hiroshima and Nagasaki; the declaration of war in Korea; the indecisions over Quemoy and Matsu in 1955; the hesitation regarding intervention in Indochina when Dienbienphu was on the verge of falling.

It is quite striking (and it is in line with Mills' conception of politics) that all the decisions he singles out as the "big decisions" are connected with *violence*. These are, it is true, the ultimate decisions a society can make: the commitment or refusal to go to war. And in this regard Mills is right. They *are* big decisions. But what is equally striking in his almost cursory discussion of these decisions is the failure to see that they are not made by the power elite. They are the decisions which, in our system, are vested constitutionally in the individual who must bear the responsibility for the choices—the President. And, rather than being a usurpation of the power of the people, so to speak, this is one of the few instances in the Constitution where such responsibility is specifically defined and where accountability is clear. Naturally, a President will consult with others, and in the instances Mills has cited, the President did. Richard Rovere has written a detailed analysis (in the *Progressive,* June, 1956) of the decisions that Mills has cited and, as Mills defines this elite, has broadly refuted the notion that a "power elite" was really involved. Few persons, other than the President, were involved in these decisions: on the atom bomb,

Stimson, Churchill, and a few physicists; on Korea, a small group of men whose counsel was divided, like Acheson and Bradley; on Quemoy and Matsu, specifically by Eisenhower; and on Dienbienphu, a broader group, the military and the Cabinet: but in this instance, "the" power elite, narrowly defined, was for intervention, while Eisenhower alone was against the intervention and decided against sending in troops, principally, says Rovere, because of the weight of public opinion.

Now it may well be that crucial decisions of such importance should not be in the hands of a few men. But short of a system of national initiative and referendum, such as was proposed in 1938–39 in the Ludlow amendment, or short of reorganizing the political structure of the country to insist on party responsibility for decision, it is difficult to see what Mills' shouting is about. To say that the leaders of a country have a constitutional responsibility to make crucial decisions is a fairly commonplace statement. To say that the power elite makes such decisions is to invest the statement with a weight and emotional charge that is quite impressive, but of little meaning.

The Question of Interests

So far we have been accepting the terms "command posts" and "power elite" in Mills' own usage. But now a difficulty enters: the question not only of *who* constitutes the power elite but how *cohesive* they are. Although Mills contends that he does not believe in a conspiracy theory, his loose account of the centralization of power among the elite comes suspiciously close to it. (It is much like Jack London's *The Iron Heel*—the picture of the American oligarchs—which so influenced socialist imagery and thought before World War I.)

C. WRIGHT MILLS AND *THE POWER ELITE*

Yet we can only evaluate the meaning of any centralization of power on the basis of what people do with their power. What *unites* them? What *divides* them? And this involves a definition of *interests*. To say, as Mills does: *"All* means of power tend to become *ends* to an elite that is in command of them. And that is why we may define the power elite in terms of power—as those who occupy the command posts" (23)— is circular.

What does it mean to say that power is an end in itself for the power elite? If the elite is cohesive and is facing another power group, the maintenance of power may be an end in itself. But is the elite cohesive? We do not know without first coming back to the question of interests. And the nature of interests implies a selection of values by a group, or part of a group, over against others, and this leads to a definition of particular privileges, and so on.

Certainly, one cannot have a power elite, or a ruling class, without a *community of interests*. Mills implies one: the interest of the elite is in the maintenance of the capitalist system as a *system*. But this is never really discussed or analyzed in terms of the meaning of capitalism, the impact of political controls on the society, or the changes in capitalism in the last twenty-five years.

But even if the interest be as broad as Mills implies, one still has the responsibility of identifying the conditions for the maintenance of the system, and the issues and interests involved. Further, one has to see whether there is or has been a *continuity of interests,* in order to chart the cohesiveness or the rise and fall of particular groups.

One of the main arguments about the importance of the *command posts* is the growing centralization of power, which would imply something about the nature of interests. Yet there is almost no sustained discussion of the forces leading to centralization. These are somewhat assumed, and hover over the book, but are never made explicit. Yet only a sustained discussion of these tendencies would, it seems to me, uncover the *locales* of power and their shifts. For example: the role of technology and increasing capital costs as major factors in the size of enterprise; forces in the federalization of power, such as the need for regulation and planning on a national scale because of increased communication, complexity of living, social and military services, and the managing of the economy; the role of foreign affairs. Curiously, Soviet Russia is not even mentioned in the book, although so much of our posture has been dictated by Russian behavior.

Since his focus is on who has power, Mills spends considerable effort in tracing the social origins of the men at the top. But, in a disclaimer toward the end of the book (280–87) he says that the conception of the power elite does not rest upon common social origins (a theme which underlies, say, Schumpeter's notion of the rise and fall of classes) or upon personal friendship, but (although the presumption is not made explicit) upon their "institutional position." But such a statement begs the most important question of all: *the mechanisms of coordination among the power holders.* One can say obliquely, as Mills does, that they "meet each other," but this tells us little. If there are "built-in" situations whereby each position merges into another, what are they? One can say, as Mills does, that the new requirements of government require increased recruitment to policy positions from outside groups.[5] But then, what groups—and what do they do?

[5] One key theoretical point, for Marxists, which Mills, surprisingly, never comes to is the question of the ultimate source of power. Is the political directorate autonomous? Is the military independent? If so, why? What is the relation of economic power to the other two? Mills writes: "Insofar as the structural clue to the power elite today lies in the enlarged military state, that clue becomes evident in the military ascendancy. The warlords have

C. WRIGHT MILLS AND *THE POWER ELITE*

At one point Mills says that the Democrats recruited from Dillon, Read, and the Republicans from Kuhn, Loeb. But the point is never developed, and it is hard to know what he means. One could equally say that in the recruitment of science advisors the Democrats took from Chicago and Los Alamos, and the Republicans from Livermore; but if this means anything, and I think it does, one has to trace out the consequences of this different recruitment in the *actions* of the different people. Mills constantly brings the story to the point where analysis has to begin—and stops.

The most extraordinary fact about American foreign policy—the most crucial area of power—has been the lack of coordination between the military and foreign-policy officials, and the failure of both to think in political terms. This is exemplified in the lack of liaison in the final days of World War II, and the nonpolitical decisions made by the U.S. generals which have had incalculable consequences for the balance of power in postwar Europe. Unlike the Soviet Union, the United States subordinated all political questions to immediate military objectives. The British, fearful of a postwar Europe dominated by the Soviet Union, were anxious in the final months of the war to push the Allied armies as fast as possible across the North German plain to Berlin—either to beat the Russians or to participate in its capture. But for the U.S. chiefs of staff, Berlin was of secondary importance.

Said General Marshall, chairman of the Joint Chiefs of Staff: "Such psychological and political advantages as would result from the possible capture of Berlin ahead of the Rus-

---

gained decisive political relevance, and the military structure is now in considerable part a political structure." (275) If so, what is one to say then about the other crucial proposition by Mills that the capitalist system in the U.S. is essentially unchanged? (See my section below on "The Continuity of Power.")

sians should not override the imperative military consideration which, in our opinion, is the destruction and dismemberment of the German armed forces."

And Ray S. Cline in *Washington Command Post: The Operations Division,* a volume in the official army history of World War II, notes the lack of "systematic co-ordination of foreign policy with military planning"—and the uncertainty— even in the fall of 1944—of State Department officials "about American foreign policy as applied to the surrender and occupation of Germany." And the Pentagon, which usually is seen as the cold political brains of U.S. foreign policy, in the negotiation on the occupation of Berlin, rejected a British suggestion for a full land corridor from West Germany to Berlin on the ground that the Soviet Union was an ally and that such a corridor was therefore unnecessary.

The European Image

How explain this image of power and policy in terms of the intents of self-conscious groups of men having fixed places in society? The peculiar fact is that while all the illustrations Mills uses are drawn from American life, the key concepts are drawn from European experiences; and this accounts, I believe, for the exotic attractiveness—and astigmatism—of the power elite idea.[6]

[6] This is a refractory problem which has distorted much of American sociological thinking. Throughout the 1930's, American intellectuals always expected that U.S. social development would inevitably follow that of Europe, particularly in the emergence of fascism. To a great extent these expectations were a product of a mechanical Marxism which saw all politics as a reflex of economic crises, and which postulated common stages of social evolution that each country would pass through. [Ed. note: In the first version of this review, Bell referred to Mills as a "mechanical Marxist."] Even as late as 1948, Harold Laski could write that "the history of the United States would, despite everything, follow the general pattern of capitalist democracy in Europe" (Harold Laski, *The American Democracy,*

For example: having defined politics and power in terms of the ultimate sanction of violence, Mills raises the provocative question: Why have the possessors of the means of violence —the military—not established themselves in power more than they have done in the West? Why is not military dictatorship the more normal form of government?

Mills' answer is to point to the role of status. "Prestige to the point of honor, and all that this implies, has, as it were, been the pay-off for the military renunciations of power . . ." (174).

Now, to the extent that this is true, this fact applies primarily to the *European* scene. On the Continent, the military did create and seek to live by a code of honor. Many European works deal with this code, and many European plays, particularly those of Schnitzler, satirize it. But does the concept apply in the United States? Where in the United States has the military (the Navy apart) been kept in check by honor? The military has not had the power—or status—in American life for a variety of vastly different reasons: the original concept of the Army as a people's militia; the populist image of the Army man—often as a "hero"; the "democratic" recruitment to West Point; the reluctance to accept conscription; the low esteem of soldiering as against money-making; the tradition of civil life, etc.

All this Mills sees and knows. But if "honor" and "violence" are not meaningful in our past, why conceptualize the problem of the military in terms of violence and honor as a general category, when the problem does not derive from the American scene in those terms? Unless Mills assumes, as many

New York: 1948, p. 17). And even so brilliant an observer as Joseph Schumpeter, in his *Capitalism, Socialism and Democracy,* could, with sleight of hand, mix American experiences with European concepts to achieve his gloomy predictions.

intellectuals did in the thirties, that we shall yet follow the European experience.

A similar pitfall can be found in the treatment of prestige. Mills says: "All those who succeed in America—no matter what their circle of origin or their sphere of action—are likely to become involved in the world of the celebrity." And further, "With the incorporation of the economy, the ascendancy of the military establishment, and the centralization of the enlarged state, there have arisen the national elite, who, in occupying the command posts, have taken the spotlight of publicity and become subjects of the intensive build-up. *Members of the power elite are celebrated because of the positions they occupy and the decisions they command"* (71).

Now by celebrities, Mills means *those names that need no further identification.* But are the relationships of celebrity, prestige, status, and power as direct as Mills makes them out to be? Certainly celebrities and glamor exist in American life, but these are the comcomitants or the necessary components, *not* of an elite, but of a *mass consumption* society. A society engaged in selling requires such a system of lure and appeal. But why assume that positions of power involve one in this system of glamor? And could even a sophisticated reader quickly identify the president and board chairman of the top ten corporations on the *Fortune* magazine list of 500 largest corporations, e.g., Standard Oil of New Jersey, A.T.&T., General Motors, etc.; the top-ranking members of military staffs, e.g., the Chairman of the Joint Chiefs of Staff, the head of the Army, the Naval Chief of Operations, Air Chief of Staff, General of S.A.C., etc., and name the members of the cabinet?

Again the confusion arises from Mills' unthinking use of older, European conceptions of prestige. In such feudal-like hierarchies, prestige was identified with *honor* and with *defer-*

ence. Those who held power could claim honor and deference. This was true in Europe. But has it been so in the United States? When Harold Lasswell first attempted in the late thirties to use deference as a key symbol, it already had a false ring. Mills, in effect, substitutes glamor or celebrity for deference, but toward the same end. But does power today carry the immediate glorification and celebration of name? It is doubtful, if, in the mass consumption society, the notions of celebrity, glamor, prestige, and power have the kind of connotations, or are linked, as Mills suggests.

History and Ideas

Now, if one is concerned with the question about changes in the source and style of power, or in the synchronization and centralization of power, one would have to examine the problem historically. Yet except in one or two instances, Mills ignores the historical dimensions. In one place he speaks of a periodization of American history wherein political power has replaced economic power. But this is too loose to be meaningful. In another place—the only concrete discussion of social change in historical terms—he cites an interesting statistic:

> In the middle of the nineteenth century—between 1865 and 1881—only 19 percent of the men at the top of government began their political career at the national level; but from 1905 to 1953 about one-third of the political elite began there, and in the Eisenhower administration some 40 percent started in politics at the national level—a high for the entire political history of the U.S. (229).

Even in its own terms, it is hard to figure out the exact meaning of the argument, other than the fact that more problems are centered in Washington than in the states and, for this reason, more persons are drawn directly to the national capital than before. Surely there is a simple explanation for much of this. During World War II, with a great need for both national unity and for specialists, more outsiders were coopted for cabinet posts and the executive branch than before. And, in 1952, since the Republicans had been out of top office for twenty years and would have fewer persons who had a career in government, they would bring in a high proportion of outsiders.

What is interesting in the use of this kind of data is the methodological bias it reveals. In using such data—and variables like lower or national levels—there is a presumption that in the different kind of recruitment one can chart differences in the character of the men at the top, and that therefore the *character of their politics* would be different too. (Mills seems to imply this but never develops the point other than to say that, today, the *political outsider* has come into the ascendant.) But as a counter-methodology, it would seem to me that one would start not with recruitment or social origins but with the *character of the politics*. Has something changed, and if so, what and why? Is the change due to differences in recruitment (differential class and ethnic backgrounds) or to some other reason? But if one asks these questions, one has to begin with an examination of *ideas and issues,* not social origins.

But Mills, at least here, is almost completely uninterested in ideas and issues. The questions in politics that interest him are: In what way have strategic positions changed, and which positions have come to the fore? Changes in power then are for Mills largely a succession of different positions. As different structural or institutional positions (i.e., military, economic, political) combine, different degrees of power are possible. The circulation of the elite—by which Pareto meant the change in the composition of groups with different "residues"—is transformed here into the succession of institutional positions.

C. WRIGHT MILLS AND *THE POWER ELITE*

But how does this apply to people? Are people—character, ideas, values—determined by their *positions?* And if so, in what way? More than that, to see political history as a shift in the power position of "institutions" rather than, say, of concrete interest groups, or classes, is to read politics in an extraordinarily abstract fashion. It is to ignore the changes in ideas and interests. This is one of the reasons why Mills can minimize, in the striking way he does, the entire twenty-year history of the New Deal and Fair Deal. For him these twenty years were notable *only* because they fostered the centralizing tendencies of the major "institutions" of society, notably the political.

In this neglect, or even dismissal of ideas and ideologies, one finds a striking parallel in Pareto's explanation of social changes in Italy. For Pareto, the rise of socialism in Italy was a mere change in the "derivations" (i.e., the masks or ideologies) while the basic combination of residues remained (No. 1704 in Pareto's notation system).

In effect, the shifts of temper from nationalism to liberalism to socialism reflected shifts in the distribution of class II residues (i.e., the residues of persistence). Thus changes in the political class meant simply the circulation of socio-psychological types. All ideologies, all philosophical claims, were masks "for mere purposes of partisan convenience in debate. [They are] neither true nor false; [but] simply devoid of meaning" (No. 1708).

Similarly, for Mills, changes in power are changes in combinations of constitutional position; and this alone, presumably, is the only meaningful reality.

> Except for the unsuccessful Civil War, changes in the power system of the United States have not involved important challenges to basic legitimations. . . . Changes in the American

structure of power have generally come about by institutional shifts in the relative positions of the political, the economic and the military orders (269).

Thus the extraordinary changes in American life, changes in the concepts of property, managerial control, responsibility of government, the changes in moral temper created by the New Deal, will become "reduced" to institutional shifts. But have there been no challenges to basic legitimations in American life? How continuous has been the system of power in the United States?

The Continuity of Power

If in his analysis of politics Mills draws from Pareto, in his image of economic power he becomes a "vulgar" Marxist. Mills notes:

> The recent social history of American capitalism does not reveal any distinct break in the continuity of the higher capitalist class. . . . Over the last half-century in the economy as in the political order, there has been a remarkable *continuity of interests,* vested in the *types* of higher economic men who guard and advance them . . . (147).

Although the language is vague, one can only say that an answer to this proposition rests not on logical or methodological arguments but on empirical grounds, and in my essay on the breakup of family capitalism in America [Chapter Two of *The End of Ideology*], I have sought to indicate an answer. For the singular fact is that in the last seventy-five years the established relations between the system of property and family, which, Malthus maintained, represented the "fundamental laws" of society, have broken down. And this has meant too the breakup of "family capitalism," which has been the social cement of the bourgeois class system.

In his summation of economic control, Mills paints an even more extraordinary picture:

> The top corporations are not a set of splendidly isolated giants. They have been knitted together by explicit associations within their respective industries and regions and in supra-associations such as the NAM. These associations organize a unity among the managerial elite and other members of the corporate rich. They translate narrow economic powers into industry-wide and class-wide power; and they use these powers, first, on the economic front, for example, with reference to labor and its organizations; and second, on the political front, for example in their large role in the political sphere. And they infuse into the ranks of smaller businessmen the views of big business (122).

This is a breathtaking statement more sweeping than anything in the old TNEC reports or of Robert Brady's theory of *Spitzenverbande* (or peak associations) in his *Business as a System of Power*. That there is some coordination is obvious; but unity of this scope—and smoothness—is almost fanciful. Mills cites no evidence for these assertions. The facts, actually, point to the other direction. Trade associations in the United States have declined; they were primarily important during wartime as a means of representing industry on government boards. The NAM has become increasingly feckless, and there has been a decline in member interest and contributions. And industry has divided on a wide variety of issues including labor policy (e.g., the large steel and auto companies have been attacked by General Electric and other firms for accepting s.u.b.—supplementary unemployment benefits).

Mills speaks of "their large role in the political sphere." But against whom are the members of the power elite united, and what kinds of issues unite them in the political sphere? I can think of only one issue on which the top corporations would be united: tax policy. In almost all others, they divide. They are divided somewhat on labor. There are major clashes in areas of self-interest, such as those between railroads, truckers, and the railroads and the airlines; or between coal and oil, and coal and natural gas interests. Except in a vague, ideological sense, there are relatively few political issues on which the managerial elite is united.

The problem of *who unites with whom on what* is an empirical one, and this consideration is missing from Mills' work. If such coordination as Mills depicts does exist, a further question is raised as to how it comes about. We know, for example, that as a consequence of bureaucratization, career lines within corporations become lengthened and, as a consequence, there is shorter tenure of office for those who reach the top. Within a ten-year period, A.T.&T. has had three executive officers, all of whom had spent thirty to forty years *within* the corporation. If men spend so much time *within* their corporate shells, how do members of the "elite" get acquainted?

In this preoccupation with elite manipulation, Mills becomes indifferent to the problems of what constitutes problems of power in the everyday life of the country. This is quite evident in the way he summarily dismisses all other questions, short of the "big decisions," as "middle level" and, presumably, without much *real* meaning. *Yet are these not the stuff of politics,* the issues which divide men and create the interest conflicts that involve people in a sense of ongoing reality: labor issues, race problems, tax policy, and the like? Is this not the meaning of power to people as it touches their lives?

The use of the term elite poses another question about the utility of its limits for discussing powers. Why use the word *elite* rather than *decision-makers,* or even *rulers?* To talk of *decision-making,* one would have to discuss policy formulation, pressures, etc. To talk of *rule,* one would have to discuss

211

the nature of rule. But if one talks of an elite, one need only discuss institutional position, and one can do so only if, as Mills assumes, the fundamental nature of the system is unchanged, so that one's problem is to chart the circulation at the top. The argument that the fundamental nature of the system —i.e., that of basic legitimations, of continuity of the capitalist class—is unchanged is a curious one, for if power has become so centralized and synchronized, as Mills now assumes, is this not a fundamental change in the system?

Yet, even if one wants to talk in terms of elites, there have been key shifts in power in American society: the breakup of family capitalism (and this is linked to a series of shifts in power in Western society as a whole), but most importantly— and obviously—the decisive role of the political arena.

From Economics to Politics

In the decade before World War I, the growing power of the trusts, the direct influence of the bankers in the economy, the ideological rise of socialism all tended to focus attention on the class system as the hidden but actually decisive element in shaping society and social change. A group of "realistic" historians, notably J. Allen Smith, and, most importantly, Charles A. Beard, began the task of reinterpreting the early colonial and constitutional struggles in economic terms. The Beard interpretation schematically, was roughly this:

The earliest struggles in American history were direct class struggles between the merchant group, represented by the Federalists, and the agrarians, represented by the Democrats. Society was split fairly cleanly between the two groups with antagonistic interests (tariff, cheap money, etc.). The unadorned way in which class conflict was discussed by the "founding fathers" could be strikingly documented in the Federalist papers. As in the later struggle between the English landed gentry and the manufacturing class over the protectionist corn laws, a decisive victory for either would have decided the basic character of the society. But that early American plutocracy, the Eastern merchants, proved to be an unstable social group that was incapable of maintaining the political initiative. So the Federalists lost. Yet the Democrats—in the face of the economic facts of life of a burgeoning capitalism—could not really win, and the "Jeffersonian revolution" was something that Jefferson found easier to promise than to execute.

But later historiography has considerably modified this crude chiaroscuro and has drawn in many subtle tones between the black and the white. As Dixon Ryan Fox, for one, in his study of politics within one state in the first four decades of the nineteenth century, *Yankees and Yorkers,* has written:

> Because of rivalries between English and Dutch, Presbyterian and Anglican, merchants and farmers, and others, party spirit early appeared in New York and persisted in changing manifestations. Yet the party lines were not closely drawn between rich and poor. So assured were the aristocrats of their social place and so various their backgrounds that they did not move as one interest; families faced each other as Capulets and Montagues. As Henry Adams has remarked, "All these Jays, Schuylers, Livingstones, Clintons, Burrs, had they lived in New England would probably have united, or abandoned the country; but being citizens of New York they quarreled." When the Tories were removed the Whigs soon split into factions, not merely two, but several, each ready for trade and compromise.

It is at this point that we find the seeds of the peculiarly American party system. The mutual defeat of attempts to establish exclusive domination left the social system undefined from the very start. It was not predominantly mercantile, slave, free, agrarian, industrial, or proletarian. The wealthy families, having lost direct political control, sought to work indirectly through the politician. But in a rapidly shifting society, whose very hugeness casts up a variety of conflicting interests, a politician can succeed only if he is a broker and the party system an agency of mediation.

This is not to deny the existence of classes or the nature of a class system. *But one cannot, unless the society is highly stratified, use the class structure for direct political analysis.* A class system defines the *mode* of gaining wealth and privilege in a society. (This mode can be land [real property], corporate title ["fictitious" property], skill [technical or managerial], mercenaries [*condottieri*], or direct political allocation [party, bureaucracy, or army], and this class system has to be legitimated, in legal forms, in order to assure its continuity. Often this wealth and privilege carries with it power and prestige, but there is no direct correlation.) But most important, whatever the mode, class analysis does not tell us directly *who* exercises the power, nor does it tell us much about the competition within that mode for power. Unless that mode and its legitimations are directly challenged, one rarely sees a class acting as a class in unified fashion. Once a specific mode is established, competition for privilege within the system is high and various and different interests develop. The growing complexity of society necessarily multiplies those interests, regional or functional, and in an open society the political arena—unless there is a conflict to overthrow the system—is a place where different interests fight it out for advantage. That is why, usually, the prism of "class" is too crude to follow the swift play of diverse political groups.

In European society, the *political* issues, especially after the French Revolution, tended to fall along class lines, but even then, any detailed analysis risked falsification of events simply by focusing the issues in gross class terms. Such a classic of Marxist political analysis as *The Eighteenth Brumaire of Louis Bonaparte* comes alive only because Marx depicts so skillfully the play of diverse group interests, as these are manipulated so imperiously by Louis Napoleon, beneath the larger façade of class interests. In the United States, so heterogeneous from the start, and striated even further by diverse ethnic, national, and religious differences, it is difficult to read the political order—which after all became an independent road to privilege for the leaders of minority groups—as a reflection of the economic order. But even where there was some rough correspondence, the play of diverse interests was immense. As late as 1892, Marx's co-worker, Friedrich Engels, wrote in a letter to his friend Sorge: "There is no place yet in America for a *third* party, I believe. The divergence of interests even in the *same* class group is so great in that tremendous area that wholly different groups and interests are represented in each of the two big parties, depending upon the locality, and almost each particular section of the possessing class has its representatives in each of the two parties to a very large degree, though *today* big industry forms the core of the Republicans on the whole, just as the big landowners of the South form that of the Democrats. The apparent haphazardness of this jumbling together is what provides the splendid soil for the corruption and the plundering of the government that flourishes there so beautifully."

At one point in later American history, the dominant business class—the plutocracy, rather than any landed squirearchy—came close to imprinting a clear mark on American politics. By the turn of the twentieth century the growing industrial class had scored a smashing economic victory. With that victory came some efforts to dissolve the structure of group interests by developing a pervasive political ideology which could also serve the emergent national feeling. One such attempt was the doctrine of imperialism in the "manifest destiny" of Beveridge and the "Americanism" of Franklin Giddings. This was alien to a heterogeneous people, or at least premature. The second and more successful effort was in the identification of capitalism with democracy. The early commercial class had feared democracy as a *political* instrument whereby the "swinish multitude" (Burke) would prepare the way for a radical despotism. The ideology of victorious industrial capitalism defined democracy almost completely in agreeable *economic* terms, as liberty of contract.

If the dominant business class was unable to exercise direct political control of the society, it could establish its ideological hegemony. While in the period from 1880 to 1912 the middle class (small farmers and businessmen, and many professionals) had supported the sporadic antitrust and antimonopoly outbursts, such opinions and movements were dissolved by the subsequent two decades of war, prosperity, and propaganda.

This unity burst with the bubble of prosperity because the ideologists of free enterprise, rugged or otherwise, did not understand the realities of the "socialized" economy that had come into being. They had failed to grasp the degree to which this market economy imposes a particular type of dependency upon everyone.

In a pure market society, as Marx once phrased it, each man thinks for himself and no one plans for all. Today it is no longer individual men who are in the market but particular collectivities, each of which tries—by administered prices, farm supports, uniform wage patterns and the like—to exempt itself from the risks of the market; inevitably, the measures each group resorts to for protection provoke governmental concern that the entire economy not be overturned in the anarchic stampede to safety.

De Tocqueville once wrote that historians who live in aristocratic ages are inclined to read all events through the will and character of heroic individuals, whereas historians of democratic times deal perforce with general causes. The dazzling aristocratic glamor of Franklin D. Roosevelt has often confused the efforts to put the New Deal period in historical perspective, and even now we lack an adequate political characterization of the era. There have been many historical analogies inspired by the flavor and verve of Roosevelt himself: e.g., Roosevelt was a temporizing Solon whose political reforms sought to stave off the revolution of propertyless masses; Roosevelt was a Tiberius Gracchus, a patrician who deserted his class to become the people's tribune; Roosevelt was a Louis Napoleon, an ambitious politician manipulating first one class and then another, while straddling them all, to maintain his personal rule. Certainly, they shed little light on the way government action gives rise to new combinations of interests and the operation of these shifting coalitions.

The public face of the New Deal was a set of sweeping social reforms, and, quite naively, some writers, and indeed, Roosevelt himself, have called the New Deal an assertion of human rights over property rights. But such terms carry little meaning, either philosophically or pragmatically. Are "support prices" for farmers a property right or a human right? In effect, what the New Deal did was to *legitimate* the idea of *group* rights, and the claim of groups, as groups, rather than individuals, for government support. Thus unions won the right to bargain collectively and, through the union shop, to enforce a group decision over individuals; the aged won pensions, the farmers gained subsidies; the veterans received benefits; the minority groups received legal protections, etc. None of these items, in themselves, were unique. Together, they added up to an extraordinary social change. Similarly, the government has

217

always had some role in directing the economy. But the permanently enlarged role, dictated on the one hand by the necessity to maintain full employment, and, on the other, by the expanded military establishment, created a vastly different set of powers in Washington than ever before in our history.

What is amazing, in retrospect, is that while the commitment to a politically managed economy could have been foreseen, we were quite badly deficient in organizing our economic thinking for it. A managed economy requires not only that we have a housekeeping budget for the government as the large spending unit, but also an economic budget that states the major magnitudes of economic interaction for society as a whole —the total amount of goods and services produced in a year's time and the total amount of income paid out. Through these figures we can chart the gaps in consumer spending and in investment and, if necessary, make up the differences by appropriate fiscal measures. Yet it was only in 1936 that the Department of Commerce brought out its first report on national income, and only in 1942 that the other side of the economic balance sheet, the gross national product, was first estimated by government. The two indexes as the pulse beat of economic health were only first combined and published together in President Roosevelt's budget message in 1945.

In the emergence of the political economy, a new kind of decision-making has taken place. In the market society, people's wants are registered by their "dollar votes," as part of the automatic interaction of supply and demand. The sum total of individual dollars-and-cents decisions, operating independently of each other, added up, as Bentham thought, to a social decision, e.g., the general consensus. Thus, when decisions on the allocation of resources operated through the market, dollars, not ideology, determined what was to be produced. In this sense, economics was the key to social power, and politics its pale reflection.

But politics, operating through the government, has more and more become the means of registering a social and economic decision. Here, instead of acting independently as in a market, the individual is forced to work through particular collectivities to enforce his will. Since in a managed economy, "politics," not dollars, determines major production, the intervention of the government not only sharpens pressure-group identifications but forces each to adopt an ideology which can justify its claims and which can square with some concept of "national interest."

The Types of Decisions

Ultimately, if one wants to discuss power, it is more fruitful to discuss it in terms of *types of decisions* rather than elites. And curiously, Mills, I would argue, ultimately agrees, for the real heart of the book is a polemic against those who say that decisions are made democratically in the United States. Mills writes:

> More and more of the fundamental issues never come to any point of decision before Congress . . . much less before the electorate (255).

> Insofar as the structural clue to the power elite today lies in the political order, that clue is the decline of politics as genuine and public debates of alternative decisions . . . America is now in considerable part more a formal political democracy (224).

Now, to some extent this is true, but not, it seems to me, with the invidious aspect with which Mills invests the judgment.

C. WRIGHT MILLS AND *THE POWER ELITE*

In many instances, even the "interested public" feels itself "trapped," so to speak, by its inability to affect events. Much of this arises out of the *security* nature of problems, so that issues are often fought out in a bureaucratic labyrinth. The decision on the H-bomb was one such issue. Here we had groups of scientists versus a section of the military, particularly SAC. Unless one assumes that everyone ever involved in decision-making is a member of the power elite—which is circular—*we have to locate the source of such decisions, for these are the central problems of a sociology of power.*

But another, equally important reason for being unable to affect events is the onset of what one can only call, inaptly, "technical decision making": the fact that once a policy decision is made, or once a technological change comes to the fore, or once some long crescive change has become manifest, a number of other consequences, if one is being "functionally rational," almost inevitably follow. Thus, shifts of power become "technical" concomitants of such "decisions," and a sociology of power must identify the kinds of consequences which follow the different kinds of decisions.

Three short examples may illustrate the point:

(1) *The federal budget as an economic gyroscope.* From 1931 to 1935, in the depth of the depression years, total federal budget expenditures of all kinds averaged 5.2 billion dollars. In the next four years, 1936 to 1940, it reached a new high of 8 billion dollars. (Income during this period was about 60 percent of expenditures.) Four years later, the federal government was spending, yearly, a staggering total of over 95 billion dollars and accumulating a national debt which more than quintupled the debt of the previous decade. The figures are in constant dollars.

More importantly, these expenditures have to be compared with gross national product (g.n.p.), the sum total of goods and services produced during a year. During the depression decade, despite the then relatively high government spending, the federal budget "consumed" and pumped back between 5 to 10 percent of g.n.p. During the war, the figure mounted to over 40 percent. But while this represented an "abnormally" high figure, in the decade and a half since the end of the war, the government has become the "consumer" of nearly one-fourth of the total g.n.p. Except for one year, 1948, the one "peacetime" year in postwar history, when the federal budget reached a "low" of 33 billion dollars (against a g.n.p. of 257 billion), the expenditures in the Korean campaign and the sums required to maintain the arms pace of the cold war has kept the federal budget at record highs. In the last half of the 1950 decade it averaged about 70 billion dollars, with g.n.p. about 325 billion dollars. In 1960, the federal budget will reach over 80 billion (estimated), and g.n.p. over 400 billion. In the 1950's, the yearly interest alone on the public debt, over 7.2 billion dollars, was greater than the *total* federal government expenditures each year during the depression.

The fact is that this enormous rise in the expenditures of the federal government was not "willed" by any one man or group of men, but arose, inevitably, as a necessary outcome of the war and its effects. And the permanent role of the federal government as the economic gyroscope of the country is due to that fact.

(2) *The "dual economy" of 1950–55.* When the Korean war broke out in 1950, the government was faced with the immediate choice of either converting existing machinery production to war goods or encouraging new plants. The decision rested on an estimate of the type of war. If it seemed as if the Korean war might spread into a general war, then the order to convert civilian facilities could be constructed to build large stockpiles of arms. The decision, based on political-military

221

estimates, was to build a "dual economy." The chief consequence, economically speaking, was the decision to speed new capital expansion by allowing firms to write off the costs of new facilities in five years, as against the normal twenty-five years. (Thus firms could deduct 20 percent of the new costs from profits and thus gain a considerable tax benefit.) This five-year tax amortization scheme encouraged an extraordinarily high rate of capital investment, undoubtedly spurred the prosperity boom of the mid-fifties, and was responsible for the overexpansion of capacity which was a contributing element to the recession of 1958–59.

(3) *Weapons technology.* The rapid emergence of new weapons decisively affects the relative weight of power and influence within the military, and within each arm of the military, of the different branches. Thus the rise of missiles reduces the importance of the battleship, once the mainstay of the navy, and of the army itself. In the new technology, for example, the missile-carrying submarine becomes a key arm of striking power, while the extension of the range of the missile makes the manned airplane obsolete. These changes in the composition of the armed forces, the requirements of new skill groups, of technicians and of technologists, mean a change in the profile of military power. Research and Development become more important than Operations, and the power of the scientist, the engineer, and the technologist grows accordingly.

All of these consequences grow out of the "big decisions" that Mills has talked about. But the fundamental policy issues which Mills mentions are primarily, as I pointed out before, decisions to be involved in war or not—or, more broadly, the question of foreign policy. And how can one discuss this question, which Mills completely evades, without discussing the cold war, *and the extent to which our posture is shaped by the Russians!* United States foreign policy since 1946—or, more specifically, since Byrnes' Stuttgart speech, which reversed our position on weakening Germany—was not a reflex of any *internal* social divisions or class issues in the United States but was *based on an estimate of Russia's intentions.*

Nor was this estimate made, in the first instance, by "the power elite." It was an estimate made by American scholarly experts, most notably by George Kennan and the policy-planning staff of the State Department. It was a judgment that Stalinism as an ideological phenomenon, and Russia as a geopolitical power, were aggressively, militarily, and ideologically expansionist, and that a policy of containment, including a rapid military build-up was necessary in order to implement that containment. This underlay Truman's Greco-Turkish policy, and it underlay the Marshall Plan and the desire to aid the rebuilding of the European economy. These policies were not a reflex of power constellations within the U.S. They were estimates of national interest and of national survival.

From the first decision, many others followed: the creation of a long-distance striking arm in the air (SAC), the establishment of a West European Defense Community (EDC, and following its failure, NATO, etc.). This is not to say that every strategic step followed inexorably from the first decision (after France rejected EDC, one had to rely more on Germany for military support), *but that the broad imperatives were clear.*

Once these broad lines were laid down, interest groups were affected, and Congress was used—often disastrously—to pass acts which gave pressure groups larger allocations of aid money (e.g., the Bland Act, pressured both by the unions and maritime industry, which provided that 50 percent of all Marshall Plan aid had to be carried in American bottoms) or to hinder the flexibility of the State Department (e.g., the Battle

223

Act, which forbade trade with the Soviet bloc and, in effect, crippled Ceylon, when it was our ally, by threatening to stop aid if Ceylon sold rubber to China).

To ignore the problems of this type of "imperative" decision-making is, it seems to me, to ignore the stuff of politics as well as the new nature of power in contemporary society. The theory of the "power elite" implies a unity of purpose and community of interest among the elite that is not proven or demonstrated. It is simply asserted.

Coda

Much of Mills' work is motivated by his enormous anger at the growing bureaucratization of life—this is his theory of history—and its abettors; and this gives the book its appeal and pathos. Many people do feel helpless and ignorant and react in anger. But the sources of helplessness ought to be made clear, lest one engage, as I think Mills does, in a form of "romantic protest" against modern life. (The Sorelian tones of power as violence, and the populist imagery of power as closed conspiracy, find disturbing echo in Mills' book.)

Complexity and specialization are inevitable in the multiplication of knowledge, the organization of production, and the coordination of large areas of political society. That these should lead to "bureaucratization" of life is not necessarily inevitable, particularly in a society of growing education, rising incomes, and multiplicity of tastes. More importantly, such ambiguous use of terms like "bureaucratization" and "power elites" often reinforces a sense of helplessness and belies the resources of a free society: the variety of interest conflicts, the growth of public responsibility, the weight of traditional freedoms (*vide* the Supreme Court, an institution that Mills fails to discuss), the role of volunteer and community groups, etc., etc.

Like the indiscriminate use by the Communists of the term "bourgeois democracy" in the thirties, or by Burnham of "managerial society" in the forties, or the term "totalitarianism" in the fifties, *particular and crucial* differences between societies are obscured. This amorphousness leads, as in the case of *The Power Elite* with its emphasis on "big" decisions, to a book which discusses power, but rarely politics. And this is curious, indeed.

PART V

In Retrospect on THE POWER ELITE

This concluding section contains two papers, the first by Mills, the second by one of the editors. The Mills rejoinder is noteworthy for the fact that it makes Mills' moral position clear and responds to criticisms having to do with the tone of the book, the nature of power, and the proper stance for a social scientist in modern America. Because Mills' reply deals primarily with questions of moral judgment and ideology, the final paper focuses on questions of a theoretical, methodological, and empirical nature. Based on recent research, it attempts to mediate some of the disputes between Mills and his critics.

Comment on Criticism

BY C. WRIGHT MILLS

Dear friends:

I hope you will forgive me if—being more interested in criticism than in critics—I don't mention names but rather bring up points.[1] I want briefly to comment on some of the criticism of *The Power Elite* not because I believe the book invulnerable to criticism nor because I want to take a crack at people who have taken one at me, but because I think the angry character of many of the reviews suggests political and moral questions that are of intellectual interest.

This anger, I believe, is due to the fact that whether it is generally right or generally wrong, the book is taken as a blow at the smooth certainties and agreeable formulas that now make up the content of liberalism. This liberalism now determines the standard view of American civilization; most reviewers are liberals of one sort or another, or at least think of themselves as such. But since they are often intelligent as well, their liberalism is rather insecure. Therefore, they are easily upset. Therefore they become very angry. Therefore, they want to wiggle out of any arguments about the liberal platitudes and qualifications to which they cling.

What is interesting is the way they wiggle.

I

One journal of liberal opinion, rather than review the book, runs a piece containing one thought: professors who

This reply to criticism appeared in Dissent, *Winter, 1957.*

[1] Ed. note: To aid the reader, the reviews from which Mills quotes will be identified.

read *White Collar* "liked every part of it except the one about professors." They thought this part "only half true, a kind of caricature."[2] So, concludes the reviewer, perhaps the pictures in *The Power Elite* of all the other groups—bureaucrats and politicians and millionaires—are also caricatures.

Of course they are. *All* concepts are "caricatures." They invite attention to selected features of some object. The question is to what extent they specify important features and to what extent they obfuscate them. This critic suggests that the test of social conceptions is whether or not those to whom they refer find them pleasantly in line with their own self-image. He suggests further that *they* should know best since it is "one kind of life that they [know] about." It is difficult to think of a more misleading test. I've never studied any group that had an adequate view of its own social position. But whether that is always true or not, merely to assume the contrary, is to assume a degree of rational self-consciousness and self-knowledge that not even eighteenth-century psychologists would allow.

II

There's one question most liberal reviewers find quite unanswerable: If the American elite is all this bad, "how come it hangs together—and, despite defects, provides people with the highest content of economic, esthetic and intellectual opportunity yet offered a population block of 165 million?"[3]

I can't really conceive, as the question assumes, that the American elite is the *author* of all the happy values of American civilization. Such an assumption makes them much more omnipotent than I've ever thought them to be. But many re-

[2] William Lee Miller, "Queen Ants and Cadillacs," *The Reporter,* May 31, 1956.

[3] A. A. Berle, Jr., "Are the Blind Leading the Blind?" in this volume.

viewers seem really to believe, and their question certainly implies, that American prosperity may be taken as proof of the virtues of the contemporary elite.

In the same vein one might ask: If the Soviet elite are such villains as all good Americans know them to be, how come in a mere thirty years they've raised an illiterate, backward, starving peasant mass into the biggest nation in the world, created one of the world's two foremost industrial plants, demonstrated for the first time in human history that classic capitalism is only one of the ways to industrialize, etc.?

In brief: such critics have swallowed the vulgar notion that the "success" of a nation, however defined, is the basis on which to judge that nation's elite. I think to state the assumption is to indicate its inadequacy.

III

To blunt the edge of an argument, contemporary critics often try to assimilate it to old stereotypes—the common coin of the lazier reviewer's mint.

To say "old stuff" or "new stuff" is equally irrelevant—unless you get very specific, as my critics in this line have not done. The argument ("It's all old stuff") equates "old" with "untrue." I don't of course accept that fashionable and easy equation. But apart from that, if this is all old stuff, where *is* the new stuff? If *The Power Elite* is about some world that's now long past, where is the image of the 1950's that stands in such irrefutable contrast? There isn't any documented image; what such reviewers are doing is wallowing in that intellectual climate, now so fashionable, which is based solely upon the fact of material prosperity. Given that, they can't conceive of *any* critical statement of a modern society being credible. That my book isn't primarily about prosperity and poverty but about power and status makes no difference to them. Having come of age in a time when poverty was the key problem, they can't really recognize any other.

The more interesting question underneath this charge of "old stuff" is how best to study the trends. Quite deliberately, of course, I have stated in *The Power Elite* an "extreme position"—which means that in order to make matters clear I try to focus on each trend just a little ahead of where it now is, and more importantly, that I try to see all the trends at once, as parts of a total structure. It is much easier for the liberal to acknowledge one trend at a time, keeping them scattered as it were, than to make the effort to see them altogether. To the literary empiricist, writing his balanced little essay, first on this and then on that, any attempt to see it whole is "extremism." Yet there is truth in one reviewer's assertion that I tend to confuse prediction with description. These two, however, are not to be sharply separated, and they are not the only ways of looking at trends. One can examine trends in an effort to answer the question: "Where are we going?"—which is of course what I have tried to do. In doing so I have tried to study history rather than to retreat into it; to pay attention to present trends without being merely journalistic; to gauge the future of these trends without being prophetic. All this is very hard to do. You've got to remember that you are dealing with historic materials; that they do change very fast; that there are countertrends. And you've always got to balance the precision of knife-edge description with the generality needed to bring out their meaning for your time. But above all, you've got to see the several major trends together—structurally, rather than as a mere scatter of happenings adding up to nothing new, in fact not adding up at all.

232

IV

"The judgment to be made of Mills," one scientific reviewer writes, "is never that what he says is true but unimportant, as can be said for much of the reporting in the social sciences; rather what he says is clearly important but not unquestionably valid."[4]

Of course the argument of *The Power Elite* is not "unquestionably valid." In the language of the social studies, it's an elaborated hypothesis, anchored, I believe, at key points to acknowledged fact. There is no other way to write now, as a social student, about such large topics.

In the social studies today there are many know-nothings who refuse to say anything, or at least really to believe anything, about modern society unless it has been through the fine little mill of The Statistical Ritual. It's usual to say that what they produce is true but unimportant. I don't think I agree with that: more and more I wonder how true it is. If you have ever seriously studied, as I have, for a year or two some thousand hour-long interviews, carefully coded and punched, you'll have begun to see how very malleable these thousands of bits of fact really are. Moreover, increasingly I come to feel that it is very important when some of the best minds among us spend their lives studying trivialities because the methods to which they are dogmatically committed don't allow them to study anything else. Much of this work, I am convinced, has become the mere following of a ritual—which happens to have gained commercial and foundation value—rather than, in the words of The Social Scientist, any "commitment to the hard [why hard?] demands of scientific social analysis."

[4] Leonard Reissman, "The Power Elite," *American Sociological Review,* August, 1956.

On the other hand, there are many literary and journalistic people who distribute larger images of the social structure in which we live. By refusing to comment on these images, much less to take them in hand, the pseudo-scientific know-nothings allow, as it were, these literary types to create and to sustain all the images that guide and all the myths that obfuscate—as the case may be—our view of social reality.

That's one feature of the intellectual situation in which I think I—along of course with others—have been trying to write. We've tried to use what we found useful of newer research techniques, but we've refused to give up the larger problems because of any initial dogma about method. Above all, we've refused to become silly about transferring the models of physical and mathematical proof into the social studies. We've kept the *problem,* whatever it is, foremost in mind and we've felt, I suppose, as working researchers rather than self-appointed Statesmen of Research, that we'd just have to work out the best methods we could as we went along trying to solve the problem. The social studies, I am convinced, will not be advanced by pontifical dogma about method or pretentious cowardice about Social Science. It will go forward out of highly self-conscious work on real problems.

v

But, then, half a dozen reviewers exclaim: "In this book, you take it upon yourself to *judge;* now really, should a sociologist judge?"

The answer is: "Does he have any choice?" If he spends his intellectual force on the petty details of elections or boy gangs or what not, he is of course as a man of intellect making himself irrelevant to the political conflicts and forces of his time. But he is also, in a tacit way and in effect, "accepting" the whole framework of the society. Only he who accepts the basic structure of his society—and is not aware of his acceptance—can turn his back on the problem of moral judgment. Now I do *not* merely assume that structure. In fact, it is my job to make it explicit and to study it as a whole. *That* is my major judgment. Because there are so many myths about American society, merely to describe it neutrally is considered, in the words of one reviewer, a "savage naturalism." Of course, I have elected to do more than that. Such judgments as I wish to make I try to make explicitly. It would not, as you know, be difficult to hide them; there's a very pretty apparatus at hand for that: the jargon of modern social science, especially sociology. (You don't write "authority," for example, which has a clean, hard edge; you write "imperative coordination," which is neutral—and Scientific too.)

Whether he wants it or not, anyone today who spends his life studying society and publishing the results is acting politically. The question is whether you face that and make up your own mind or whether you conceal it from yourself and drift morally. Most social scientists are today uneasily liberal. They conform to the prevailing tone of liberal American politics and the accompanying fear of any passionate commitment. *This,* and not "scientific objectivity" is what is really wanted by those who complain about "value judgments."

VI

Teaching, by the way, I do not regard as altogether in the same case as writing. When you publish a book it becomes a public property; your only responsibility to your reading public is to make it as good a book as you can, and you are the sole judge of that. But you have further responsibilities when you are teaching. To some extent your students are a captive audience, and to some extent they are dependent upon you. If you are worth a damn as a teacher, you are something of a model to them. Your job—and it is your prime job—is to reveal to them just how a supposedly self-disciplined mind works. The art of teaching is the art of thinking out loud. In a book you are trying to persuade others of the result of your thinking; in a classroom you are trying to show others how one man thinks—and at the same time reveal what a fine feeling you get when you do it well. You ought then, it seems to me, to make very, very explicit the assumptions, the facts, the methods, the judgments. You ought not to hold back anything, but you ought to take it very slowly and at all times and repeatedly make clear what the full range of moral alternatives are before you give your own choice. To write that way would be enormously dull, and impossibly self-conscious. That's one reason why very successful lectures don't usually print well.

VII

What I suppose has to be called "highbrow" criticism tends to pay less attention to the content of a book than to its publication as an event and a stratagem. As for content, I must say such "highbrow" reviews of *The Power Elite* as I've seen seem in rather complete agreement with it. They don't question the general idea I've constructed; they restate and accept my view of the newer relations of property and the state; they see quite clearly that the intellectual target of my attack is the classic liberal image of modern American society.

Basic agreement, however, is often hidden by the surface tone of the "highbrow" review. Considering the book as an event, one such reviewer makes the point that (like all other products) radical criticism in America can become a "salable commodity."[5] Of course. And so can reviewers' criticism of radical criticism. The only surefire way to avoid this situation is silence or suicide. Considering the book as political strategy, they make the point that it is negative in that it offers no "saving myth." Quite true. But then they call this "posturing." I don't quite see why, especially since they seem to agree with my judgment of the intellectual and moral character of the power elite as well as my statement of the mass society. The "highbrow" style, it seems to me, often consists merely of telling the revolutionaries they are not revolutionary enough, the theologians they are not theologically pure, the Freudians that they disregard The Founder's biases. Perhaps the Craving For Authenticity stands in place of, or at least in the way of, a passion to know what's what. Writing for me has always been, first of all, an effort to state what is so, as I see it. When there's no public that might accept the ideas *and* act upon them with consequence, one still has to go ahead and try to say what's so. That's all one can usefully say of the weary complaint about possible misuse of radical criticism.

VIII

But the salient point about so much "highbrow" reviewing is that in it presentation simply runs away with belief. Such reviewers ignore their own agreement or disagreement with the book at hand and adopt a tone. It is a tone which assumes superior accomplishment without ever revealing it; it is an attempt to turn all questions, in particular the question of truth, into matters of taste. In such magazines as *Partisan Review* one finds writers who have made a real thing out of such pretension; in fact, it has become the very token of what is some-

[5] Philip Rieff, "Socialism and Sociology," in this volume.

times called "brilliant." In the post-war period it has gone very well with the ostentatious boredom with political questions of larger scope—which is to say, with conservatism.

In "highbrow" reviews of *The Power Elite* this posture doesn't come off because—for one thing—the "highbrows" try to stand outside or above the book, but in fact they have no place to stand. The tone they imitate from one another is therefore obviously a mere surface manner rather than intrinsic to some point of view that is truly their own. The key to this posture is simply a lack of moral confidence. The way to overcome it is also clear: to take on a substantive job of work, one that forces you to deal imaginatively with a mass of facts. Were they to do that, such critics might come to see more of the world they live in, as well as in the work of writers they read, than "strategies of presentation." In the meantime, in striving to be intellectually fastidious, they only succeed in displaying moral weakness.

IX

Contemporary reviewers make wide use of the *ad hominum* argument: anyway, it's all resentment, these shrewd psychologists conclude—the implication being that therefore it's all a little personal show and nothing else.

Now, I take "resentment" to mean that I want to be like somebody else but can't be, so I dislike them. This of course is the expected imputation to make of any critical book about the higher circles. It is also cheap and easy in that it merely *assumes* that the book's author shares the values of those about whom he writes and therefore wants them for himself.

So far as the social fact of their existence and its consequence goes, my liking or disliking the power elite, whether it shows in the book or not, is altogether irrelevant. That's the foremost point. For it means that were I just dying to become a millionaire, this would not in itself affect the truth or falsity of what I've written about the millionaires in American society.

But I certainly am not aware of any desire to be more like the rich in the sense that I *am* sometimes aware of wanting to be more like some of the crack mechanics I know. Of course, although it means something to me, the comparison is a little unreal. I'm a third type of a man—and on the whole glad to be such.

x

One type of reasonable liberal broadly accepts my "account of who holds the power in American society" but complains that I really don't say *"what* the elite does with its power . . ."[6] This, of course, is to ask for a full-scale American history of our times, military, economic and political. And this I clearly have not done nor attempted to do in *The Power Elite.* An account of the power elite, in one volume at least, must work from examples. Seemingly realizing this, such reviewers then object to the examples I use as ". . . the most obvious ones conceivable." They are of course the big events of our time which have involved major decisions: Hiroshima, Korea, etc. And, of course, they *are* obvious. Should I seek out esoteric ones? But I think such reviewers have the notion—although they certainly didn't get it from my book—that, if there's anything to the idea, the power elite *must* be all the time secretly at work doing secret things that nobody knows about. They then complain that I don't tell what these things are. Of course, my idea of the power elite is not of that order. It is an inter-

[6] This section is directed toward Dennis Wrong's "Power in America," in this volume.

pretation of well-known historical events, not a notion of a secret cabal making decisions. Such decisions do enter into it, but they are by no means its defining characteristic. Naturally I sought examples that were not questionable; it is their interpretation that we are arguing about.

This line of reflection permits reasonable liberals to accept much of my account with a little moral shrug which helps bury the consequences of accepting it. They do so by reiterating a few of my points with the comment that "most modern governments" are of this sort. This of course is merely to accept the facts as if they were inevitable and obvious while refusing to confront the democratic problem of responsibility, in fact any problems of democracy, to which they lead.

A second objection along the same line is that I don't really say "what are the interests on the basis of which the power elite decides policy." This again is either to ask for a detailed history—this time in large part a psychological one—or it is to assume that there must be some one all-embracing, unifying interest, in short, that the unity of the elite must be based on conscious interests, or even ideology. This, I believe, is too rationalistic a means of interpretation. It is possible to say, as I do, that socially their decisions run to a maintenance of the status quo and personally, to a consolidation of their personal stake, both materially and ideally, in it. But this, of course, is a quite formal assertion which holds of other groups as well as of those on top.

One key to such elite unity as exists lies in the "coincidence" of the several structural trends I've traced; another is the psychological and status facts on which I've spent so many pages. Only third and last have I brought into the picture the explicit following of explicitly known interests. The whole idea of the power elite is set up and presented in this way in order to avoid the kind of "conspiracy" theory into which some reviewers, with a rather crude lack of theoretical acuteness, try to force a much more complicated and quite different view.

Yet one reviewer, for example, believes that I am "hinting" at an idea needed by my argument but which I can't really accept—the idea of an elite interest in "a permanent war economy." The fact is I don't hint at all. I think it obvious that war and the preparation for war as we know it is a perfectly marvelous way of solving and of ditching all sorts of problems confronted by the several members of the power elite, as well as by many other people.

XI

Some of the most interesting reviews I've seen are given over to consideration of the several pivotal decisions which I've used to illustrate the nature of decision-making in our time: Hiroshima, Dienbienphu, etc. Such reviewers typically acknowledge the only points I felt the need to make in connection with these examples: that they *are* pivotal and that very few persons indeed had any real say-so about them. "In any case," one acknowledges, "the first atomic bomb was dropped on the responsibility of one man who was the beneficiary of very sketchy advice from a handful of other men."[7] Exactly. And on Korea: "This decision was made in the course of a few hours by a few men." Just so.

But such reviewers seem to think that this refutes my idea of the power elite because (1) not a little crowd, but often only a few men, are in on such decisions; (2) these men don't always agree but are divided in their counsel; (3) in their decisions, they sometimes take into account the state of public opinion or the policy of other countries; (4) sometimes the decision made is "taken against the better judgment of the

[7] Richard Rovere, "The Interlocking Overlappers," in this volume.

power elite." Each of these points I readily accept, indeed I've stated them myself, and nothing in my conception of the power elite, or in the nature of the big decisions of our time, is upset by them.

The power elite is *not* a homogeneous circle of a specified number of men whose solidified will continuously prevails against all obstacles. Accordingly, I take such discussion of these pivotal events as an interesting and informed carrying on of the kind of social history I've urged, in which the idea of the power elite is refined and elaborated.

XII

The most important problem for political reflection in our time has to do with the problem of responsibility. I'm really sorry that only one reviewer takes up what is of course the chief moral theme of *The Power Elite*. He puts his point this way:

Mills sees himself standing outside society. Even though he's "generally humanistic in outlook," he makes a rigid distinction between life and history. "The tragic view of life is barred to them [people like Mills] . . . Feeling no personal responsibility—I do not mean accountability in the social and political sense but rather involvement in the tragic and comic sense—their view is almost certain to be irresponsible."[8]

Here is my answer to this:

Yes, I do feel that I stand, with most other people, outside the major history-making forces of my epoch, but at the same time I feel that I am among those who take the consequences of these forces. That is why I do *not* make a rigid distinction between "life and history," and that is one major reason why I am a political man. No one is outside society; the question is where you stand within it.

[8] We have been unable to locate the source of this comment.

The "tragic view of life," at least as it seems to be meant in this review, is not "barred" to me. Having examined it carefully, I have rejected it as a political blind alley, as sociologically unreal, and as morally irresponsible. It is a romanticism which in his social and personal loneliness the American adolescent finds very attractive, but it is not a mood that will stand up to even a little reflection. It is a way of saying to oneself: "We're all in this together, the butcher and the general and the ditch digger and the Secretary of the Treasury and the cook and the President of the United States. So let's all feel sad about one another, or if we're up to it, let's just see it all as one great comedy." But "we" are *not* all in this together—so far as such decisions as are made and can be made are concerned. "We" are *not* all in this together—so far as bearing the consequences of these decisions is concerned. To deny either statement is to deny the facts of power, in particular the fact that different men hold very different portions of such power as is now available. Only if all men everywhere were actors of equal power in an absolute democracy of power could we seriously hold the "tragic view" of responsibility.

The difference between this "tragic view" and the romantic pluralism of ordinary balance-of-power theories is that, being more politically sophisticated, the tragedians generalize the "we" to the generically human and in so doing try to shove it beyond the political sphere. But I'm afraid the distinction between "political accountability" and "tragic responsibility" which they make will not hold up. Certainly not today, certainly not in the United States today. If it did hold up it would offer a convenient escape from the frustrations of politics, and at the same time provide a grand view of one's own role in human affairs. But, in fact, it is nothing more than a shallow form of fatalism, which, adorned with a little liberal rhetoric, leads to political irresponsibility.

C. WRIGHT MILLS AND *THE POWER ELITE*

XIII

I've seen only two reviews in which the reviewer tries to pigeonhole the book from the left of it. One of them borders on an obstinate silliness over words like "capitalism" and "class"—words that have become clichés by which True Radicals try to retain the insurgency of their political adolescence yet avoid thinking freshly about what might be going on in the world today. Such a reviewer is likely to ask: "If the contemporary trends in corporate business power and its influence in government are as here suggested, why pretend that government and business are any longer importantly apart?"[9] Why indeed? Since the war, neither business nor government can be understood as a separate realm of power. That is not enough for the True Radicals. They want to believe that the corporations and the state are identical, that they have become one big structure. Well, if not that, what do they mean? If they want me merely to evoke the good old party emotions that flood up in some people when they are told that the state is "a committee of the ruling class," I am sorry, I can't oblige. I don't believe it is quite that simple.

A second question occurs to the True Radicals. "Well," they ask (as if they'd just thought of it and all alone), are you implying "that big business is increasingly in the position to dominate political democracy?" Of course. And I not only imply it; I spell it out in detail. Nevertheless, they continue: "Mills' failure to deal with the meanings for democracy of the impressive power trends he analyzes is the colossal loose-end of *The Power Elite*." In fact, one of the major themes of the book is that many key decisions are made outside the parliamentary mechanism which thus drops to a secondary position,

[9] This section is in answer to Robert S. Lynd, "Power in the United States," in this volume.

to the middle levels of power. On this level, there is very often a semi-organized stalemate. That is the key meaning of the power elite for democracy. But that's no answer for the True Radicals, for, you see, I've not used the old romantic words loosely enough to make them feel happy.

XIV

Several reviewers assert that I don't "really know what power is," but one radical critic spells this out: I put too much emphasis on force.[10] Well, I do believe that in the last resort, coercion is the "final" form of power, but I also believe—despite Hungary and Suez—that we are not constantly at the last resort. *Authority* (or power that is made legitimate by the beliefs of the obedient) and *manipulation* (power that is wielded unbeknown to the powerless)—along with *coercion*—make up the major and well-known types of power which must constantly be sorted out when we think about the elite. The point that is relevant to this criticism, I believe, is that authority is no longer so explicit as it was, say in the medieval epoch, and that along with this, the ideology (justification or legitimations of power) of ruling groups is no longer so relevant to understanding phenomena of modern power. For many of the great decisions of our time, mass "persuasion" has *not* been "necessary"; the fact is simply accomplished. Further, more often than not such ideologies as are available for the power elite are neither taken up nor used by them. In modern times, ideology, and hence legitimate authority, arises as a response to effective debunking, to thoroughgoing criticism; in the United States such opposition has not been recently available, has not been effective enough to create the felt need for ideologies of rule. As a result, there has come about neither acceptance nor

[10] This and the following two sections are directed to Eugene V. Walter, "The Power Elite: Two Views," *Dissent*, Fall, 1956.

rejection of the old symbols of authority, but simply political indifference. This—and I use the word with care—spiritual condition seems to me the key to much modern malaise, as well as the key to many political features of the power elite in the United States. What we've recognized as conviction is not necessary, in either the ruling or the ruled, for the structure of power as well as its elite formations to persist and even flourish. So far as ideologies are concerned, that is one of the interpretative guides I've found most helpful in trying to understand the nature of contemporary types of power.

XV

Another complaint from the left is that all this business of the elite does not jibe with true "radical values." Such criticism is more likely to be buttressed by general statements about the "latent political bias" of "elite theory" than by concrete reference to *The Power Elite*. But what are "radical values"? "For radical criticism to have any meaning it must utter its judgments from some moral norm that transcends the system, or from some standard that recognizes an immanent, unfulfilled, potential in the existing state of things." I want to make very clear that in so far as this is the meaning, I am *not* a Radical Critic and never have been. I have never found either a transcendent or an immanent ground for moral judgment. The only moral values I hold I've gotten from right inside history; in fact they are values proclaimed by many and, within the possibilities of various life-ways, practiced by small circles in western history whose members I've taken as models of character. Moral judgment, I suppose, is a matter of wanting to generalize and to make available for others those values you've come to choose. Foremost among them is the chance of truth. Simple descriptions of elite persons and groups can be politically neutral, but I don't think they usually are. When little is known, or only trivial items publicized, or when myths prevail, then plain description becomes a radical fact—or at least is taken to be radically upsetting.

The study of elite groups, at least as I have carried it on, does not blind one "to the real potential for fundamental social change . . ." After all, the only "potential" mentioned by critics who make this charge ends up merely as the commonplace thought that "prosperity" and "contemporary trends" will not last forever. Surely. But no writer about such topics as these is writing "forever"; one writes for now. I don't of course believe that the contemporary power elite is here "forever." War and the preparation for war, is one of its major conditions, although not its only one. I don't suppose it could survive a really disastrous slump, but I don't see the conditions of such a slump in the immediately foreseeable future. Let us not be so urgent for hope of fundamental change that we slip over into the falsely wise mood of This Too Shall Pass, as many "radical" philosophers border on doing. The fundamental political error of so much "radicalism" is its tendency, borrowed directly from the optimistic bourgeois notion of progress, to confuse the cry for hope with the metaphysics of history.

XVI

But the "radical" criticism goes deeper: it holds that there is some "latent ideological bias" in "the elite theory" and that it's this bias that's against "radical values," whatever they are. My trouble here is that I don't really understand what is meant by "the elite theory." There is no such thing. Merely to study elite groups is not automatically to accept some one definite theory of elites. Do the critics mean Pareto's theory of the circulation of the elite? I don't accept that. Michels' iron law of oligarchy? I think it's a fairly good description of what has in fact happened in most mass organization. But what is "the hidden ideological bias" in "the elite theory" or in empirical work on elite groups? Do they mean only that "elite theory" reduces power to "a conquest theory of politics"? If so, then certainly I do not hold "the elite theory." I don't think history is merely a succession of elites which, one after the other, conquer the institutional means of power. That is an omnipotent theory of the elite and an elite theory of history from which I have been very careful to dissociate my view. The structural mechanics of institutions must indeed be given due weight. My point, in this connection, is simply that the shape of these institutions—for example, their extreme centralization—makes the action and the policies, of those who exercise such human control over them and through them as nowadays exists, more consequential, more relevant to an understanding of the history of our times—than, let us say, in the model society of the Jeffersonian scatter.

The study of elites does not rule out an acceptance of the kind of structural view one finds, for example, in Marx. In fact, one must pay attention to both. The historical structure of opportunity is more important, I hold, than "the seizure of power" by elites of which some critics talk so much. The relation of institutional structure and elite formations is of course a two-sided play. Institutions, as I've repeatedly documented, select and form those who come to their top. In fact, sometimes the norms of selection and the shaping influences of institutional structures are more important to understanding human affairs and even the affairs of the powerful than the actual circles of men on top at any given time. I believe that is true just now, for example, in many corporations. But it's also true, given the shape of major institutions in the United States today, that those at the top are more than privileged persons: to a varying extent, in different historical situations, they are also powerful with all the means of power now at their disposal.

XVII

Many reviewers of *The Power Elite*—liberal, radical and highbrow—complain that the book is "too pessimistic" or "too negative." Only one of them it seems to me, has been self-conscious enough to be altogether honest about this: he writes that he does not "respond more readily" to the book "in part, no doubt, because [its] conclusions are gloomy . . ."[11] What many reviewers really want, I think, is less of a program than a lyric upsurge—at least at the end. They want a big thump on the intellectual and political back. They want a sturdy little mood of earnest optimism, out of which we step forward all nice and fresh and shining. But the world I'm trying to understand does not make me politically hopeful and morally complacent, which is to say, I find it difficult to play the cheerful idiot. Many people tend, often without knowing it, to judge a position in terms of optimism-pessimism, the pessimistic being not nearly so good as the optimistic. Personally, as you know, I'm a very cheerful type, but I must say that I've never been able to make up my mind whether something is so or not in terms of whether or not it leads to good cheer. First you try to get it straight, to make an adequate statement. If it's gloomy, too bad; if it's cheerful, well fine. Anyway, just now isn't it obvious that it's not at all a question of what "we're" going to do; the question is what are a lot of other people doing? In the meantime, the charges of irresponsibility, the pseudo-crying

[11] Marcus Cunliffe, "American Trends," *Encounter,* July, 1956.

for a program, are really signs of fear, of an incapacity to face facts as they are, even if these facts are decidedly unpleasant— and so irrelevant to the truth or falsity of my views.

Yours truly,
C. Wright Mills

Svanemollevej 64
Copenhagen, Denmark

THE POWER ELITE *and Its Critics*

BY G. WILLIAM DOMHOFF

Introduction

Mills' reply to his critics dealt quite explicitly with questions of values, mood, and the nature of power. However, it did not give adequate answers in all instances to the methodological, theoretical, and empirical criticisms leveled against *The Power Elite*. Not only is this to be expected in such a short reply, but many of the most important substantive critiques had not appeared when Mills wrote. The purpose of this essay, then, will be to discuss some of these major substantive disputes and to adjudicate each one insofar as it is possible on the basis of new arguments and more recent empirical research. The primary emphasis will be on the differences between pluralist and Marxist critics on almost every issue, with Mills' own position sometimes closer to the one side, sometimes closer to the other. The pluralists are those who see a variety of interest groups determining major decisions in American society. They include those Mills defined as liberals, along with the highbrows Rovere and Bell. By Marxist critics we mean those Mills called radicals. It should be noted, however, that Rovere and Bell have been influenced by Marxism.

G. William Domhoff teaches psychology at the University of California, Santa Cruz. He is the author of Who Rules America? (*Englewood Cliffs, New Jersey: Prentice-Hall, 1967*).

C. WRIGHT MILLS AND *THE POWER ELITE*

Mills' Methodological Approach

Mills' reviewers, pluralist and Marxist alike, were unanimous in criticizing his approach to the problem of power in modern America, which was to study the structure and personnel of the major institutional hierarchies of the country. The pluralists favored a decision-making analysis, a weighing of the arguments and outcomes on a variety of key political issues to determine how and why the decisions were made. Such a study would show, the pluralists felt, that most decisions are made—after taking a variety of factors and interest groups into account—in a way that tends to satisfy the major concerns of all sides of the issue and to provide a long-run balance and stability to the society. They were especially annoyed that Mills would only mention important decisions in passing, and that most of these decisions were military ones that were made by the President. By way of challenge, they called on Mills to show that decisions were made by his power elite on the basis of interests that put them in at least some degree of opposition to other groups in the society. They further challenged Mills to show that these decisions by federal authorities were made in the interests of any special group rather than in the interests of the society as a whole.

The Marxist critics felt that to study the structure and personnel of major institutions did not go far enough; the institutions and their leaders must in turn be related to socioeconomic classes. They pointed out that if Mills had done so, he would have been in a better position to answer the claim by pluralists, noted above, that decision-makers had no interests or goals that would set them off from the rest of the population. Demonstrating that the power elite was made up of rich capitalists and their employees, said the Marxists, would be to show that leaders from other social classes might react differently in certain of the crucial situations encountered by the power elite. In short, Marxists did not so much reject Mills' approach, as did the pluralists; they merely said that he did not go far enough with it.

Mills answered his Marxist critics by saying that an institutional analysis does not rule out a class analysis, but the fact remains that he did not relate the two in any detailed empirical fashion.

As to the pluralist criticisms of his approach, Mills answered first by pointing out that the decisions he mentioned were only examples to show that a few people were involved in decisions which had enormous consequences for millions of people. As far as Mills was concerned, his pluralist critics, by admitting this fact, had granted the point which most concerned him in choosing his particular examples. But Mills also had something much more profound to say to these critics. In terse fashion he made another point in his reply to his critics that is only recently being emphasized by sophisticated advocates of this approach: a study of any specific decision requires a full-scale history of our time. As Raymond A. Bauer, who collaborated on a decision-making study of tariff policy, put it:

> However, we have treated the process involving the formation of a particular decision as a closed system which can for practical purposes be isolated for analysis. Regrettably this cannot be done. The parties involved in any policy issues have other responsibilities and obligations. They also have a past and a future. One of the fallacies of treating the policy process as decision making is that it assumes that someone is aware of the problem, that he can devote full time and attention to it, and that the issue has a clear-cut beginning and end. In practice, other events compete for his resources, including time, attention, and energy. Other issues raise the question of other interests and values involved in the policy issue that somehow

253

has captured our attention. I have coined the phrase "the envelope of events and issues" to refer to those events and issues which must be considered as the context within which to analyze a given policy problem.[1]

If Bauer's "envelope of events and issues" does not imply a full-scale history, it comes very close to it.

An example of the ambiguities of a decision-making approach can be seen in recent research on one of the big decisions mentioned by Mills, the decision to drop the atomic bomb. Rovere in particular argues in his review that we can make an adequate analysis of this decision, which is generally held to have been based upon military considerations and the desire to spare American troops. However, a more recent study of previously unpublished diaries, relevant testimony, and memoirs of the decision-makers suggests that this decision may have been affected by factors that were not apparent to those who criticized Mills and emphasized the need for a decision-making analysis. With a number of quotes from such important advisers to President Truman as Henry Stimson, Joseph Clark Grew, James Forrestal, Vannevar Bush, and James F. Byrnes, and a closely reasoned argument which correlates policy changes with A-bomb developments, Gar Alperovitz suggests that a major consideration in dropping the bomb may have been a desire to reverse tacit concessions made to Russia in Eastern Europe and to keep Russia from entering the war against Japan (and thus occupying Manchuria) as it had promised to do.[2] Alperovitz quotes several major military fig-

[1] Raymond A. Bauer, "Social Psychology and the Study of Policy Formation," *American Psychologist,* October, 1966, p. 937.

[2] Gar Alperovitz, *Atomic Diplomacy: Hiroshima and Potsdam* (New York: Simon and Schuster, 1965). See also his very important review of Herbert Feis's *The Atomic Bomb and the End of World War II* in *The New York Review of Books,* June 15, 1967. See also David Horowitz' *The Free*

ures in the U.S., Britain, and France as saying (some before the event, some after) that the war with Japan was all but over and such a bomb was not necessary. He further notes that the commander in the Pacific, Douglas MacArthur, was not even consulted about the advisability of this military maneuver.

Whether Alperovitz is right or not cannot be determined at this time, for many of the documents needed for further support were refused him by the government—an example of one of the limitations on a decision-making analysis. But a rather skeptical review by the eminent British political scientist Max Beloff makes the point we want to stress: "Meanwhile, it is useful to be reminded how little we really know about the historical decisions that matter most."[3]

The Unity of the Power Elite

Mills' views on the unity of the power elite were unacceptable to both his pluralist and Marxist critics. Due to his methodological approach, they said, he could not show that the leaders of the separate institutions were in any way unified. The pluralists then concluded that there was no cohesiveness to the power elite; they saw competition rather than unity. They believed that a study of the decision-making process would document this lack of unity as well as a lack of decision-making power within any one elite group. The Marxists, while agreeing that Mills did not convincingly demonstrate the unity of the power elite, claimed that he could have done so if he had

World Colossus (New York: Hill and Wang, 1965), especially pp. 55–58; and Lloyd C. Gardner, *Economic Aspects of New Deal Diplomacy* (Madison: University of Wisconsin, 1964), pp. 320–321. For a review by a political writer for the magazine *Science* which contradicts Rovere's emphasis on scientists in determining this decision, see Elinor Langer, "Scientists and Policy at Ground Zero," *The Nation,* September 6, 1965.

[3] Max Beloff, "Prelude to the Cold War," London *Observer,* February 27, 1966.

taken a socioeconomic class approach, if he had argued that an interest in maintaining a highly profitable private enterprise system which favored them—which made them a privileged class—was the glue of the power elite. At the same time, one of the Marxists added, a class approach would have permitted Mills to deal with the possibility of opposing cliques within the upper class.

Mills responded to this general criticism by pointing out to the pluralists that he had given reasons and evidence for power elite unity and by resisting the Marxists' suggestion that there was one "key" basis to the unity of the elite. He suggested that structural trends of the society, similar socioeconomic status, and similar psychological experiences in large institutions all formed the basis for the unity. He also pointed out that differences of opinion within the power elite did not contradict his thesis.

Although the pluralists and Marxists seem to be making a similar criticism, the answers to them are in each case different. The pluralists are raising an empirical question: where is adequate evidence for the unity of these separate hierarchies. As will be seen in our concluding section, this challenge is readily met even if Mills did not do it to their satisfaction. The Marxists, on the other hand, are asking a theoretical question: how are the separate institutional hierarchies in fact united. They then insist that the basis of this unity is in the means of production and the property relations of the society. However, as Aptheker makes clear, really speaking for all Marxists on this point, they do not claim that this is the only reason. Simple economic self-interest or psychological greed are caricatures of Marxism. But even knowing that, Mills was not ready to grant their point and capitulate to historical materialism as the "Archimedean" point of social structure and social psychology, to use a term from an excellent discussion of Marxian social psychology by the late Paul A. Baran.[4] As Mills made even clearer in his later critique of Marxism in *The Marxists,* he saw no compelling reasons to relegate his other factors to a secondary importance. While this may seem a matter of emphasis, it is a point of concern to Marxists. Historical materialism is their rock. We do not presume to adjudicate this age-old dispute.

The Warlords

No critic denied the right of any arm—corporate, political, or military—of Mills' power elite to be included among the powerful. However, they did disagree about the relative importance he gave to each of the three. For example, pluralists said he underestimated the political directorate, Marxists that he underestimated the corporate rich. With these problems we will be concerned in a moment, but first we will deal with a criticism that was almost unanimous: Mills overestimated the role of the military. On this point we agree with the critics. Events and data of the years since Mills wrote have made clear the subordinate role of military men within the power elite.[5] Civilians—in particular the corporate rich—have dominated the defense department, and the number of military men in important roles in the business world has been greatly exaggerated. However, this does not mean that Mills was wrong in emphasizing the military definition of reality that has been increasingly accepted by the power elite. As Sweezy put it in his review, the corporate rich can see no other way out of their problems than military ones. As compared with the years be-

---

[4] Paul A. Baran, *Marxism and Psychoanalysis* (New York: Monthly Review Press, 1960), p. 50.

[5] See, for example, Morris Janowitz, *The Professional Soldier* (New York: The Free Press, 1960); and Jack Raymond, *Power at the Pentagon* (New York: Harper and Row, 1964).

257

fore 1940, this is a momentous change in the shape of the American polity, but it is not the same as saying that the warlords of Washington should be considered on an equal footing with their corporate and political masters.

But even if pluralists and Marxists agreed that Mills overestimated the importance of the military, they disagreed as to why Mills made this wrong analysis. Sweezy believed it was because Mills made too much of an external factor—the menace of Soviet Russia—and of factors internal to the military—code of honor, military metaphysics, and a desire for a place in the sun. He suggested that the real answer can be found in the internal dynamics of the corporate political economy, a permanent war economy being the only method acceptable to the corporate rich for saving monopoly capitalism from overproduction, underconsumption, depression, unemployment, stagnation, and political unrest. This economic theory—which Sweezy does not find in *The Power Elite*—is said to be implicit by a pluralist critic, Dennis Wrong, who then labels the notion "incredible" and instead points to the belligerency of certain foreign countries. Similarly, Daniel Bell argues that Mills underestimates the importance of Russian initiatives in determining the rise of the military and military thinking.

It seems to us that Mills relies on both factors. At the same time, it is also true that he did not make himself very clear on this point. There is no one paragraph or chapter where he deals with the question directly. His clearest expression of any one position is in the chapter on the warlords: "For the first time, the American elite, as well as effective sections of the underlying population, begin to realize what it means to live in a military neighborhood, what it means to be technically open to catastrophic attack upon the national domain" (183). Ninety-two pages later he notes that "The seemingly permanent military threat places a premium on the military," but that is the extent of his comments on external factors. By the same token, the closest he comes to an economic motivation for maintaining the permanent war economy is when he quotes the *New York Times* columnist Arthur Krock as saying that certain events support "the thesis that immediate prosperity in this country is linked to a war economy and suggests desperate economic problems that may arise on the home front" (216). He perhaps implies it in two other brief comments embedded in other contexts: "Underneath the whole prosperity of the 'forties and 'fifties, of course, is the structural fact of the war economy" (149); "War is, of course, the health of the corporate economy . . . and moreover, political legitimations of the most unquestionable sort—national security itself—are gained for corporate economic activities" (167). However, if Mills' position on the "economic factor" is equivocal in the book, it is nonetheless quite clear in his answer to critics: war and preparing for war are "perfectly marvelous ways of solving and ditching all sorts of problems" for the power elite.

Unfortunately, it is difficult to go beyond theoretically based arguments on these matters to the point where weight can be given to the possible variables. We think economic, ideological, psychological (mutual suspicion), and military (threats to Western commercial colonies and dependencies by national liberation movements, not Soviet threats to the United States) factors were operating, but the question is the importance of each type.[6]

[6] For evidence on the U.S. role in fomenting and maintaining the cold war, which opposes the standard emphasis on Russian initiatives, see Horowitz, *The Free World Colossus,* and Carl Oglesby, "Vietnamese Crucible," *Containment and Change* (New York: Macmillan, 1967).

C. WRIGHT MILLS AND *THE POWER ELITE*

The Corporate Rich

Pluralists and Marxists disagreed as to how Mills was wrong in the emphasis he gave to the corporate rich. For the pluralists, the managerial revolution is accepted as the most important fact of modern-day private enterprise, and the rise of the political directorate since the New Deal is seen as an effective check on the wealth and power that are now divided between corporate owners and corporate managers. Thus, for example, Parsons states that the rich did not consolidate their position and are losing some of their wealth to inheritance taxes and income taxes. These two notions are also the basis for understanding Daniel Bell's viewpoint, which is most succinctly expressed in the conclusion to his essay on "The Breakup of Family Capitalism."[7] This particular essay describes two "silent revolutions" in the relationship between power and social class. Inheritance is no longer the avenue to power, wealth is no longer the basis of power. The new keys to understanding power are in education, technical skill, and political position. The decline in importance of inheritance and wealth as the avenue and basis, respectively, for power means that the social upper class of wealthy businessmen and their descendants is no longer a ruling class. "Today," says Bell, "there is an upper class and a ruling group." Upper classes still have differential privileges which they can pass along, but they do not rule. The technical-intellectual elites (including the corporate managers) and the political directorate do that.[8] And one basic reason why members of the

[7] See *The End of Ideology* (New York: The Free Press, 1960), especially p. 42.

[8] This argument is now almost as widely accepted as that of the "managerial revolution" in the 1950's. For recent examples, see Suzanne Keller, *Beyond the Ruling Class* (New York: Random House, 1964), and J. K.

upper class do not rule is that the death of family capitalism and the rise of managerial capitalism has robbed them of a community of interest and a continuity of interest.

Contrary to the pluralists, Marxist critics believed that Mills, for all his excellent remarks on the corporate rich, still underestimated their importance. The Marxists would raise this group into a position of leadership within the power elite. They claim that the corporate elite are the operating arm of a ruling class which sets the standards by which men move into positions of prominence within the political directorate and the military establishment. They would emphasize even more than Mills that the managerial revolution has really been an institutionalization of the capitalist function and a slight reorganization of the ownership class.

Since there is a great deal of new information about the corporate rich which bears on this all-important dispute among Mills, pluralists, and Marxists, we will withhold our comments on it until a final section in which we try to synthesize the various views.

The Political Directorate

The question of the political directorate once again finds the pluralists and the Marxists at odds as to how and why Mills is wrong. Indeed, the nature of the state and its role is an old and crucial argument in the long-standing disagreements between pluralists and Marxists. The pluralists are unanimous in believing that the political directorate is even more autonomous than Mills would hold. Parsons states that business opposition to the government would be "impossible to understand" without the assumption that the federal government is the most

---

Galbraith, *The New Industrial State* (Boston: Houghton Mifflin, 1967). We will comment on it later in this essay.

important of the institutions constituting the power elite. The key to understanding the pluralist position on this issue is the theory that the New Deal significantly altered the relationship between the upper class and the federal government. For them, it is a classic demonstration of their thesis that the government is responsive to all interests in society and that it functions to redress the claims of all parties. They point to the rise of organized labor, subsidies to farmers, TVA, laws restricting businessmen, and many other changes as evidence for the rise of a political directorate that is at once powerful and at the same time at least somewhat autonomous of the corporate rich.

Mills' answer to the pluralists was empirical rather than theoretical. That is, he did not see the government as the inevitable captive of a ruling socioeconomic class. He agreed that the big political man was important during the thirties, but claimed that a military-industrial complex pushed this political directorate aside during World War II. As to labor, Mills too at one time saw them as "the new men of power," but decided that they sunk to the middle levels of power during the late forties and early fifties.

Marxists, of course, took just the opposite position from the pluralists *vis-à-vis* the political directorate. They found it to be the "errand boy of the corporate rich," a finding which Mills characterized as "too simple." On this point, it seems to us, the Marxists and Mills are operating at different levels of abstraction. The Marxists mean that big businessmen control "in general" and "in the long run." In another context, Sweezy —who made the comment about the political directorate being "errand boys"—has written that "protection of private property" is the essence of "ruling class" and that to claim that "the state always and everywhere and automatically serves the interests of the ruling class" is a "vulgar Marxism." He then goes on to list the main weaknesses of such a vulgar Marxism:

1. There are conflicts between the true long-run interests of the ruling class as a whole and the short-run interests of particular segments of it.

2. Because it wears ideological blinkers which distort its view of reality the ruling class often does not see clearly what its true long-run interests are and hence acts on a false conception of ruling-class interests.

3. Under certain circumstances, other classes or segments of classes can force the state to make concessions to their interests.

Sweezy then concludes:

There are naturally limits to all these qualifications and it doubtless remains true that *in general* the state serves the interests of the ruling class. But in any given situation the range of alternatives is wide and the course to be followed by the state is far from mechanically predetermined. The whole subject, in other words, is enormously complicated and difficult; and so far as I am aware, it has nowhere been satisfactorily dealt with either theoretically or empirically.[9]

That the vulgar Marxism decried by Sweezy and Mills was not the Marxism of Marx or Engels is clear. Nor does Aptheker's lengthy discussion suggest any tendency toward an oversimplification of this concept. It would seem to us that the Marxists were justified in demanding more from Mills than a footnote in Chapter 12 in rejecting the concept "ruling class." Whether it fits all societies is one question, and whether it fits modern America is another, but it seems fair to say that Mills did not put it to a detailed empirical test.[10]

[9] Paul M. Sweezy, "Has Capitalism Changed?" in Shigeto Tsuru (ed.), *Has Capitalism Changed?* (Tokyo: Twanami Shotin Co., 1961), pp. 87–90.
[10] See T. B. Bottomore, *Elites and Society* (New York: Basic Books, 1964).

C. WRIGHT MILLS AND *THE POWER ELITE*

The Power of Experts

Interwoven throughout the pluralist critique of the power elite concept are a set of criticisms that must be both generalized and made more explicit, for the general notion that encompasses these criticisms is an old and important one. It has to do with the rise in importance of expertise in a technological society. In the words of Parsons, "responsibility" is tied to "competence." Complex modern society, says this argument, is run by groups of technical-intellectual elites drawn originally from diverse socioeconomic backgrounds. They make their decisions on the basis of their skills in the best interests of their institution, profession, or nation, rather than on the basis of narrow personal and socioeconomic class interests. The thesis of the managerial revolution can be seen as one example of this trend toward a meritocracy which has led us "beyond the ruling class." Such an argument is used by Parsons, for example, when he stresses the role of corporate managers and corporate lawyers, and when he points to the rise of the educational establishment as a supplier of competence to corporation and government. It is used by Bell when he notes the importance of education and technical skill, and it is seen in Rovere when he states that parts of the intelligentsia and technological-managerial classes are more important than Mills admits.

Mills was well aware of this phenomenon and summarized it very succinctly in the fourth paragraph of his opening chapter: "The power elite are not solitary rulers. Advisers and consultants, spokesmen and opinion-makers are often the captains of their higher thought and decision" (4). Mills would argue, however, that to advise a decision-maker is not the same as being one, and that the power of the power elite is best seen when they must choose among the conflicting suggestions of their hired experts. Nor, contrary to Parsons, was Mills un-

aware of the independent importance of corporation lawyers—
he noted their crucial role several times.[11] The argument
between Mills and his critics on this score, then, would be one
of degree.

The Mass Society

Contrary to the criticisms concerning the concept of a
power elite, the critics did not break along pluralist-Marxist
lines in their reaction to the other side of Mills' theoretical
coin, his characterization of the lower levels of American society as a "mass society." Among the pluralists, Riesman (via
Kornhauser) and Berle accepted it, but Parsons thought it
considerably overstated. Parsons is joined in this negative
judgment by the Marxist Aptheker and the ex-radicals Bell and
Rovere, who offer as one piece of contrary evidence the alleged role of public opinion in preventing the power elite from
moving into Vietnam militarily in 1954.[12] Parsons would see

[11] "Accordingly, the lawyer is becoming a pivotal figure in the giant
corporation" (131). "The inner core of the power elite also includes men
of the higher legal and financial types from the great law factories and investment firms, who are almost professional go-betweens of economic, political, and military affairs, and who thus act to unify the power elite" (289).
"Not the trade associations but the higher cliques of lawyers and investment
bankers are the active political heads of the corporate rich and the members
of the power elite" (291).

[12] See Marvin Gurtov, *The First Vietnam Crisis* (New York: Columbia
University Press, 1967), for a detailed scholarly account of this decision.
The major factors preventing a gradual escalation, beginning with air support, were French fears that they would lose influence in the region, American reluctance to support unilaterally an anti-colonial war, British refusal
to join in a united action, and American military opinion (with the exception of Admiral Radford) that air support was not enough and our ground
strength was insufficient to risk a land war in Asia. Most political scientists
seem to agree that public opinion has very little effect on foreign policy. In
any case, polls in May and September of 1953 and April of 1954 showed
52 to 60 percent in favor of sending air support and 59 to 65 percent in
favor of sending American troops if necessary. On this latter point, see
Kenneth N. Waltz, "Electoral Punishment and Foreign Policy Crisis," in
James N. Rosenau (ed.), *Domestic Sources of Foreign Policy* (New York:
The Free Press, 1967).

265

reason for doubting Mills' notion of a powerless, atomized mass in the facts on kinship ties and well-organized voluntary associations, while Aptheker would emphasize the power of labor unions and blue-collar workers in general.

On this problem, a Millsian answer to Parsons has been set down by Andrew Hacker in "Power To Do What?", an essay which undertakes to answer some of the criticisms of *The Power Elite:*

> In the realms of public education and popular culture, in civil liberties and civil rights, and often in local government—in all these areas majority sentiment prevails. . . . Indeed, the elite has no real interest in or objection to democracy in the areas that have been mentioned here. . . . In short, the elite is content to let the public blow off steam on certain questions.[13]

As to Aptheker's emphasis on the power of the working class, Mills would probably answer with his oft-quoted phrase —labor metaphysic. He thought the role of the blue-collar worker greatly exaggerated by the Marxists. Furthermore, according to Mills, the classical "worker" is fast being replaced by the white-collar employee, who has a different psychology and political outlook even though he is a wage or salary earner with no income-producing property who is hired and fired by a profit-making businessman.[14]

[13] In Irving L. Horowitz (ed.), *The New Sociology* (New York: Oxford University Press, 1964), p. 135. For the opinion that the power elite may not care about most local decisions, see also Robert A. Dahl, "Business and Politics: A Critical Appraisal of Political Science," in *Social Science Research on Business* (New York: Columbia University Press, 1959), pp. 32–33; and Scott Greer and Peter Orleans, "Political Sociology," *Handbook of Modern Sociology* (Chicago: Rand, McNally, 1964), p. 827.

[14] C. Wright Mills, *White Collar* (New York: Oxford University Press, 1951), and C. Wright Mills, *The Marxists* (New York: Dell, 1962). For an excellent discussion of this and related points, see also Ralph Miliband, "Mills and Politics," in Irving L. Horowitz (ed.), *The New Sociology* (New York: Oxford University Press, 1965).

An Attempt at Synthesis

This final section will be an attempt to integrate the various views on the higher circles of power in American society in the light of recent research. As we have seen, both pluralists and Marxists were in agreement in rejecting Mills' theory that the military, corporate rich, and political directorate form a power elite which is more or less united on the basis of inevitable structural necessities of modern society and similar socioeconomic, institutional, and psychological backgrounds. The Marxists favored a ruling-class theory, which states that a social upper class of business owners and corporate managers dominates the crucial decisions made by the political directorate and hence the military, which is under the wing of the Department of Defense. This model in effect raises one member of Mills' power elite, the corporate rich, to a position of primacy and ties it to the socioeconomic class described in Mills' excellent chapter on the Metropolitan 400.

The pluralists attacked the power elite concept from the other direction, claiming that the three groups Mills singled out were not so tightly knit as to form a power elite and that there were other groups with significant power. These other groups include labor, farmers, small businessmen, and various professional groups. Furthermore, said the pluralists, the corporate rich, political directorate, and military establishment are in reality made up of sub-groups with as many conflicts as agreements. This pluralistic model does not necessarily argue that all interest groups have an equal amount of power on all issues, but only that no one group (corporate rich) or trio of groups (power elite) are in the position of dominating policy on a wide variety of issues.

There are new data that bear on this power-elite versus ruling-class versus interest-group argument. They allow us to

267

suggest a synthesis of the three views in which the idea of a "power elite" forms the conceptual bridge between the Marxist and pluralist positions without denying the data stressed by either. The first set of studies concerns the upper class as a social class. The most noteworthy of these efforts have been produced by E. Digby Baltzell, a sociologist of upper-class origins who holds to Tocquevillian values and has different aims from the pluralists and Marxists in putting forth his analysis of the American social structure. Baltzell finished his training at Columbia during Mills' tenure there and went on to publish his dissertation in 1958 under the title *Philadelphia Gentlemen: The Making of a National Upper Class*. The book has been reissued as a paperback under the title *An American Business Aristocracy,* which better captures Baltzell's thesis that a national upper class of rich businessmen and their descendants came into existence in the last part of the nineteenth century as a result of the national corporate economy and the national transportation-communication network. Baltzell followed this book six years later with *The Protestant Establishment,* which tells of the demise of one ruling clique within the upper class, a ruling clique of prejudiced, conservative Protestant industrialists and bankers who were replaced by a more ethnically and religiously representative establishment made up of other elements—both older and newer—of the upper class.

The first merit of Baltzell's work is that it establishes empirically the existence of a national upper class which interacts and intermarries. Baltzell shows the importance of private schools, Ivy League colleges, gentlemen's clubs, summer resorts, and boards of directors in understanding this upper class. The second merit of his work is that it combines an institutional and class analysis in the fashion advocated by Mills' radical critics. That is, after showing that the *Social Register* is a good index of upper-class standing, he demonstrated that leading businessmen, lawyers, and civic leaders are part of this class. Most of the data in *An American Business Aristocracy* concern the major institutions of Philadelphia, but they also show that 20 percent of America's "elite" in 12 major cities in 1940 —as defined by being listed in *Who's Who in America*—were in the *Social Register*. If Baltzell's work is not definitive, primarily because he did not deal in more detail with upper-class control of political and governmental institutions, it is certainly provocative enough to invite further studies based upon it.

In writing *Who Rules America?*, I was reacting in part to the challenge provided by Baltzell's findings. Building on the work of both Baltzell and Mills, I developed six criteria of upper-class membership and then studied the sociological backgrounds of major institutional leaders, political campaign donors, and decision-makers. This study showed that the less-than-one-percent who make up the American upper class contribute anywhere from 25 percent to 62 percent of the directors and partners of the largest banks, law firms, and corporations, and that these men and their hired employees dominate the philanthropic foundations, the boards of trustees of leading universities, the largest opinion-forming associations, the largest of the mass media, and the executive branch of the federal government. Two of the most important findings of *Who Rules America?* concerned the relationship between the old-line members of the upper class and the control of the corporate economy. On the one hand, it is clear that many members of the upper class continue to acquire the expertise necessary to function in the complex world of modern corporations and law firms. On the other hand, it is clear that rising executives are assimilated into the social institutions of the upper class. This would seem to support Mills in lumping these seemingly disparate groups as the corporate rich, thus refuting the claims of those who emphasize the managerial revolution and the supposed loss of economic power, continuity of interest, and community of interest by the upper class.

There are other recent studies which support the idea of a relatively unified corporate rich as opposed to a "managerial revolution." First, surveys show that more corporate executives own stock than any other occupational group.[15] This suggests that those not originally stockholders soon become so through special stock-option plans and the utilization of insider's information. Thus, rising executives are not only assimilated socially, but economically as well. Another line of evidence concerning the essential oneness of the corporate rich concerns testimony by social observers in a position to know. Lucy Kavaler's *The Private World of High Society,* an excellent snapshot of present-day upper-class life, contains several statements by members of the upper class testifying that successful corporate executives are accepted into exclusive clubs and invited to in-group social functions. In a similar vein, our recently completed questionnaire study based upon returns from society editors of leading newspapers around the country also suggests that the most exclusive social clubs and events often assimilate rising executives. However, our study revealed that there are a few cities where this is less the case, so it is easy to see why there would be confusion on this point among researchers who base their conclusions on limited experience. For example, a society editor in New Haven reported that many successful executives have a hard time reaching the innermost circles there, thus corroborating Dahl's statements about that city.[16]

A second set of important studies that have appeared in

[15] For this and other relevant information see Earl F. Cheit (ed.), *The Business Establishment* (New York: Wiley and Sons, 1964), especially Cheit's own chapter.

[16] Robert A. Dahl, *Who Governs?* (New Haven: Yale University Press, 1961), pp. 67–69.

recent years concerns wealth and income distribution in the United States. These studies suggest that there has been very little, if any, change in these important indicators of social structure and political power. Economist Robert Lampman's examination of the estates of deceased individuals worth $60,000 or more shows that the top one percent of society has not been losing its wealth, and its share may even be increasing since the early 1950's. This top one percent owns at least 25–30 percent of all wealth that is privately held and more importantly, 75–80 percent of the corporate stock that is privately held.[17] Furthermore, according to an interview study with a sample of top wealth-holders in a large midwestern city, these figures may be an underestimate.[18]

Another economist's work, Herman Miller's *Rich Man, Poor Man,* shows that the income share of the top levels of society has remained steady over the past twenty years after a gradual decline from his base-line year of 1929.[19] According to Gabriel Kolko,[20] this small decline may be exaggerated due to the many nontaxable ways that the higher levels of society are rewarded—the "higher emoluments," in Mills' terms. These include tax-free municipal bonds (the income from which is grossly under-reported because it is not taxable),[21] expense accounts, company yachts, company airplanes, company resorts, free medical care, special insurance policies, deferred compensations, and other such amenities. To these findings on

[17] Robert Lampman, *The Share of Top Wealth-Holders in National Wealth* (Princeton: Princeton University Press, 1962).

[18] George Katona and John B. Lansing, "The Wealth of the Wealthy," *Review of Economics and Statistics,* February, 1964.

[19] Herman Miller, *Rich Man, Poor Man* (New York: Signet Books, 1964).

[20] Gabriel Kolko, *Wealth and Power in America* (New York: Praeger, 1962).

[21] George Lent, *Ownership and Tax Exempt Securities, 1913–1953,* National Bureau of Economic Research, New York, 1953.

income can be added Miller's statement that taxes do not redistribute income in refuting the claim by Parsons and others that the wealthy are losing out economically.

A third set of recent findings of considerable relevance concerns the unity and interaction of the men who supposedly constitute the power elite. The first of these is Floyd Hunter's *Top Leadership, USA,* wherein he attempts to ascertain whether or not there is a national power structure by means of his reputational method, which entails asking a great many people supposedly in a position to know whom they think to be the top leaders of the country. Names that recur frequently are chosen by Hunter as top leaders. Reading through the several hundred persons and their institutional affiliations, it is safe to say that they are by and large people who were members of Mills' power elite during the 1950's. One hundred of these men were further studied by means of interviews. Among the questions asked of each man was whether or not he knew any of the other ninety-nine. The results show that a great many of those interviewed were known personally to each other, a finding which reinforces the notion of an interacting national power structure.

Data from *Who Rules America?* are relevant to the question of the unity of the various institutions of the power elite. These data show that the same men who run the corporate world are also active in foundations, associations, and political parties. The data further show that these men are appointed to positions in the executive branch of the federal government. This is particularly true in regard to foreign affairs, defense, finance, and commerce. To provide evidence for this governmental role from a study of attitudes toward tariff policy, 32 percent of a sample of 166 big businessmen (executives in firms with 10,000 or more employees) had served in either a policy-level government job (20 percent), a foreign-affairs government job (8 percent), or an overseas government job (4 percent).[22]

Finally, there are new data on experts which tend to indicate that their presence does not require alterations in a power elite theory. The most general of these data are presented by Baltzell, in *An American Business Aristocracy,* who shows that two very important types of experts, those dealing with financial and legal matters, are for the most part well-educated and hard-working members of the upper class. This point has been further reinforced by Irwin O. Smigel's comprehensive study of large corporate law firms.[23] Baltzell also demonstrates that members of the upper class are a considerable proportion in other areas of expertise, such as architecture and medicine.

If empirical studies are clear in suggesting that a formidable amount of expertise is lodged within the upper class, they also seem to indicate that members of the upper class and their high-level corporation executives finance and control the universities, foundations, institutes, and associations which train and are repositories for the experts. This control over the sources of expertise implies at the very least the power to select, train, and encourage those who will become experts. Among several lines of evidence tending in this direction, there

[22] Raymond A. Bauer, Ithiel de Sola Pool, and Lewis A. Dexter, *American Business and Public Policy* (New York: Atherton Press, 1963), p. 168. For detailed evidence on how members of the power elite control the issue-area of foreign policy, see the forthcoming *The Corporations and the Cold War,* edited by David Horowitz. For a detailed demonstration of how one subgroup within the corporate elite controls those aspects of government essential to it, see Robert Engler, *The Politics of Oil* (New York: Macmillan, 1961).

[23] Irwin O. Smigel, *The Wall Street Lawyer* (New York: The Free Press, 1964).

are detailed studies of two major areas of expertise which make the point very well. The first concerns the role of foundations in fostering American scholarship on the non-Western world:

> Foundation encouragement and support of the development of non-Western studies in American higher education has been crucial if not decisive . . . Of the many foundations, the Rockefeller Foundation, the Carnegie Corporation, and especially the Ford Foundation have contributed the lion's share in support of graduate training and research programs at major universities, of the recruitment and training of graduate students through national fellowship programs, of research by individual scholars and by groups of them, and of efforts by undergraduate colleges to add non-Western studies to the mainstream of liberal learning.[24]

Tracing the history of involvement in these areas, Beckmann shows that university grants have gone to a small handful of elite universities, while big research grants have gone to individuals and specially created institutes at an even smaller group of institutions.

Similar findings are presented in a historical study of policy-oriented research organizations. It indicates that the most respected organizations active in the investigation of alternative economic and political policies, such as the National Bureau of Economic Research, The Brookings Institution, the Twentieth Century Fund, the National Planning Association, and the Committee for Economic Development, were founded, financed, and managed by leading members of the corporate rich. The Carnegie Corporation and Rockefeller Foundation were especially important in organizing and maintaining several of these groups:

[24] George M. Beckmann, "The Role of the Foundations," *The Annals of the American Academy of Political and Social Science,* November, 1964, p. 12.

The relationship of government to the foundations is an interesting one. The government, for example, created and directed the National Research Council (as it had the National Academy of Science) but confidently relied on foundation support to sustain their long-run operation. The NBER could undertake some of the most important of its early (and later) work because of the ability of Secretary of Commerce [Herbert] Hoover to acquire Carnegie money for this private organization. Foundation executives were in at the organization of many of these groups (the Carnegie Corporation actually founded the Institute of Economics) and were strongly represented on the directional bodies of nearly all of them.[25]

It would seem likely, then, that experts have not displaced those Mills called the power elite, but that members of the power elite have financed, encouraged, and utilized the experts trained in the universities, foundations, institutes, and associations of which they are trustees and directors.

If Baltzell's work and the recent empirical findings of others are taken as a starting point, the divergent views of Mills and his critics on the nature of the power structure can be incorporated into a larger framework. It can be suggested, as the Marxists claim, that there is a national upper class of rich businessmen and their descendants whose members control corporations, foundations, the largest of the mass media, major

[25] David Eakins, "The Development of Corporate Liberal Policy Research, 1885–1965," Ph.D. dissertation, University of Wisconsin, 1966. Eakins also studied the proposals and reports presented by these groups throughout the past 40 to 50 years. He is able to show a considerable similarity between their suggestions and later government legislation. The Twentieth Century Fund, for example, seems to have had a close connection with certain New Deal welfare legislation, while the National Planning Association and the Committee for Economic Development seem to have played a key role during the forties and fifties on legislation dealing with employment, foreign aid, and taxation. For details on the CED and its history see also Karl Schriftgiesser, *Business Comes of Age* (New York: Harper and Brothers, 1960).

275

opinion-forming associations, and, through campaign financing and their presence in key cabinet and advisory positions, the executive branch of the federal government. Recalling studies which show middle-class control in many local communities, it also can be suggested, as the pluralists claim, that there is considerable political diversity on the American scene. And it can be agreed that there is a power elite, defined by Mills as the men who control the major institutions and make decisions of at least national consequence.

However, contrary to Mills, we wish to suggest that the corporate elite, who, according to recent research, control those institutions considered "major" by Mills, form the controlling core of the power elite. The interests and unity of the power elite are thus determined primarily by the interests of the corporate rich, with the factors mentioned by Mills contributing in a secondary fashion. According to this view, the power elite can be defined more explicitly as "politically, economically, and culturally active members of the social upper class and high-level employees in institutions controlled by members of the upper class." While this definition is formally different from that utilized by Mills, it leads empirically to designating the same persons he did as members of the power elite.

Defined in this way, the concept of a "power elite" is the bridge between the Marxist and pluralist positions. On the one hand, it is a necessary concept because not all national leaders are members of the upper class. In this sense, it is a modification and extension of the concept of a "ruling class."[26] On the

[26] It is likely that the occupations of these non-upper-class members of the power elite are the primary determinants of their attitudes and values, thus dealing with the supposed problem that they have middle-class origins. For a computerized empirical study of attitudinal and social background data which shows how well present occupation and present political affiliation predict attitudes in large samples of French and German leaders who

other hand, empirical studies on community power, viewed in the light of this redefinition, suggest that Mills was right to say that the power elite is directly involved mainly in decisions of national and international consequence. Coupled with the already-cited suggestion by Hacker, Dahl, and others that most local decisions do not seem to affect the interests of the power elite, this emphasis on national-level power leaves the concept free to coexist with the findings on the variety of power structures that are present on community or local levels.

In claiming that important national decisions are controlled by a power elite which has its roots in and serves the interests of the American upper class, several caveats must be added. The control is not complete; other groups sometimes have their innings, particularly when these groups are well-organized and angry. Nor is the power elite always united in its policies; there are long-standing disagreements between its moderate and conservative wings on some issues, as manifested, for example, in the arguments between the Committee for Economic Development and the National Association of Manufacturers.[27] Nor does the power elite automatically act in its best interests; to read case studies of specific decisions is to be aware that lack of information, misunderstandings, and personality clashes may lead to mistakes on issues that must be decided in a hurry. For all of these reasons, there is a degree of conflict and complexity in this country of 38,000 governments and 200 million people that lends a certain credence to the portrait of diversity drawn by most observers.

were interviewed, see Lewis J. Edinger and Donald D. Searing, "Social Background in Elite Analysis: A Methodological Inquiry," *American Political Science Review,* June, 1967.

[27] See David S. McLellan and Charles E. Woodhouse, "The Business Elite and Foreign Policy," *Western Political Quarterly,* March, 1960; and Charles E. Woodhouse and David S. McLellan, "American Business Leaders and Foreign Policy: A Study in Perspectives," *The American Journal of Economics and Sociology,* July, 1966.

C. WRIGHT MILLS AND *THE POWER ELITE*

Conclusion

With or without alterations and qualifications, *The Power Elite* stands as tall in the light of recent events as it did in 1956 when it crashed in on the Great American Celebration with its detailed description and provocative indictment of the structure of power in modern America. Not only did it present a new conception of how the United States is ruled, but it forced pluralists and Marxists to rethink, make explicit, and defend their own positions. It is a landmark of political sociology that will be read with more than mere historical interest for many years to come, a beacon to the intellectual craftsmen on whom Mills placed his hopes for the rational and humane world he passionately sought.